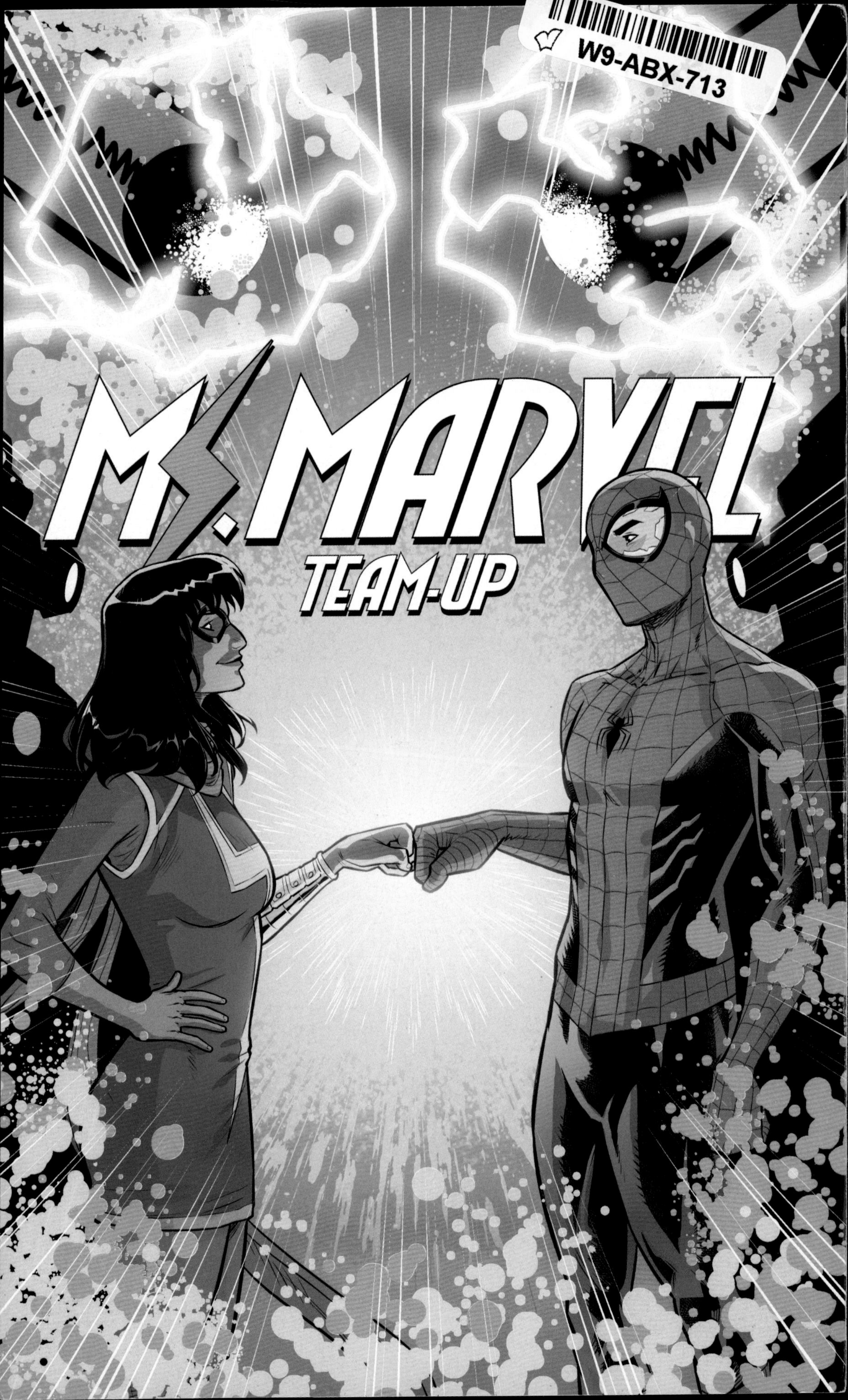
MS. MARVEL
TEAM-UP

WHEN A STRANGE TERRIGEN MIST DESCENDED UPON JERSEY CITY, KAMALA KHAN WAS IMBUED WITH POLYMORPH POWERS. USING HER NEW ABILITIES TO FIGHT EVIL AND PROTECT JERSEY CITY, SHE BECAME...

MS. MARVEL

PETER PARKER WAS BITTEN BY A RADIOACTIVE SPIDER AND GAINED THE PROPORTIONAL SPEED, STRENGTH AND AGILITY OF A SPIDER, ADHESIVE FINGERTIPS AND TOES AND THE UNIQUE PRECOGNITIVE AWARENESS OF DANGER CALLED "SPIDER-SENSE"! HE BECAME THE CRIMEFIGHTING SUPER HERO CALLED...

SPIDER-MAN

BORN TO A KREE MOTHER AND A HUMAN FATHER, FORMER AIR FORCE PILOT CAROL DANVERS BECAME A SUPER HERO WHEN A KREE DEVICE ACTIVATED HER LATENT POWERS. NOW SHE'S AN AVENGER AND EARTH'S MIGHTIEST HERO...

CAPTAIN MARVEL

COLLECTION EDITOR **JENNIFER GRÜNWALD**
ASSOCIATE MANAGING EDITOR **KATERI WOODY**
VP PRODUCTION & SPECIAL PROJECTS **JEFF YOUNGQUIST**

SVP PRINT, SALES & MARKETING **DAVID GABRIEL**
EDITOR IN CHIEF **C.B. CEBULSKI**
PRESIDENT **DAN BUCKLEY**

CAITLIN O'CONNELL ASSISTANT EDITOR
MARK D. BEAZLEY EDITOR, SPECIAL PROJECTS
JAY BOWEN BOOK DESIGNER

SVEN LARSEN DIRECTOR, LICENSED PUBLISHING
JOE QUESADA CHIEF CREATIVE OFFICER
ALAN FINE EXECUTIVE PRODUCER

MS. MARVEL TEAM-UP. Contains material originally published in magazine form as MARVEL TEAM-UP #1-6. First printing 2019. ISBN 978-1-302-91831-6. Published by MARVEL WORLDWIDE, INC., a subsidiary of MARVEL ENTERTAINMENT, LLC. OFFICE OF PUBLICATION: 135 West 50th Street, New York, NY 10020. © 2019 MARVEL No similarity between any of the names, characters, persons, and/or institutions in this magazine with those of any living or dead person or institution is intended, and any such similarity which may exist is purely coincidental. **Printed in Canada.** DAN BUCKLEY, President, Marvel Entertainment; JOHN NEE, Publisher; JOE QUESADA, Chief Creative Officer; TOM BREVOORT, SVP of Publishing; DAVID BOGART, Associate Publisher & SVP of Talent Affairs; DAVID GABRIEL, VP of Print & Digital Publishing; JEFF YOUNGQUIST, VP of Production & Special Projects; DAN CARR, Executive Director of Publishing Technology; ALEX MORALES, Director of Publishing Operations; DAN EDINGTON, Managing Editor; SUSAN CRESPI, Production Manager; STAN LEE, Chairman Emeritus. For information regarding advertising in Marvel Comics or on Marvel.com, please contact Vit DeBellis, Custom Solutions & Integrated Advertising Manager, at vdebellis@marvel.com. For Marvel subscription inquiries, please call 888-511-5480. **Manufactured between 10/4/2019 and 11/5/2019 by SOLISCO PRINTERS, SCOTT, QC, CANADA.**

10 9 8 7 6 5 4 3 2 1

MS. MARVEL TEAM-UP

ISSUES #1-3

WRITER	**EVE L. EWING**
ARTISTS	**JOEY VAZQUEZ** WITH **MOY R.** (#3)
COLORIST	**FELIPE SOBREIRO**
COVER ART	**STEFANO CASELLI** & **TRÍONA FARRELL**

ISSUES #4-6

WRITER	**CLINT McELROY**
ARTIST	**IG GUARA**
COLOR ARTIST	**FELIPE SOBREIRO**
COVER ART	**ANNA RUD** & **EDUARD PETROVICH**

LETTERER	**VC's CLAYTON COWLES**
ASSISTANT EDITOR	**SHANNON ANDREWS BALLESTEROS**
EDITOR	**ALANNA SMITH**
EXECUTIVE EDITOR	**TOM BREVOORT**

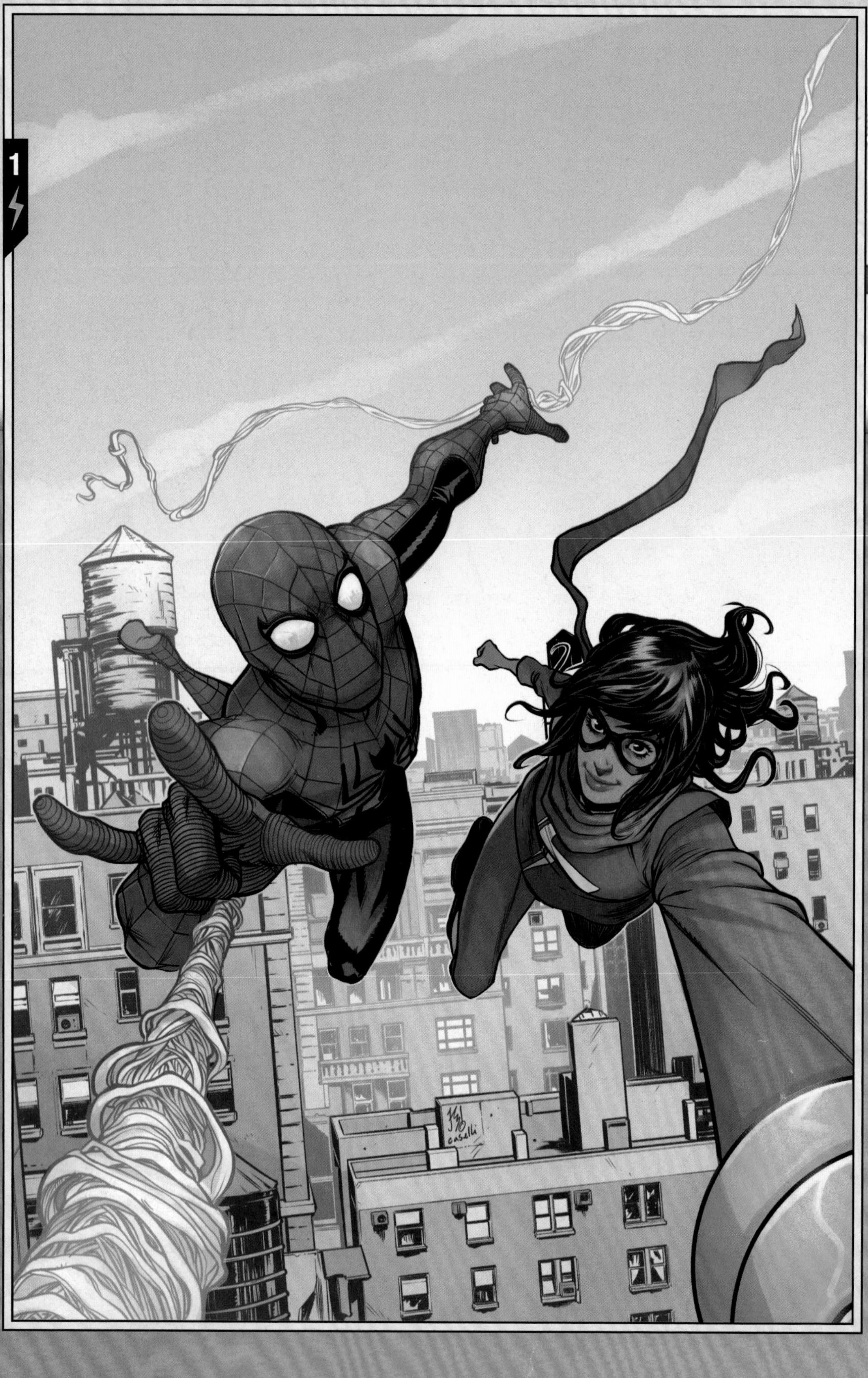
1

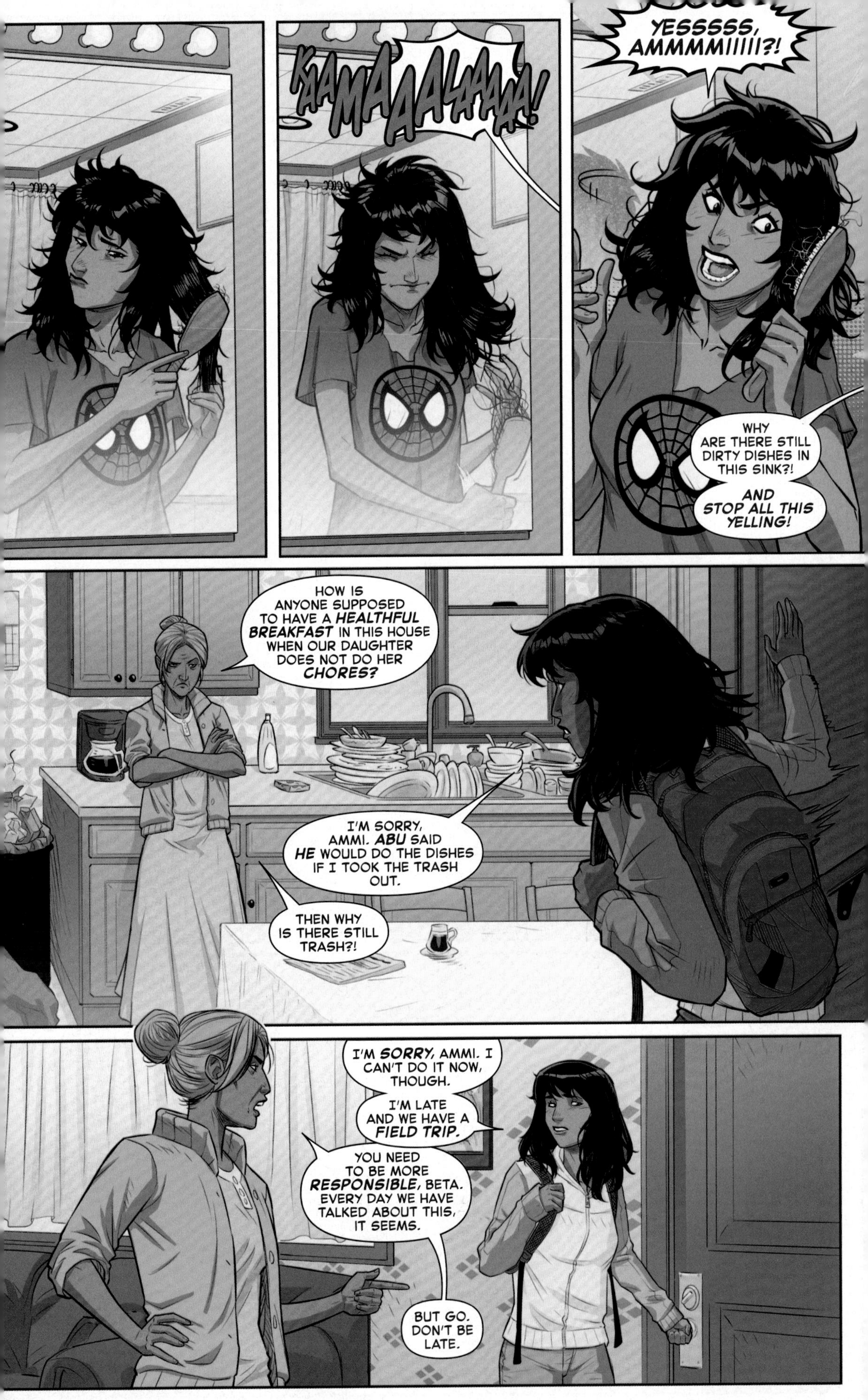
KAAMAAAALAAAAA!
YESSSSS, AMMMMIIIII?!
WHY ARE THERE STILL DIRTY DISHES IN THIS SINK?!
AND STOP ALL THIS YELLING!
HOW IS ANYONE SUPPOSED TO HAVE A HEALTHFUL BREAKFAST IN THIS HOUSE WHEN OUR DAUGHTER DOES NOT DO HER CHORES?
I'M SORRY, AMMI. ABU SAID HE WOULD DO THE DISHES IF I TOOK THE TRASH OUT.
THEN WHY IS THERE STILL TRASH?!
I'M SORRY, AMMI. I CAN'T DO IT NOW, THOUGH.
I'M LATE AND WE HAVE A FIELD TRIP.
YOU NEED TO BE MORE RESPONSIBLE, BETA. EVERY DAY WE HAVE TALKED ABOUT THIS, IT SEEMS.
BUT GO. DON'T BE LATE.

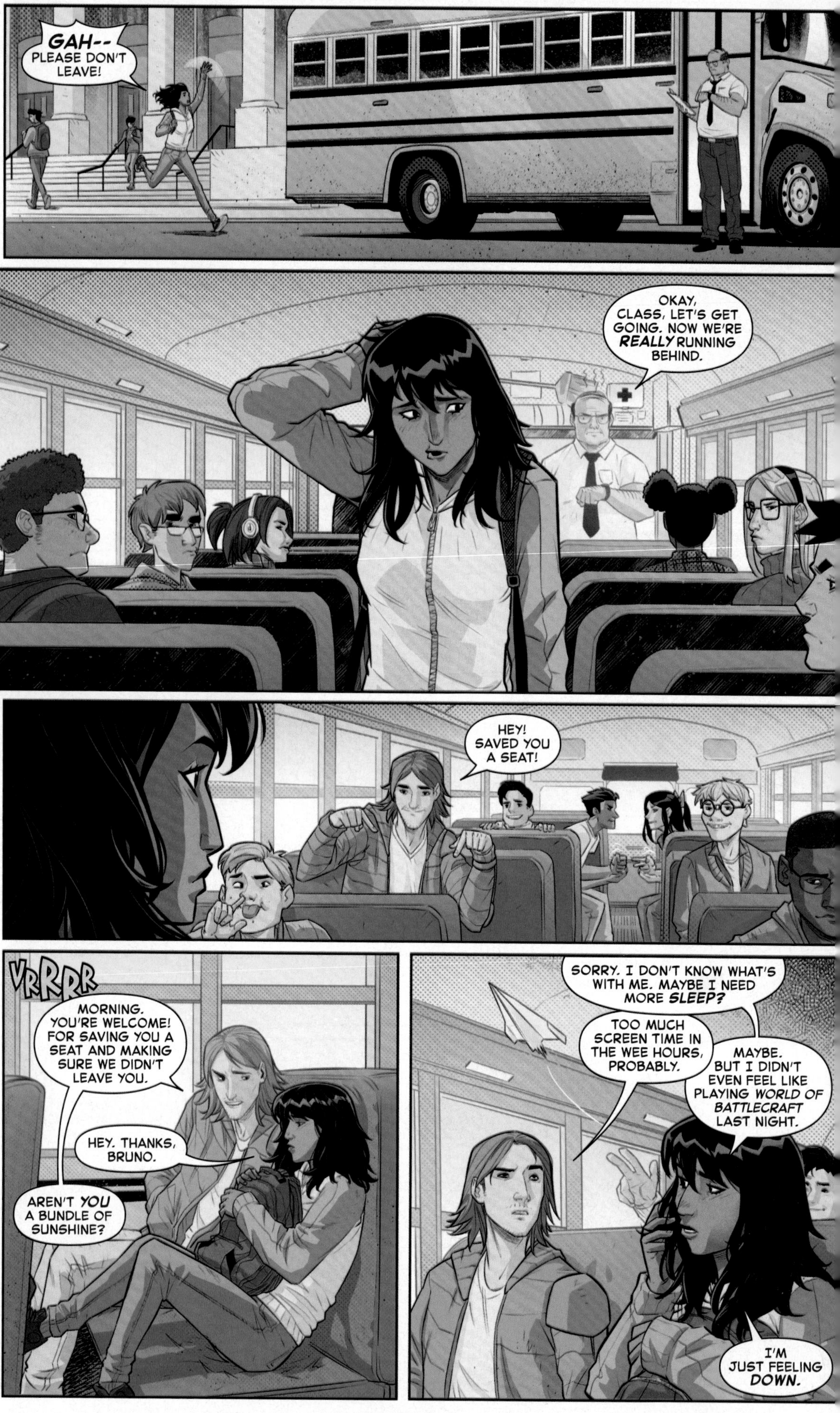
GAH-- PLEASE DON'T LEAVE!
OKAY, CLASS, LET'S GET GOING. NOW WE'RE *REALLY* RUNNING BEHIND.
HEY! SAVED YOU A SEAT!
VRRRR
MORNING. YOU'RE WELCOME! FOR SAVING YOU A SEAT AND MAKING SURE WE DIDN'T LEAVE YOU.
HEY. THANKS, BRUNO.
AREN'T *YOU* A BUNDLE OF SUNSHINE?
SORRY. I DON'T KNOW WHAT'S WITH ME. MAYBE I NEED MORE *SLEEP?*
TOO MUCH SCREEN TIME IN THE WEE HOURS, PROBABLY.
MAYBE. BUT I DIDN'T EVEN FEEL LIKE PLAYING *WORLD OF BATTLECRAFT* LAST NIGHT.
I'M JUST FEELING *DOWN.*

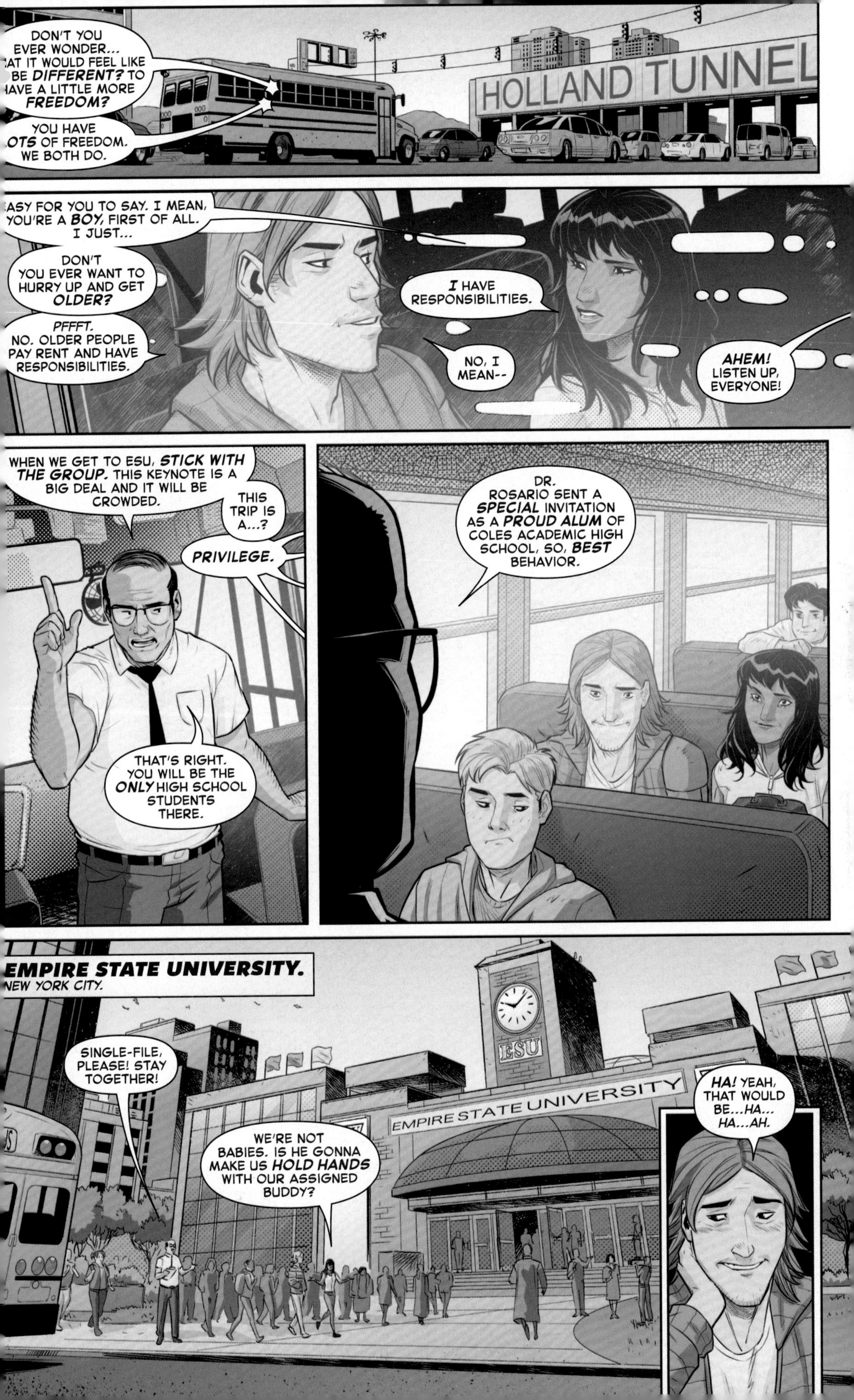

DON'T YOU EVER WONDER... AT IT WOULD FEEL LIKE BE DIFFERENT? TO AVE A LITTLE MORE FREEDOM?
YOU HAVE OTS OF FREEDOM. WE BOTH DO.
HOLLAND TUNNEL
ASY FOR YOU TO SAY. I MEAN, YOU'RE A BOY, FIRST OF ALL. I JUST...
DON'T YOU EVER WANT TO HURRY UP AND GET OLDER?
PFFFT. NO. OLDER PEOPLE PAY RENT AND HAVE RESPONSIBILITIES.
I HAVE RESPONSIBILITIES.
NO, I MEAN--
AHEM! LISTEN UP, EVERYONE!
WHEN WE GET TO ESU, STICK WITH THE GROUP. THIS KEYNOTE IS A BIG DEAL AND IT WILL BE CROWDED.
THIS TRIP IS A...?
PRIVILEGE.
THAT'S RIGHT. YOU WILL BE THE ONLY HIGH SCHOOL STUDENTS THERE.
DR. ROSARIO SENT A SPECIAL INVITATION AS A PROUD ALUM OF COLES ACADEMIC HIGH SCHOOL, SO, BEST BEHAVIOR.
EMPIRE STATE UNIVERSITY.
NEW YORK CITY.
ESU
EMPIRE STATE UNIVERSITY
SINGLE-FILE, PLEASE! STAY TOGETHER!
WE'RE NOT BABIES. IS HE GONNA MAKE US HOLD HANDS WITH OUR ASSIGNED BUDDY?
HA! YEAH, THAT WOULD BE...HA... HA...AH.

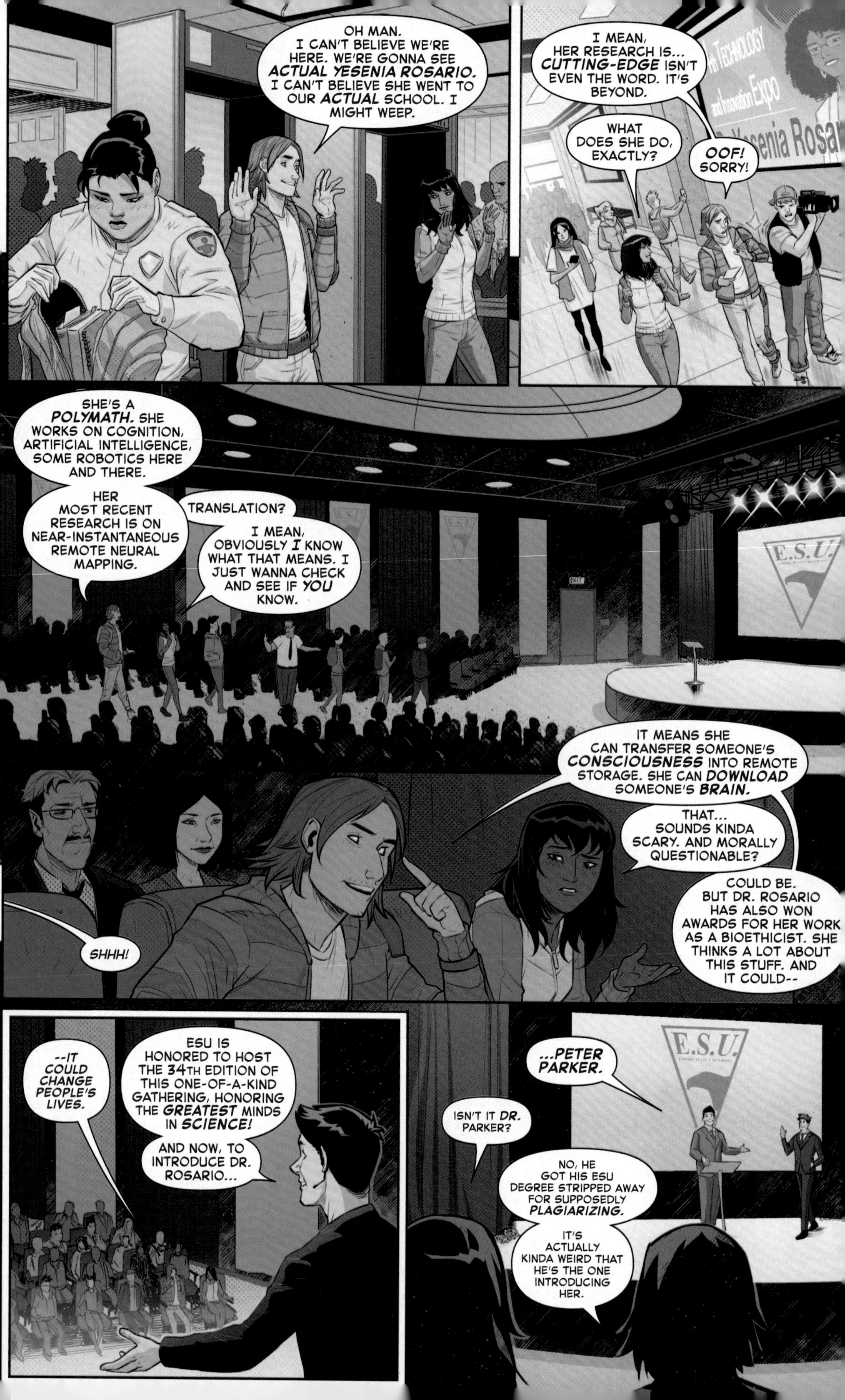
OH MAN. I CAN'T BELIEVE WE'RE HERE. WE'RE GONNA SEE ACTUAL YESENIA ROSARIO. I CAN'T BELIEVE SHE WENT TO OUR ACTUAL SCHOOL. I MIGHT WEEP.
I MEAN, HER RESEARCH IS... CUTTING-EDGE ISN'T EVEN THE WORD. IT'S BEYOND.
WHAT DOES SHE DO, EXACTLY?
OOF! SORRY!
SHE'S A POLYMATH. SHE WORKS ON COGNITION, ARTIFICIAL INTELLIGENCE, SOME ROBOTICS HERE AND THERE.
HER MOST RECENT RESEARCH IS ON NEAR-INSTANTANEOUS REMOTE NEURAL MAPPING.
TRANSLATION?
I MEAN, OBVIOUSLY I KNOW WHAT THAT MEANS. I JUST WANNA CHECK AND SEE IF YOU KNOW.
E.S.U.
IT MEANS SHE CAN TRANSFER SOMEONE'S CONSCIOUSNESS INTO REMOTE STORAGE. SHE CAN DOWNLOAD SOMEONE'S BRAIN.
THAT... SOUNDS KINDA SCARY. AND MORALLY QUESTIONABLE?
COULD BE. BUT DR. ROSARIO HAS ALSO WON AWARDS FOR HER WORK AS A BIOETHICIST. SHE THINKS A LOT ABOUT THIS STUFF. AND IT COULD--
SHHH!
--IT COULD CHANGE PEOPLE'S LIVES.
ESU IS HONORED TO HOST THE 34TH EDITION OF THIS ONE-OF-A-KIND GATHERING, HONORING THE GREATEST MINDS IN SCIENCE!
AND NOW, TO INTRODUCE DR. ROSARIO...
E.S.U.
...PETER PARKER.
ISN'T IT DR. PARKER?
NO, HE GOT HIS ESU DEGREE STRIPPED AWAY FOR SUPPOSEDLY PLAGIARIZING.
IT'S ACTUALLY KINDA WEIRD THAT HE'S THE ONE INTRODUCING HER.

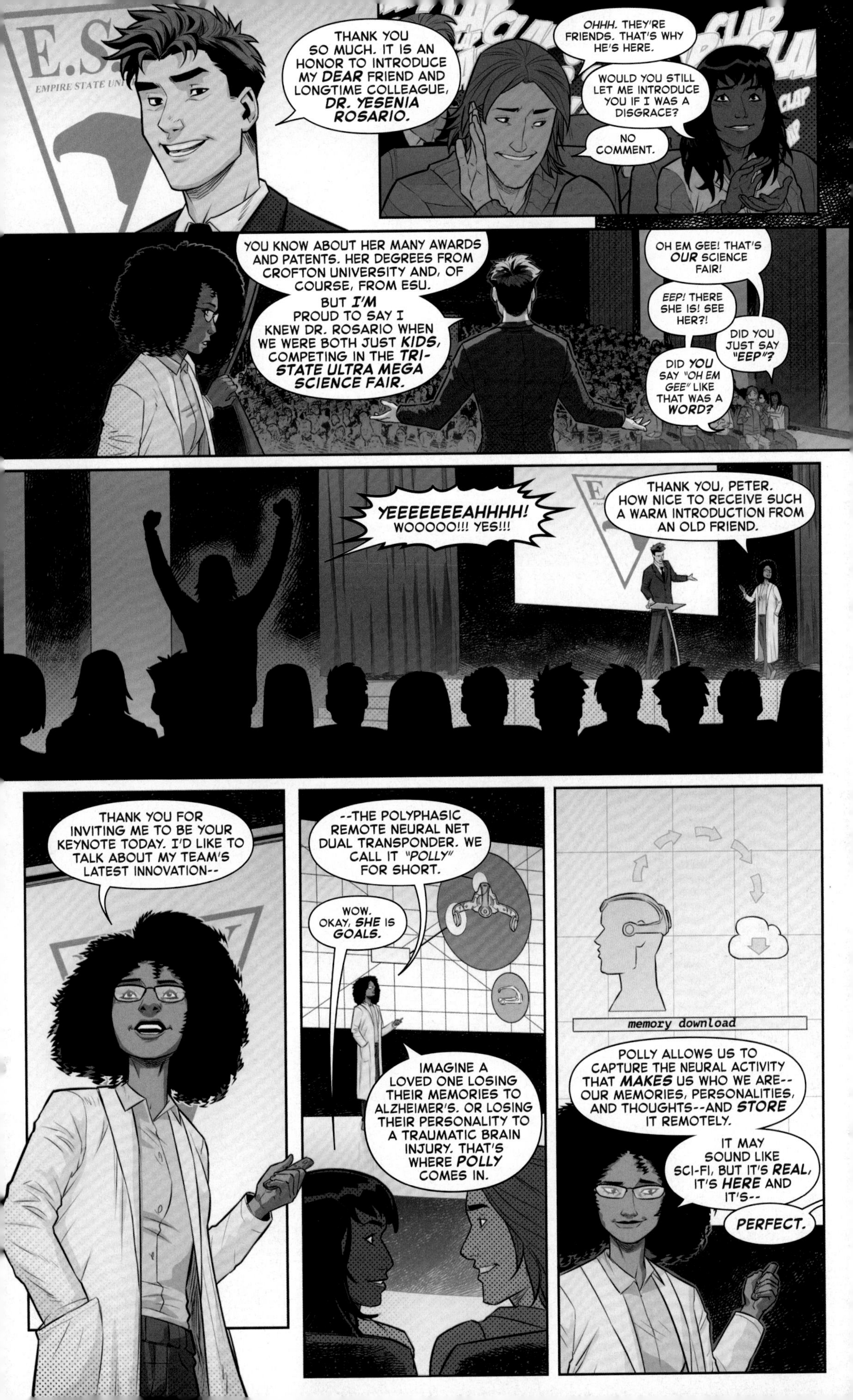
E.S.
EMPIRE STATE UNI
THANK YOU SO MUCH. IT IS AN HONOR TO INTRODUCE MY DEAR FRIEND AND LONGTIME COLLEAGUE, DR. YESENIA ROSARIO.
CLAP CLAP
OHHH. THEY'RE FRIENDS. THAT'S WHY HE'S HERE.
WOULD YOU STILL LET ME INTRODUCE YOU IF I WAS A DISGRACE?
NO COMMENT.
YOU KNOW ABOUT HER MANY AWARDS AND PATENTS. HER DEGREES FROM CROFTON UNIVERSITY AND, OF COURSE, FROM ESU.
BUT I'M PROUD TO SAY I KNEW DR. ROSARIO WHEN WE WERE BOTH JUST KIDS, COMPETING IN THE TRI-STATE ULTRA MEGA SCIENCE FAIR.
OH EM GEE! THAT'S OUR SCIENCE FAIR!
EEP! THERE SHE IS! SEE HER?!
DID YOU JUST SAY "EEP"?
DID YOU SAY "OH EM GEE" LIKE THAT WAS A WORD?
YEEEEEEEAHHHH! WOOOOO!!! YES!!!
THANK YOU, PETER. HOW NICE TO RECEIVE SUCH A WARM INTRODUCTION FROM AN OLD FRIEND.
THANK YOU FOR INVITING ME TO BE YOUR KEYNOTE TODAY. I'D LIKE TO TALK ABOUT MY TEAM'S LATEST INNOVATION--
--THE POLYPHASIC REMOTE NEURAL NET DUAL TRANSPONDER. WE CALL IT "POLLY" FOR SHORT.
WOW. OKAY, SHE IS GOALS.
IMAGINE A LOVED ONE LOSING THEIR MEMORIES TO ALZHEIMER'S. OR LOSING THEIR PERSONALITY TO A TRAUMATIC BRAIN INJURY. THAT'S WHERE POLLY COMES IN.
memory download
POLLY ALLOWS US TO CAPTURE THE NEURAL ACTIVITY THAT MAKES US WHO WE ARE--OUR MEMORIES, PERSONALITIES, AND THOUGHTS--AND STORE IT REMOTELY.
IT MAY SOUND LIKE SCI-FI, BUT IT'S REAL, IT'S HERE AND IT'S--
PERFECT.

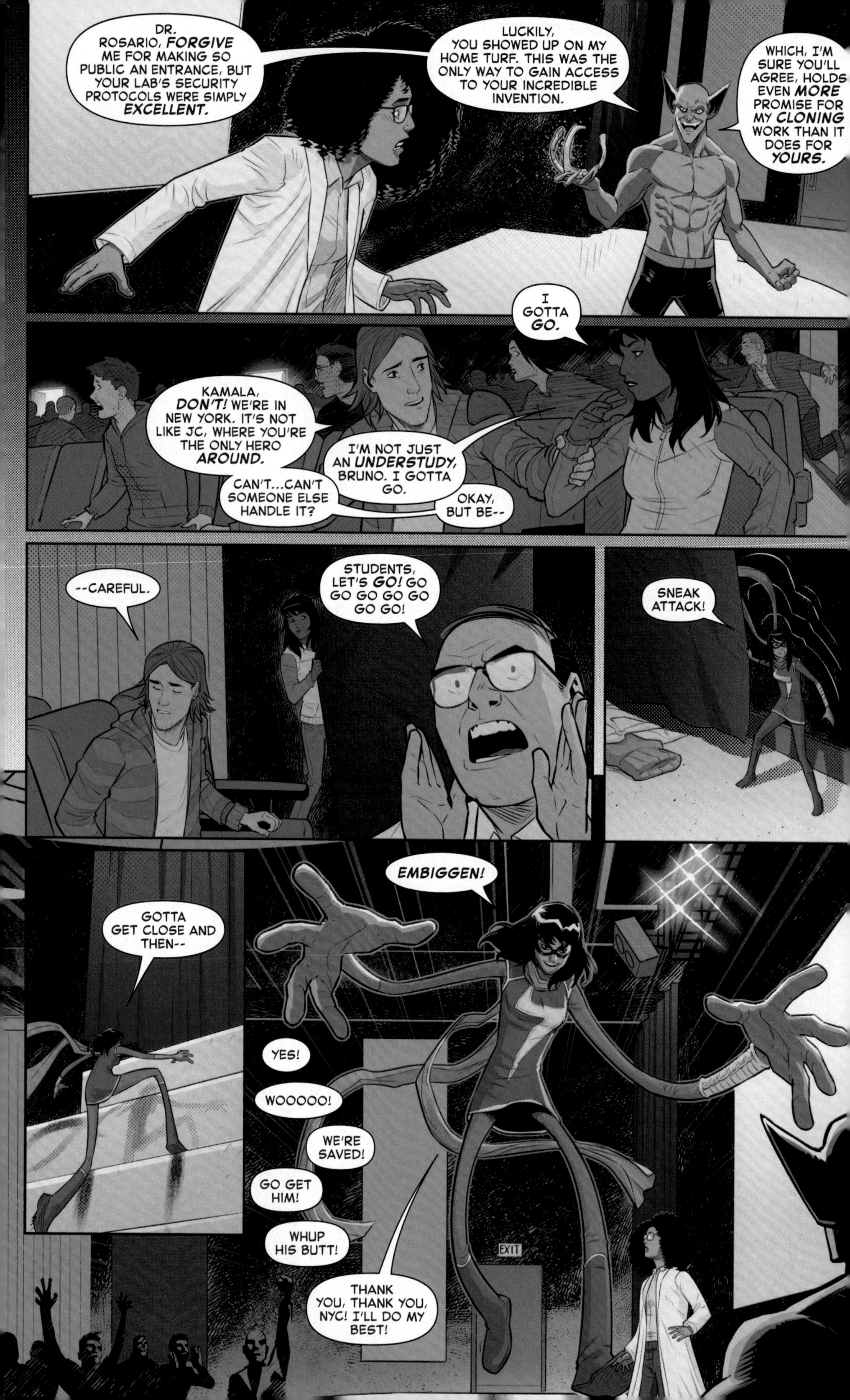
DR. ROSARIO, FORGIVE ME FOR MAKING SO PUBLIC AN ENTRANCE, BUT YOUR LAB'S SECURITY PROTOCOLS WERE SIMPLY EXCELLENT.
LUCKILY, YOU SHOWED UP ON MY HOME TURF. THIS WAS THE ONLY WAY TO GAIN ACCESS TO YOUR INCREDIBLE INVENTION.
WHICH, I'M SURE YOU'LL AGREE, HOLDS EVEN MORE PROMISE FOR MY CLONING WORK THAN IT DOES FOR YOURS.
I GOTTA GO.
KAMALA, DON'T! WE'RE IN NEW YORK. IT'S NOT LIKE JC, WHERE YOU'RE THE ONLY HERO AROUND.
I'M NOT JUST AN UNDERSTUDY, BRUNO. I GOTTA GO.
CAN'T...CAN'T SOMEONE ELSE HANDLE IT?
OKAY, BUT BE--
--CAREFUL.
STUDENTS, LET'S GO! GO GO GO GO GO GO GO!
SNEAK ATTACK!
GOTTA GET CLOSE AND THEN--
EMBIGGEN!
YES!
WOOOOO!
WE'RE SAVED!
GO GET HIM!
WHUP HIS BUTT!
THANK YOU, THANK YOU, NYC! I'LL DO MY BEST!
EXIT

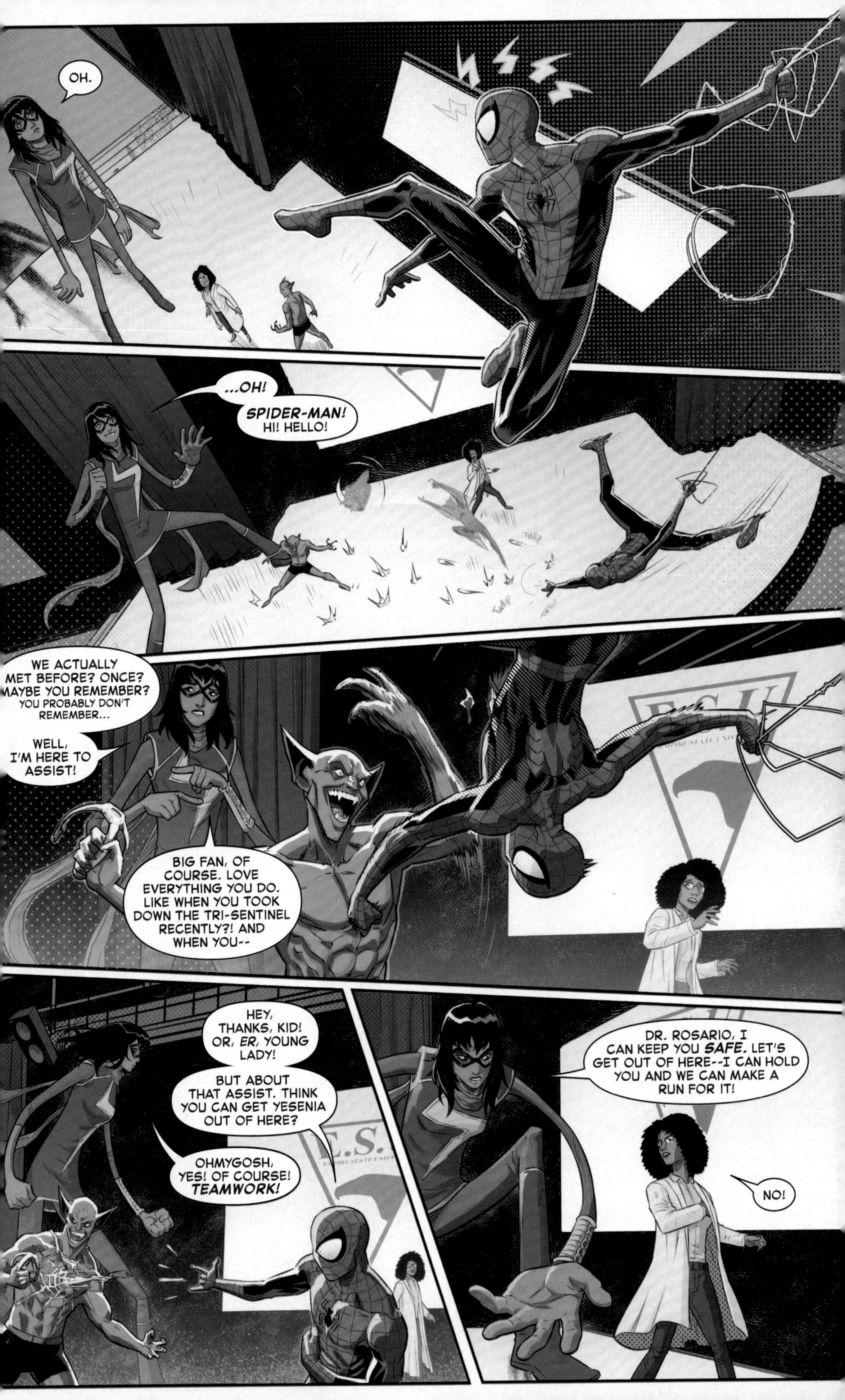
OH.
...OH! SPIDER-MAN! HI! HELLO!
THWIP
THWIP
THWIP
WE ACTUALLY MET BEFORE? ONCE? MAYBE YOU REMEMBER? YOU PROBABLY DON'T REMEMBER...
WELL, I'M HERE TO ASSIST!
BIG FAN, OF COURSE. LOVE EVERYTHING YOU DO. LIKE WHEN YOU TOOK DOWN THE TRI-SENTINEL RECENTLY?! AND WHEN YOU--
E.S.U.
EMPIRE STATE UNIV
HEY, THANKS, KID! OR, ER, YOUNG LADY!
BUT ABOUT THAT ASSIST. THINK YOU CAN GET YESENIA OUT OF HERE?
OHMYGOSH, YES! OF COURSE! TEAMWORK!
DR. ROSARIO, I CAN KEEP YOU SAFE. LET'S GET OUT OF HERE--I CAN HOLD YOU AND WE CAN MAKE A RUN FOR IT!
NO!

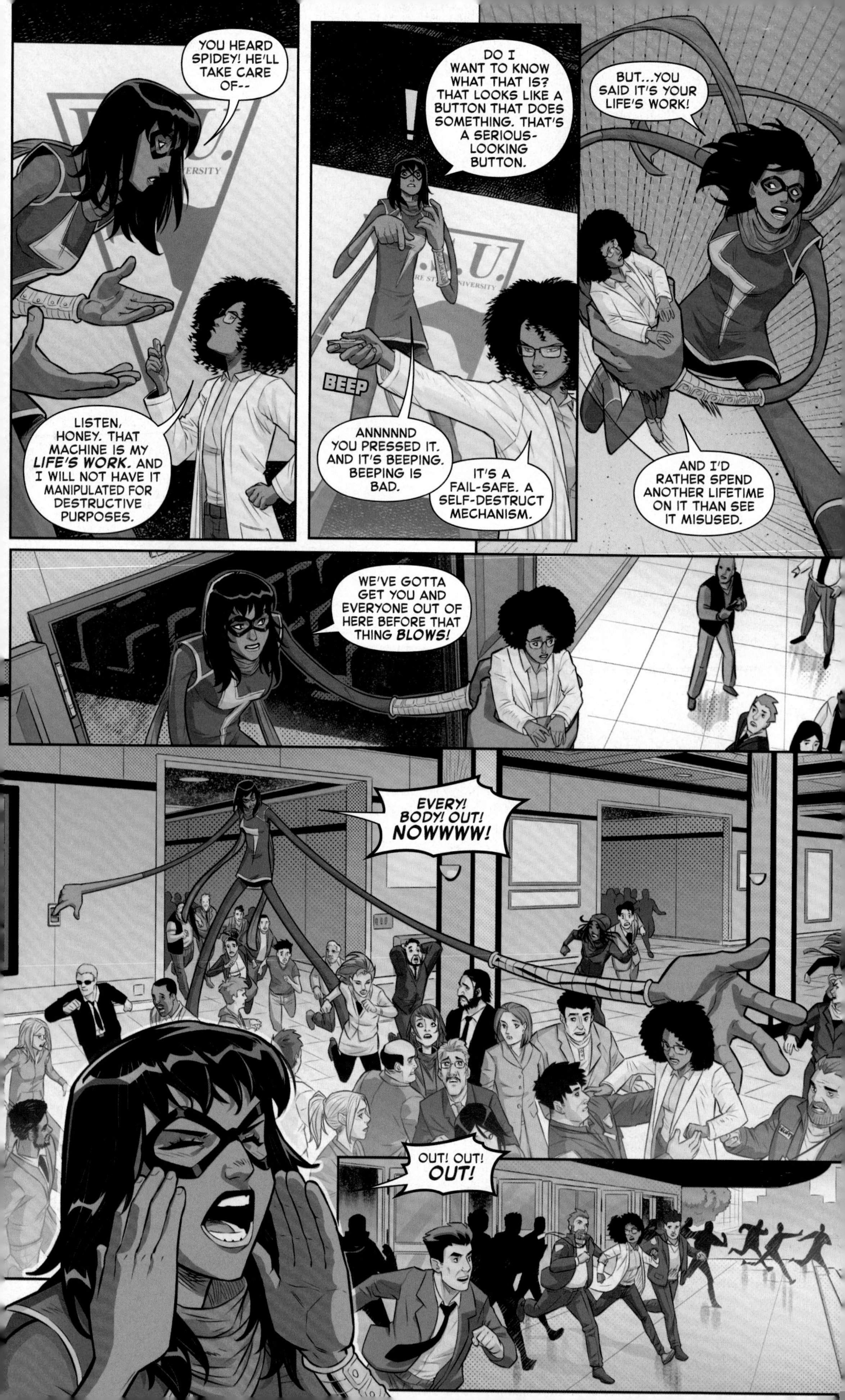
YOU HEARD SPIDEY! HE'LL TAKE CARE OF--
LISTEN, HONEY. THAT MACHINE IS MY LIFE'S WORK. AND I WILL NOT HAVE IT MANIPULATED FOR DESTRUCTIVE PURPOSES.
DO I WANT TO KNOW WHAT THAT IS? THAT LOOKS LIKE A BUTTON THAT DOES SOMETHING. THAT'S A SERIOUS-LOOKING BUTTON.
BEEP
ANNNNND YOU PRESSED IT. AND IT'S BEEPING. BEEPING IS BAD.
IT'S A FAIL-SAFE. A SELF-DESTRUCT MECHANISM.
BUT...YOU SAID IT'S YOUR LIFE'S WORK!
AND I'D RATHER SPEND ANOTHER LIFETIME ON IT THAN SEE IT MISUSED.
WE'VE GOTTA GET YOU AND EVERYONE OUT OF HERE BEFORE THAT THING BLOWS!
EVERY! BODY! OUT! NOWWWW!
OUT! OUT! OUT!

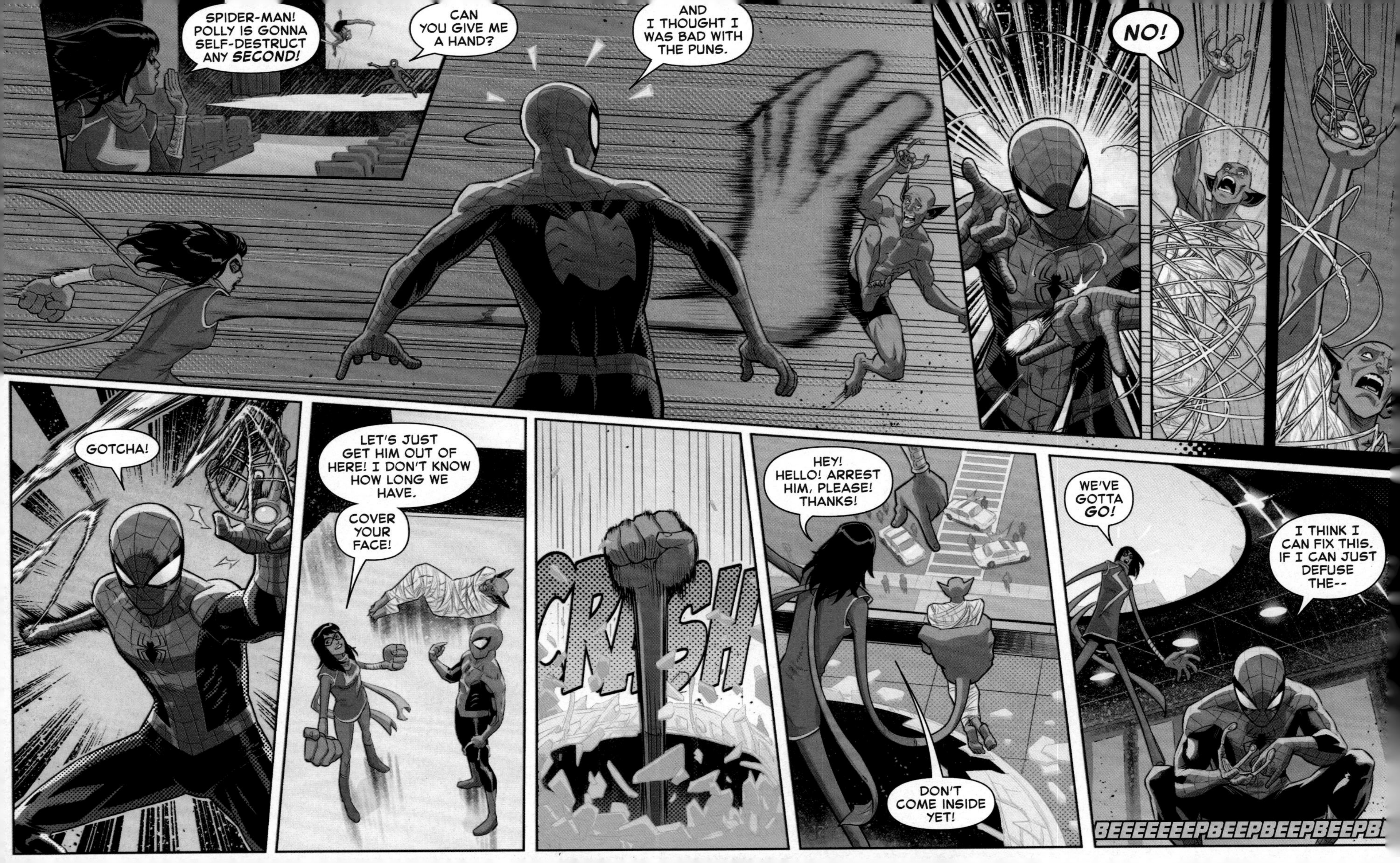
SPIDER-MAN! POLLY IS GONNA SELF-DESTRUCT ANY SECOND!
CAN YOU GIVE ME A HAND?
AND I THOUGHT I WAS BAD WITH THE PUNS.
NO!
GOTCHA!
LET'S JUST GET HIM OUT OF HERE! I DON'T KNOW HOW LONG WE HAVE.
COVER YOUR FACE!
CRASH
HEY! HELLO! ARREST HIM, PLEASE! THANKS!
DON'T COME INSIDE YET!
WE'VE GOTTA GO!
I THINK I CAN FIX THIS. IF I CAN JUST DEFUSE THE--
BEEEEEEEPBEEPBEEPBEEPB

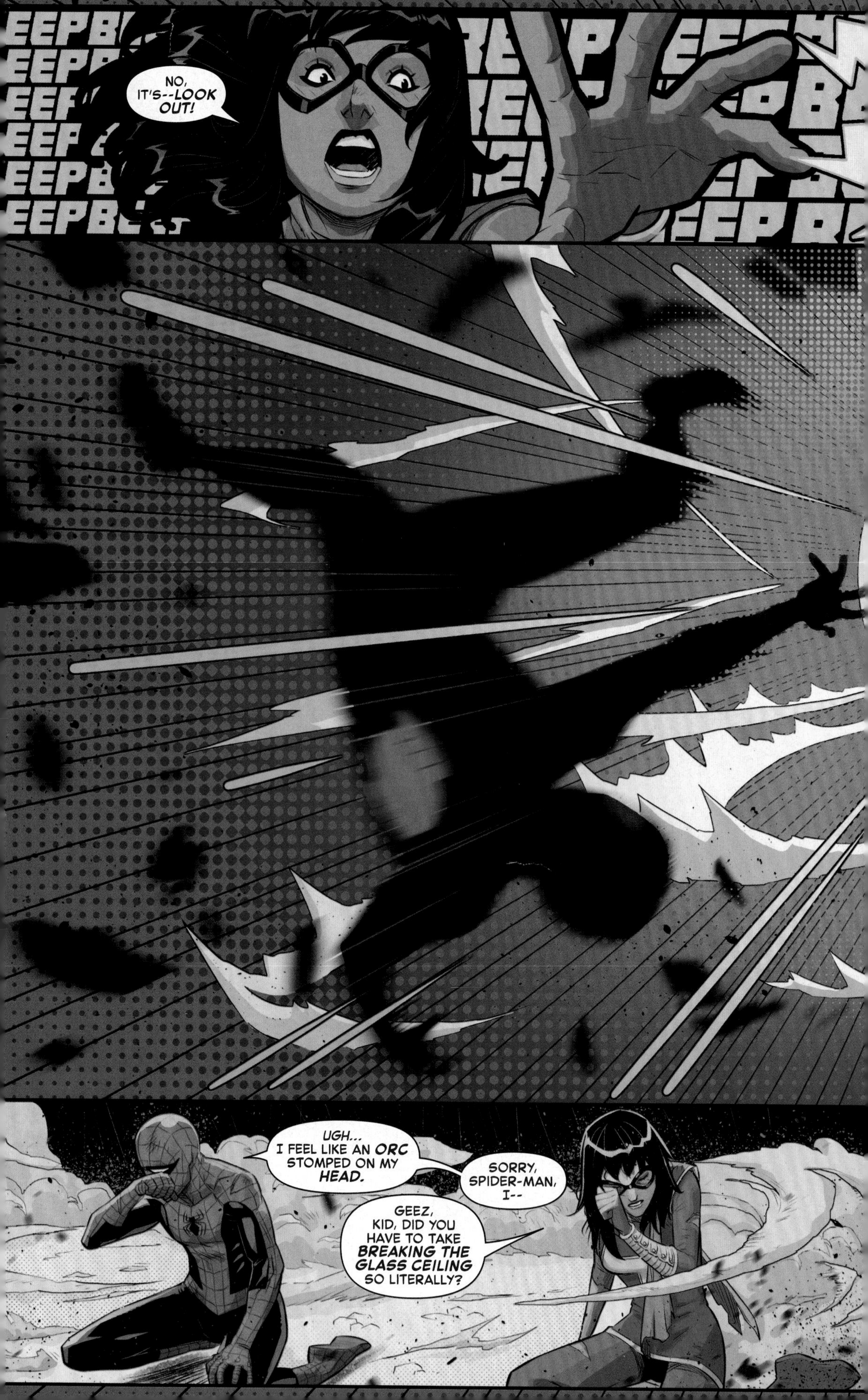
NO, IT'S--LOOK OUT!
UGH... I FEEL LIKE AN ORC STOMPED ON MY HEAD.
SORRY, SPIDER-MAN, I--
GEEZ, KID, DID YOU HAVE TO TAKE BREAKING THE GLASS CEILING SO LITERALLY?

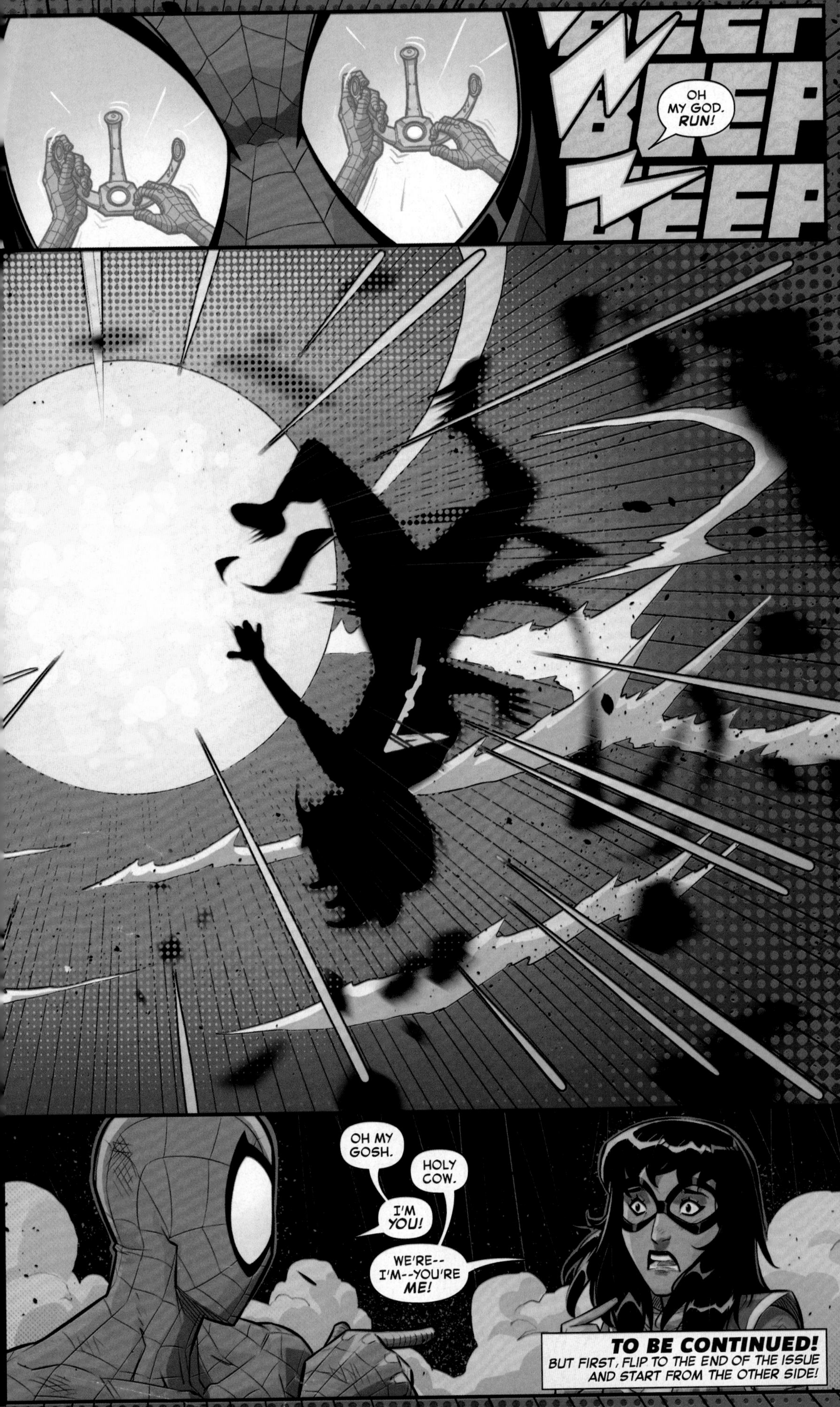
OH MY GOD. RUN!
OH MY GOSH.
HOLY COW.
I'M YOU!
WE'RE-- I'M--YOU'RE ME!
TO BE CONTINUED!
BUT FIRST, FLIP TO THE END OF THE ISSUE AND START FROM THE OTHER SIDE!

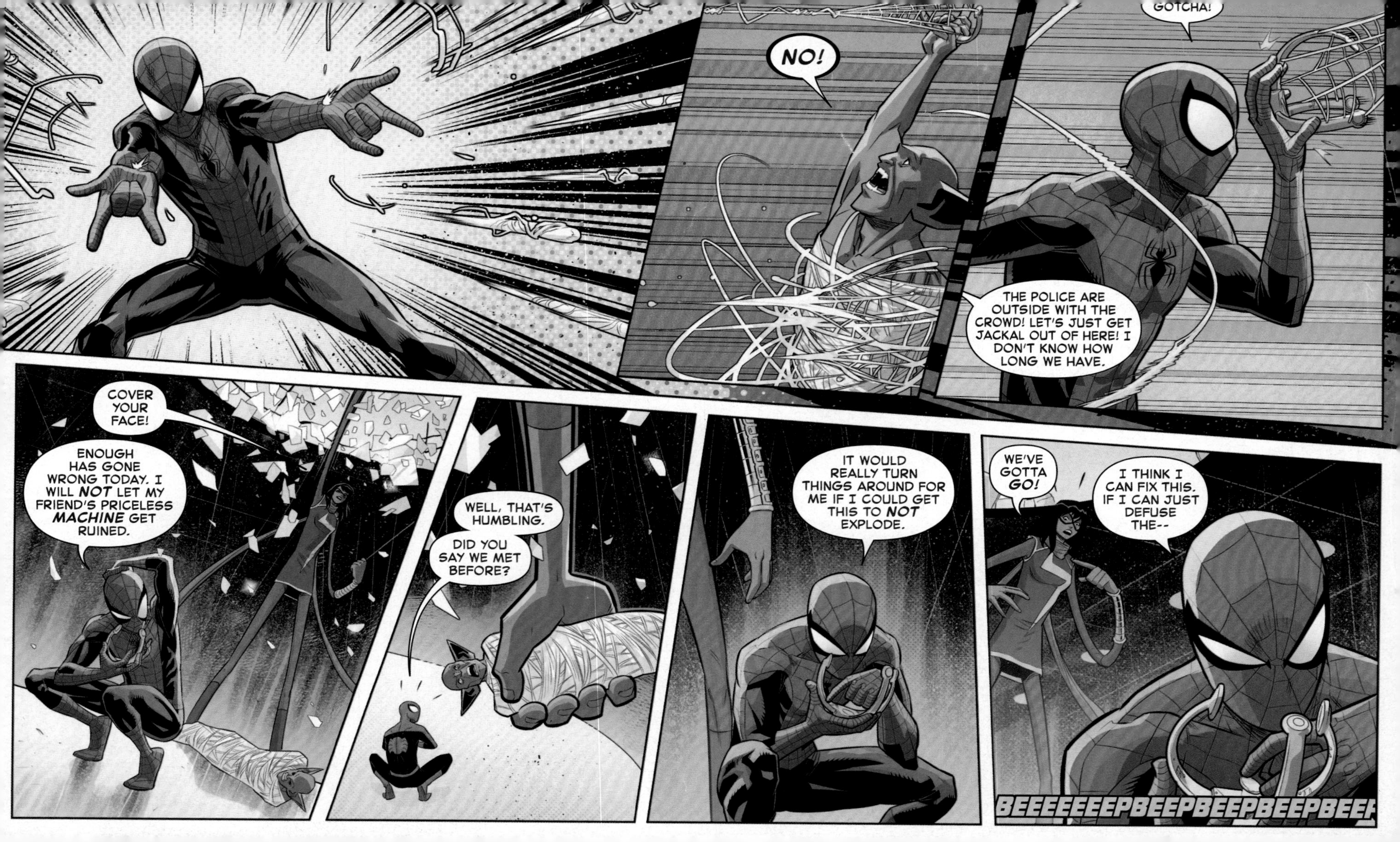
NO!
GOTCHA!
THE POLICE ARE OUTSIDE WITH THE CROWD! LET'S JUST GET JACKAL OUT OF HERE! I DON'T KNOW HOW LONG WE HAVE.
COVER YOUR FACE!
ENOUGH HAS GONE WRONG TODAY. I WILL **NOT** LET MY FRIEND'S PRICELESS ***MACHINE*** GET RUINED.
WELL, THAT'S HUMBLING.
DID YOU SAY WE MET BEFORE?
IT WOULD REALLY TURN THINGS AROUND FOR ME IF I COULD GET THIS TO ***NOT*** EXPLODE.
WE'VE GOTTA ***GO!***
I THINK I CAN FIX THIS. IF I CAN JUST DEFUSE THE--
BEEEEEEEPBEEPBEEPBEEPBEEPBEEP

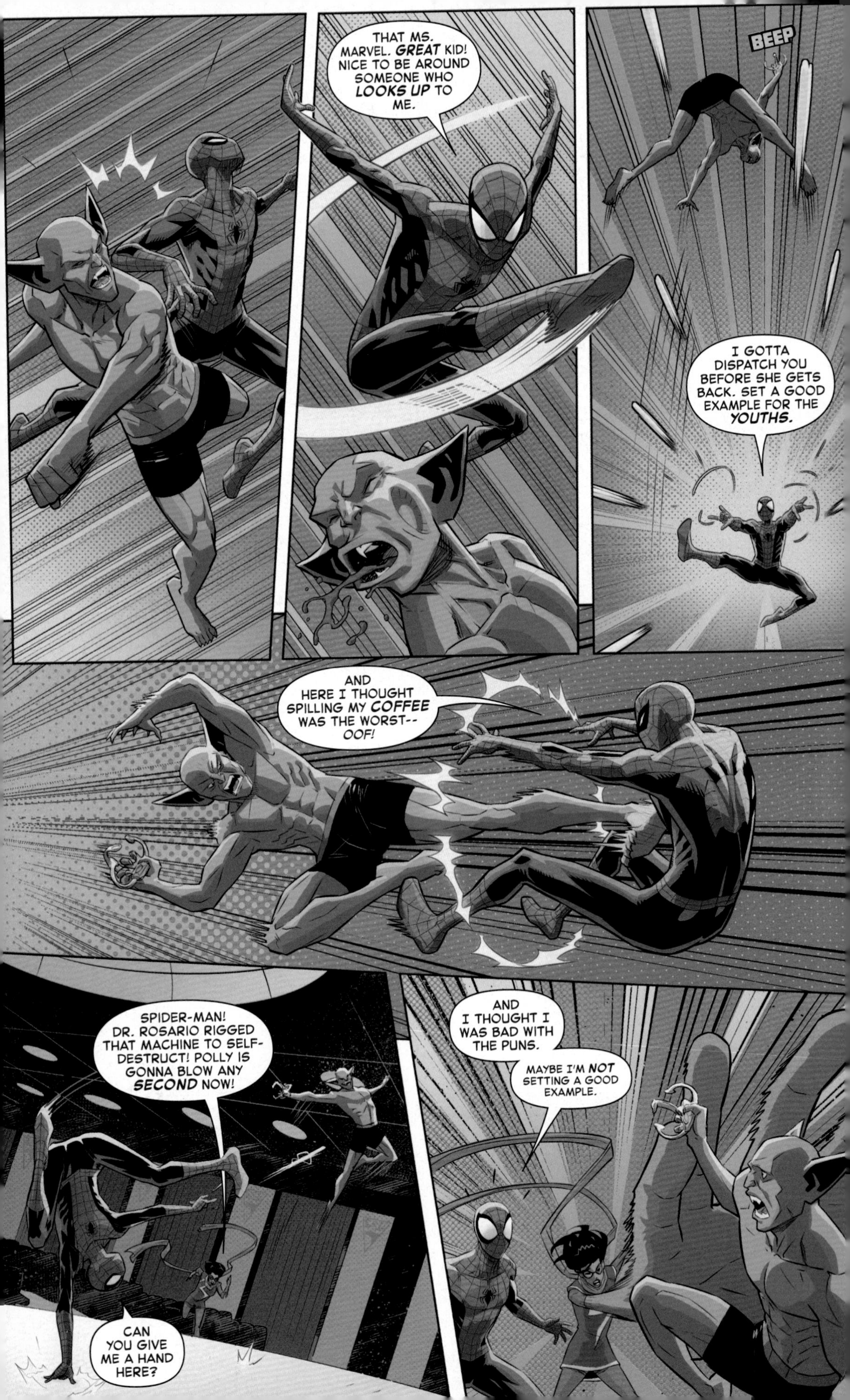
THAT MS. MARVEL. GREAT KID! NICE TO BE AROUND SOMEONE WHO LOOKS UP TO ME.
BEEP
I GOTTA DISPATCH YOU BEFORE SHE GETS BACK. SET A GOOD EXAMPLE FOR THE YOUTHS.
AND HERE I THOUGHT SPILLING MY COFFEE WAS THE WORST-- OOF!
SPIDER-MAN! DR. ROSARIO RIGGED THAT MACHINE TO SELF-DESTRUCT! POLLY IS GONNA BLOW ANY SECOND NOW!
CAN YOU GIVE ME A HAND HERE?
AND I THOUGHT I WAS BAD WITH THE PUNS.
MAYBE I'M NOT SETTING A GOOD EXAMPLE.

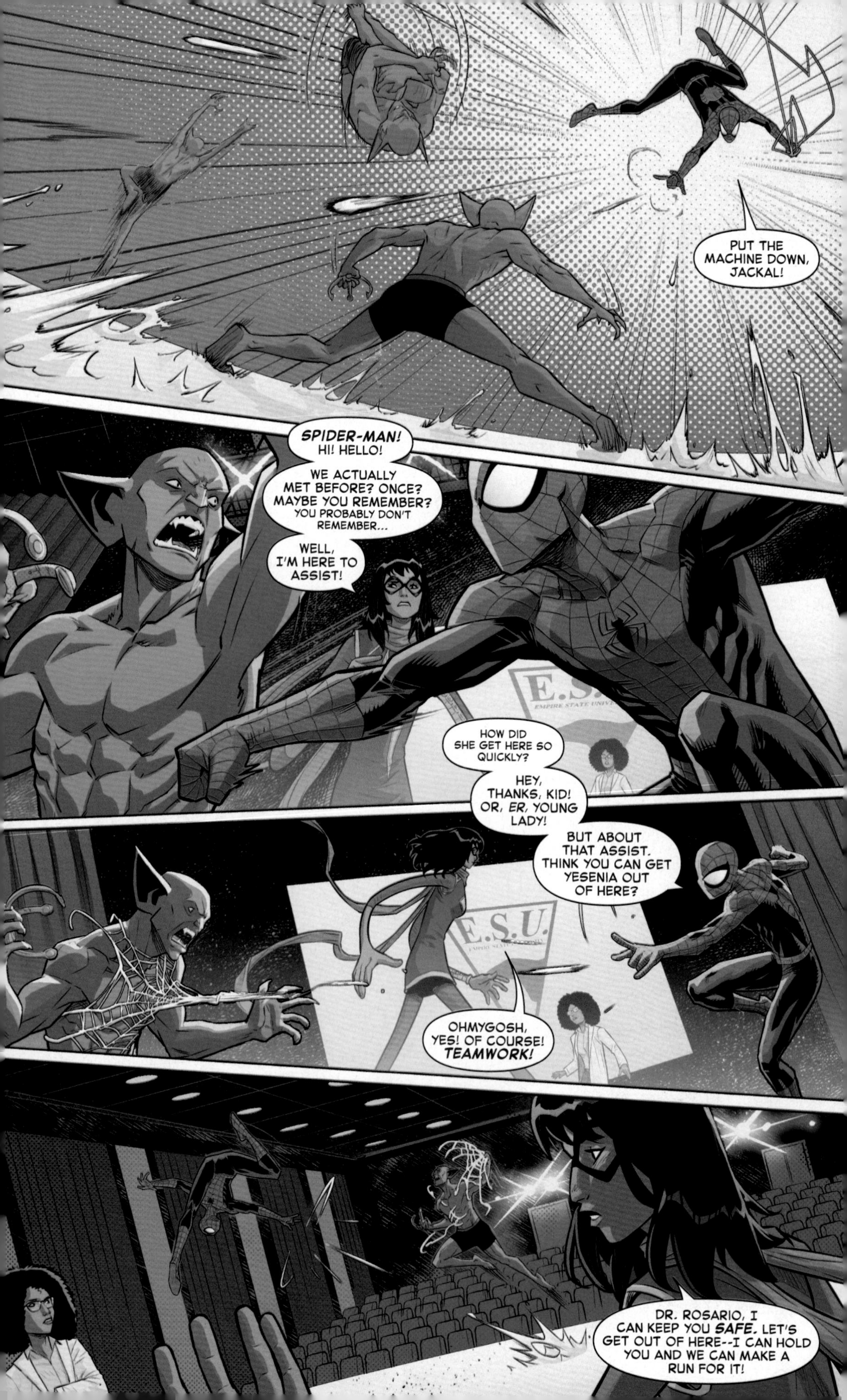
PUT THE MACHINE DOWN, JACKAL!
SPIDER-MAN! HI! HELLO!
WE ACTUALLY MET BEFORE? ONCE? MAYBE YOU REMEMBER? YOU PROBABLY DON'T REMEMBER...
WELL, I'M HERE TO ASSIST!
E.S.U.
EMPIRE STATE UNIV
HOW DID SHE GET HERE SO QUICKLY?
HEY, THANKS, KID! OR, *ER*, YOUNG LADY!
BUT ABOUT THAT ASSIST. THINK YOU CAN GET YESENIA OUT OF HERE?
E.S.U.
OHMYGOSH, YES! OF COURSE! ***TEAMWORK!***
DR. ROSARIO, I CAN KEEP YOU ***SAFE.*** LET'S GET OUT OF HERE--I CAN HOLD YOU AND WE CAN MAKE A RUN FOR IT!

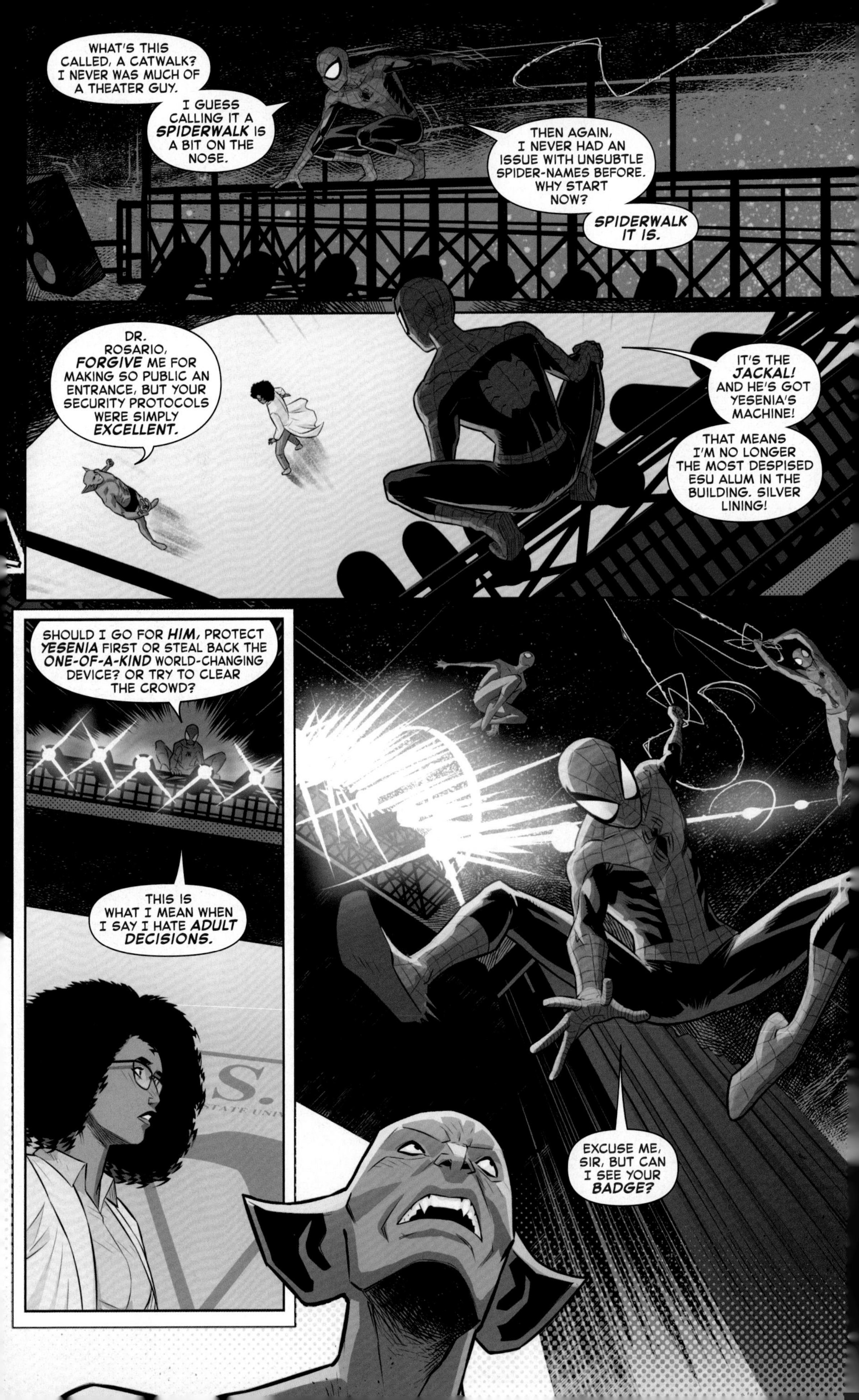
WHAT'S THIS CALLED, A CATWALK? I NEVER WAS MUCH OF A THEATER GUY.
I GUESS CALLING IT A *SPIDERWALK* IS A BIT ON THE NOSE.
THEN AGAIN, I NEVER HAD AN ISSUE WITH UNSUBTLE SPIDER-NAMES BEFORE. WHY START NOW?
SPIDERWALK *IT IS.*
DR. ROSARIO, *FORGIVE* ME FOR MAKING SO PUBLIC AN ENTRANCE, BUT YOUR SECURITY PROTOCOLS WERE SIMPLY *EXCELLENT.*
IT'S THE *JACKAL!* AND HE'S GOT YESENIA'S MACHINE!
THAT MEANS I'M NO LONGER THE MOST DESPISED ESU ALUM IN THE BUILDING. SILVER LINING!
SHOULD I GO FOR *HIM,* PROTECT *YESENIA* FIRST OR STEAL BACK THE *ONE-OF-A-KIND* WORLD-CHANGING DEVICE? OR TRY TO CLEAR THE CROWD?
THIS IS WHAT I MEAN WHEN I SAY I HATE *ADULT DECISIONS.*
EXCUSE ME, SIR, BUT CAN I SEE YOUR *BADGE?*

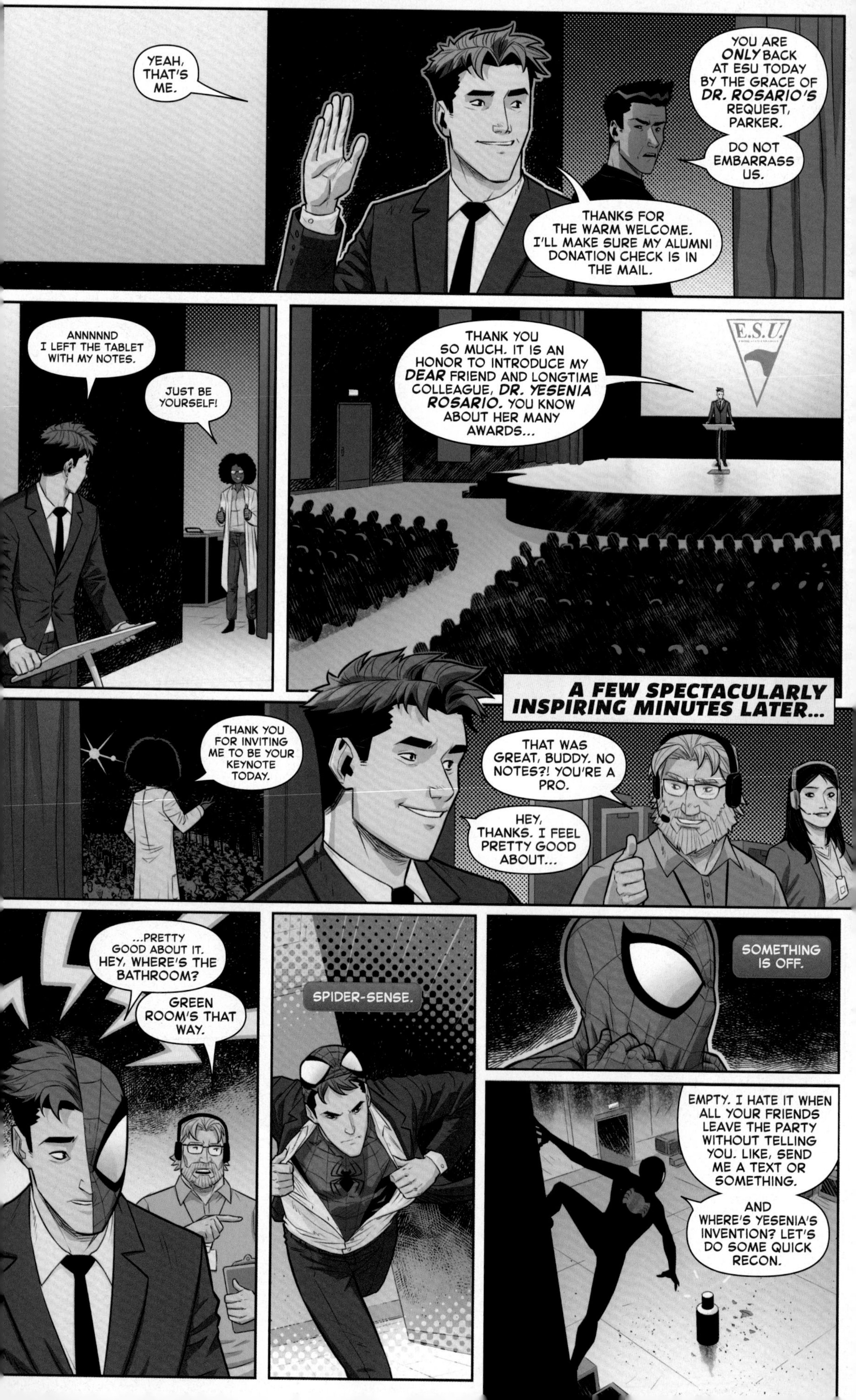
YEAH, THAT'S ME.
YOU ARE ONLY BACK AT ESU TODAY BY THE GRACE OF DR. ROSARIO'S REQUEST, PARKER.
DO NOT EMBARRASS US.
THANKS FOR THE WARM WELCOME. I'LL MAKE SURE MY ALUMNI DONATION CHECK IS IN THE MAIL.
ANNNNND I LEFT THE TABLET WITH MY NOTES.
JUST BE YOURSELF!
THANK YOU SO MUCH. IT IS AN HONOR TO INTRODUCE MY DEAR FRIEND AND LONGTIME COLLEAGUE, DR. YESENIA ROSARIO. YOU KNOW ABOUT HER MANY AWARDS...
E.S.U.
A FEW SPECTACULARLY INSPIRING MINUTES LATER...
THANK YOU FOR INVITING ME TO BE YOUR KEYNOTE TODAY.
THAT WAS GREAT, BUDDY. NO NOTES?! YOU'RE A PRO.
HEY, THANKS. I FEEL PRETTY GOOD ABOUT...
...PRETTY GOOD ABOUT IT. HEY, WHERE'S THE BATHROOM?
GREEN ROOM'S THAT WAY.
SPIDER-SENSE.
SOMETHING IS OFF.
EMPTY. I HATE IT WHEN ALL YOUR FRIENDS LEAVE THE PARTY WITHOUT TELLING YOU. LIKE, SEND ME A TEXT OR SOMETHING.
AND WHERE'S YESENIA'S INVENTION? LET'S DO SOME QUICK RECON.

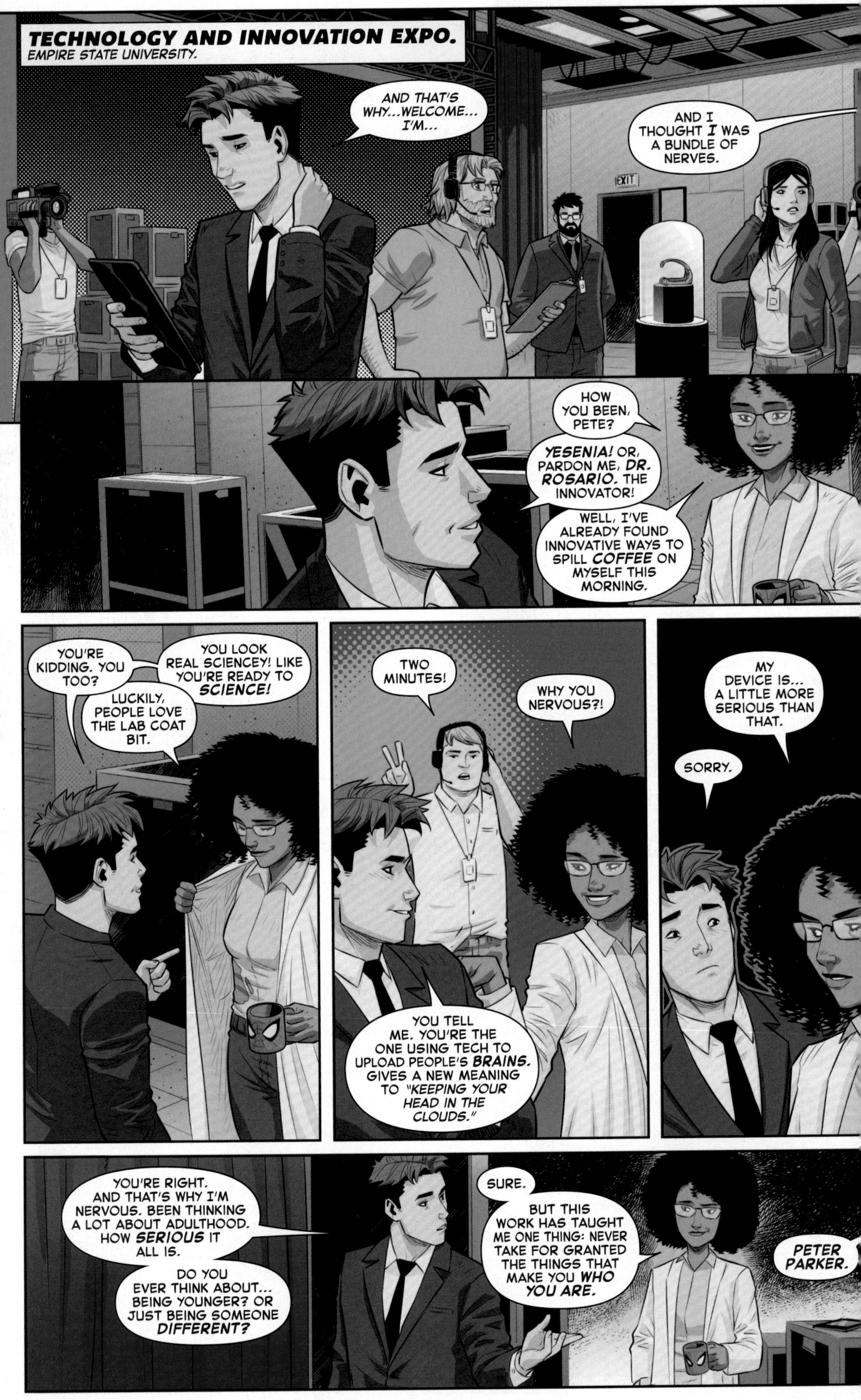
TECHNOLOGY AND INNOVATION EXPO.
EMPIRE STATE UNIVERSITY.
AND THAT'S WHY...WELCOME... I'M...
AND I THOUGHT I WAS A BUNDLE OF NERVES.
EXIT
HOW YOU BEEN, PETE?
YESENIA! OR, PARDON ME, DR. ROSARIO. THE INNOVATOR!
WELL, I'VE ALREADY FOUND INNOVATIVE WAYS TO SPILL COFFEE ON MYSELF THIS MORNING.
YOU LOOK REAL SCIENCEY! LIKE YOU'RE READY TO SCIENCE!
YOU'RE KIDDING. YOU TOO?
LUCKILY, PEOPLE LOVE THE LAB COAT BIT.
TWO MINUTES!
WHY YOU NERVOUS?!
YOU TELL ME. YOU'RE THE ONE USING TECH TO UPLOAD PEOPLE'S BRAINS. GIVES A NEW MEANING TO "KEEPING YOUR HEAD IN THE CLOUDS."
MY DEVICE IS... A LITTLE MORE SERIOUS THAN THAT.
SORRY.
YOU'RE RIGHT. AND THAT'S WHY I'M NERVOUS. BEEN THINKING A LOT ABOUT ADULTHOOD. HOW SERIOUS IT ALL IS.
DO YOU EVER THINK ABOUT... BEING YOUNGER? OR JUST BEING SOMEONE DIFFERENT?
SURE.
BUT THIS WORK HAS TAUGHT ME ONE THING: NEVER TAKE FOR GRANTED THE THINGS THAT MAKE YOU WHO YOU ARE.
PETER PARKER.

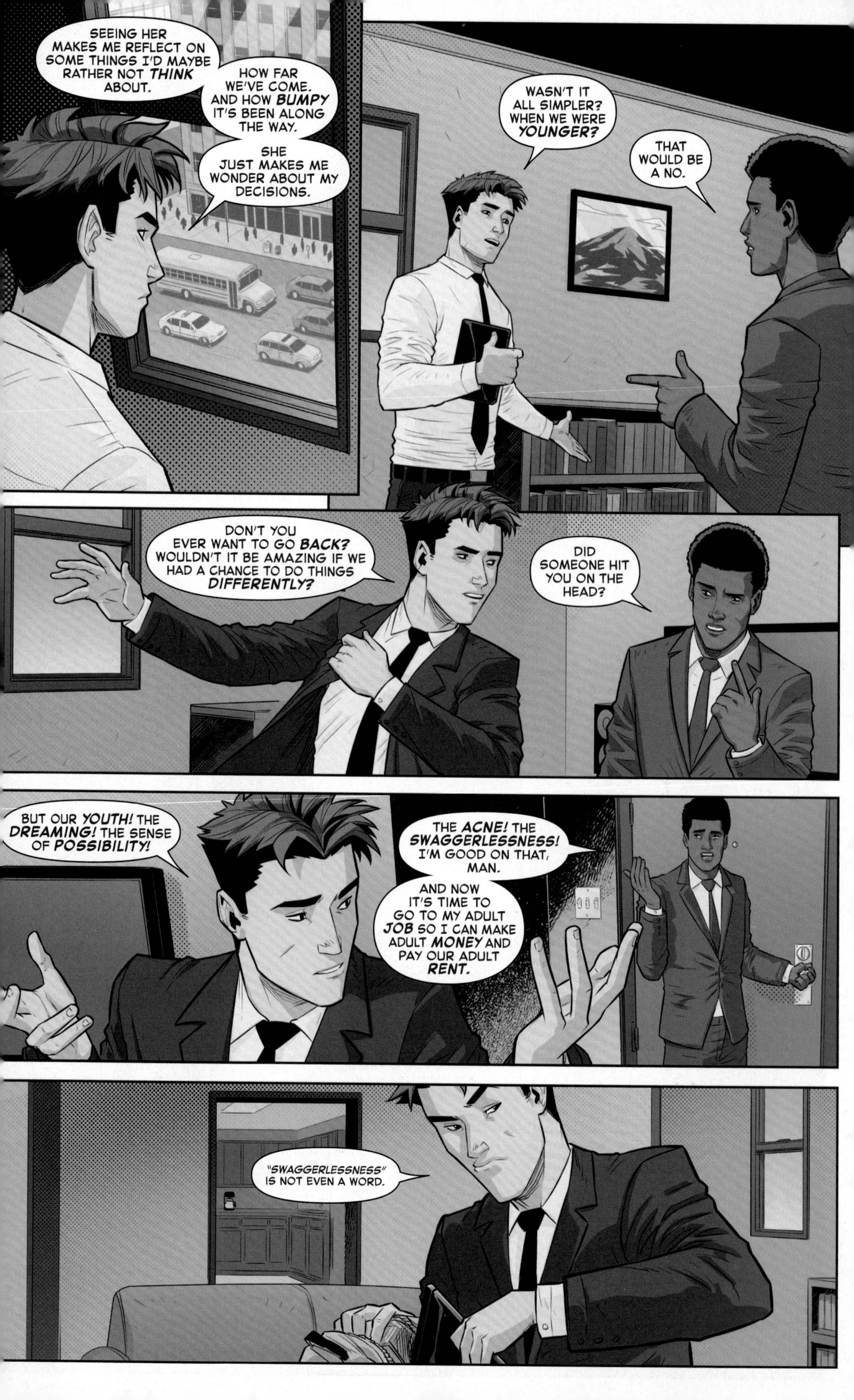
SEEING HER MAKES ME REFLECT ON SOME THINGS I'D MAYBE RATHER NOT *THINK* ABOUT.
HOW FAR WE'VE COME. AND HOW *BUMPY* IT'S BEEN ALONG THE WAY.
SHE JUST MAKES ME WONDER ABOUT MY DECISIONS.
WASN'T IT ALL SIMPLER? WHEN WE WERE *YOUNGER?*
THAT WOULD BE A NO.
DON'T YOU EVER WANT TO GO *BACK?* WOULDN'T IT BE AMAZING IF WE HAD A CHANCE TO DO THINGS *DIFFERENTLY?*
DID SOMEONE HIT YOU ON THE HEAD?
BUT OUR *YOUTH!* THE *DREAMING!* THE SENSE OF *POSSIBILITY!*
THE *ACNE!* THE *SWAGGERLESSNESS!* I'M GOOD ON THAT, MAN.
AND NOW IT'S TIME TO GO TO MY ADULT *JOB* SO I CAN MAKE ADULT *MONEY* AND PAY OUR ADULT *RENT.*
"SWAGGERLESSNESS" IS NOT EVEN A WORD.

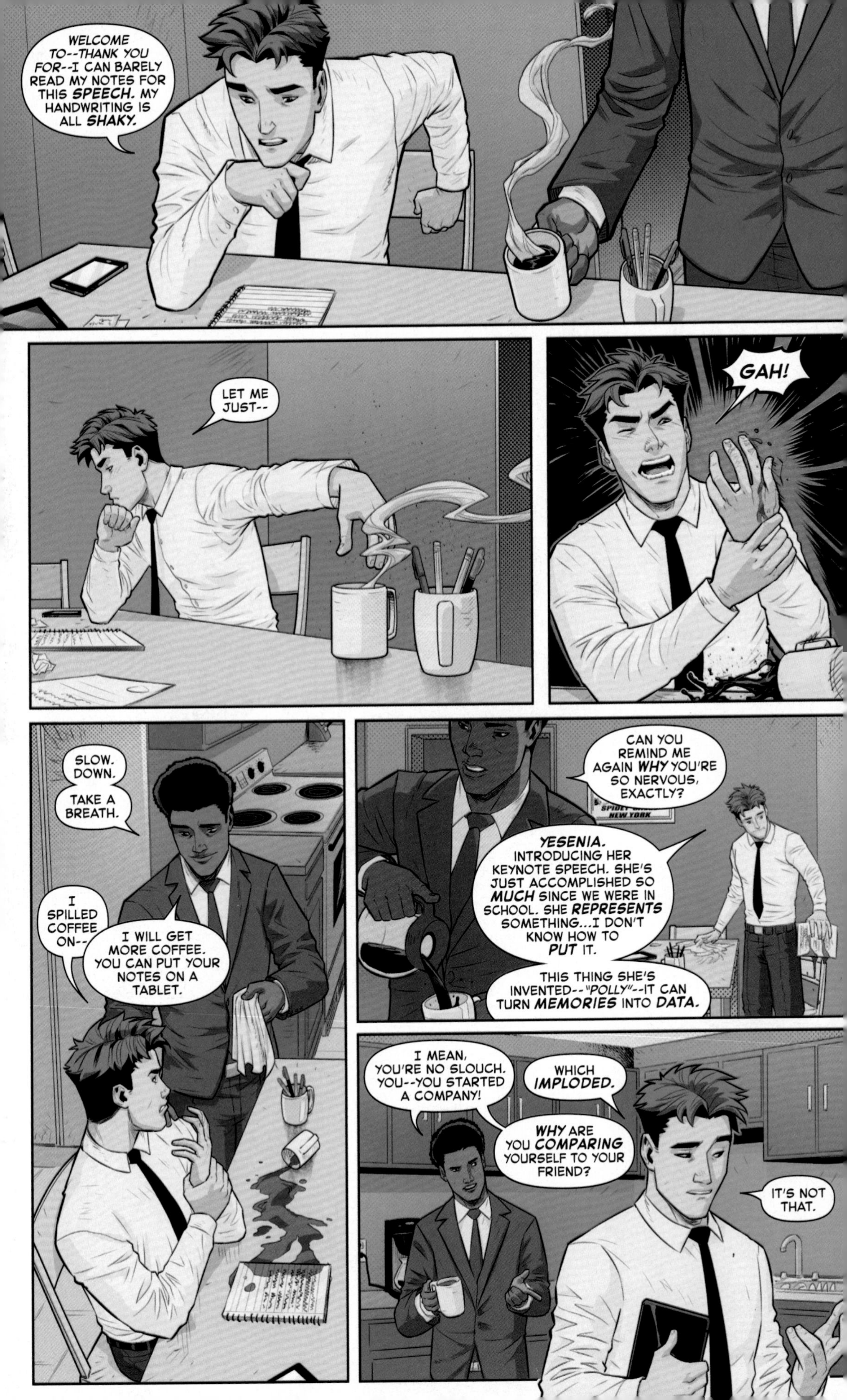
WELCOME TO--THANK YOU FOR--I CAN BARELY READ MY NOTES FOR THIS SPEECH. MY HANDWRITING IS ALL SHAKY.
LET ME JUST--
GAH!
SLOW. DOWN.
TAKE A BREATH.
I SPILLED COFFEE ON--
I WILL GET MORE COFFEE. YOU CAN PUT YOUR NOTES ON A TABLET.
CAN YOU REMIND ME AGAIN WHY YOU'RE SO NERVOUS, EXACTLY?
YESENIA. INTRODUCING HER KEYNOTE SPEECH. SHE'S JUST ACCOMPLISHED SO MUCH SINCE WE WERE IN SCHOOL. SHE REPRESENTS SOMETHING...I DON'T KNOW HOW TO PUT IT.
THIS THING SHE'S INVENTED--"POLLY"--IT CAN TURN MEMORIES INTO DATA.
NEW YORK
I MEAN, YOU'RE NO SLOUCH. YOU--YOU STARTED A COMPANY!
WHICH IMPLODED.
WHY ARE YOU COMPARING YOURSELF TO YOUR FRIEND?
IT'S NOT THAT.

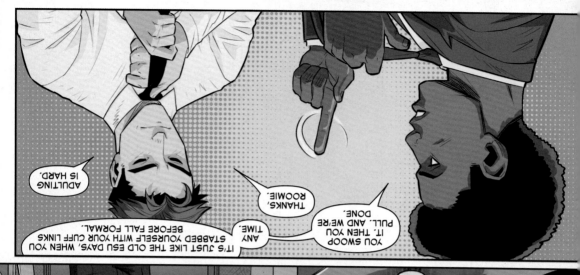

ADULTING IS HARD.

THANKS, ROOMIE.

YOU SWOOP IT, THEN YOU PULL, AND WE'RE DONE.

ANY TIME.

IT'S JUST LIKE THE OLD ESU DAYS, WHEN YOU STABBED YOURSELF WITH YOUR CUFF LINKS BEFORE FALL FORMAL.

I DO NOT.

DO YOU WANT MY HONEST ANSWER?

ISN'T JACKET-AND-NO-TIE THE PREFERRED LOOK THESE DAYS, RANDY?

NAH, THAT'LL JUST GIVE ME JITTERS. I'M ALREADY SO NERVOUS.

THERE'S STILL SOME COFFEE IF YOU WANT.

YOU ASKED ME TO TELL YOU WHEN IT WAS TIME TO GO TO THE CONFERENCE.

AND IT WAS TIME TO GO TEN MINUTES AGO.

YES?

YO, PETE!

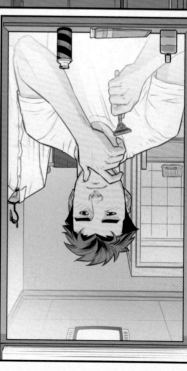

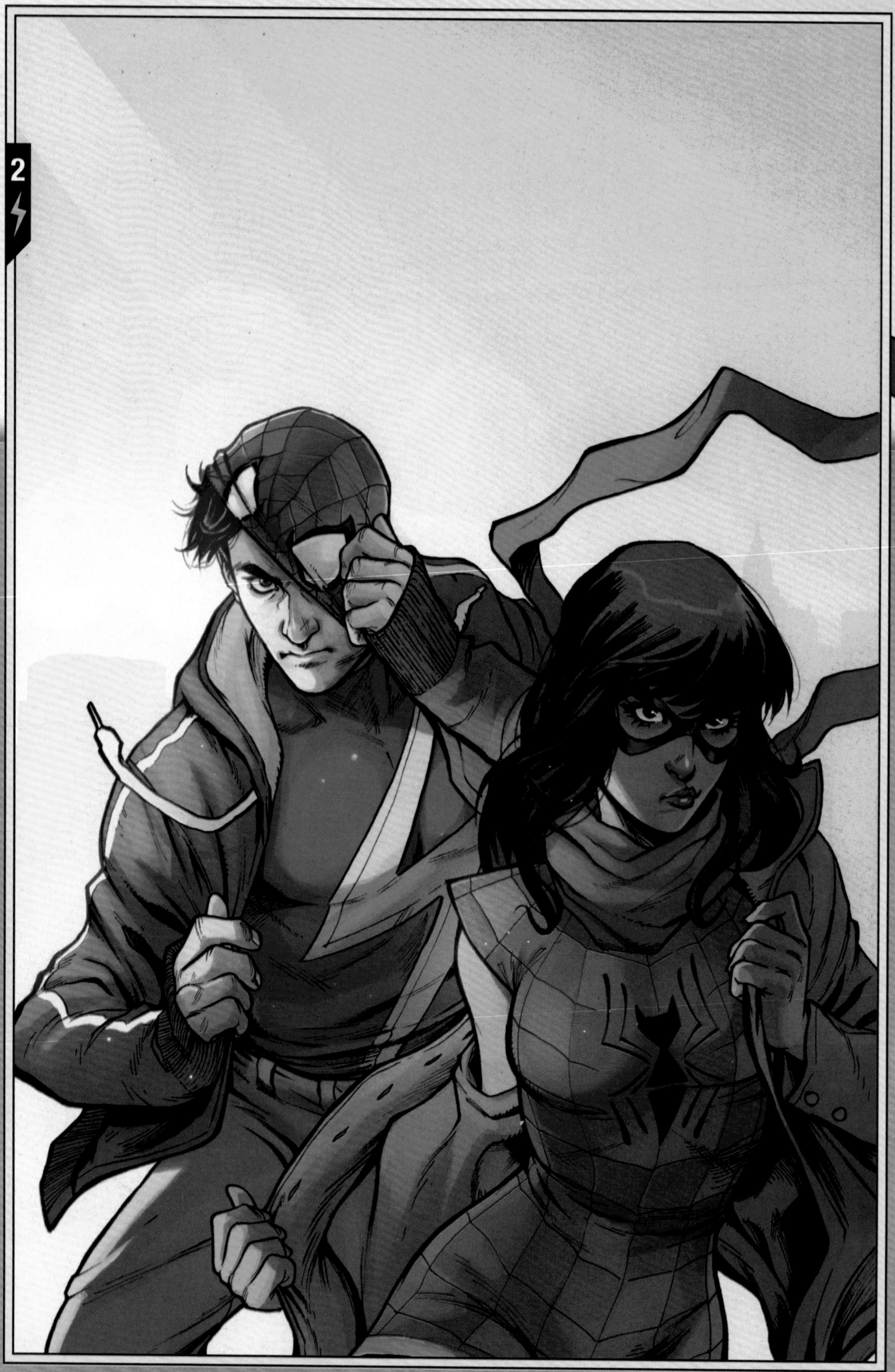
2

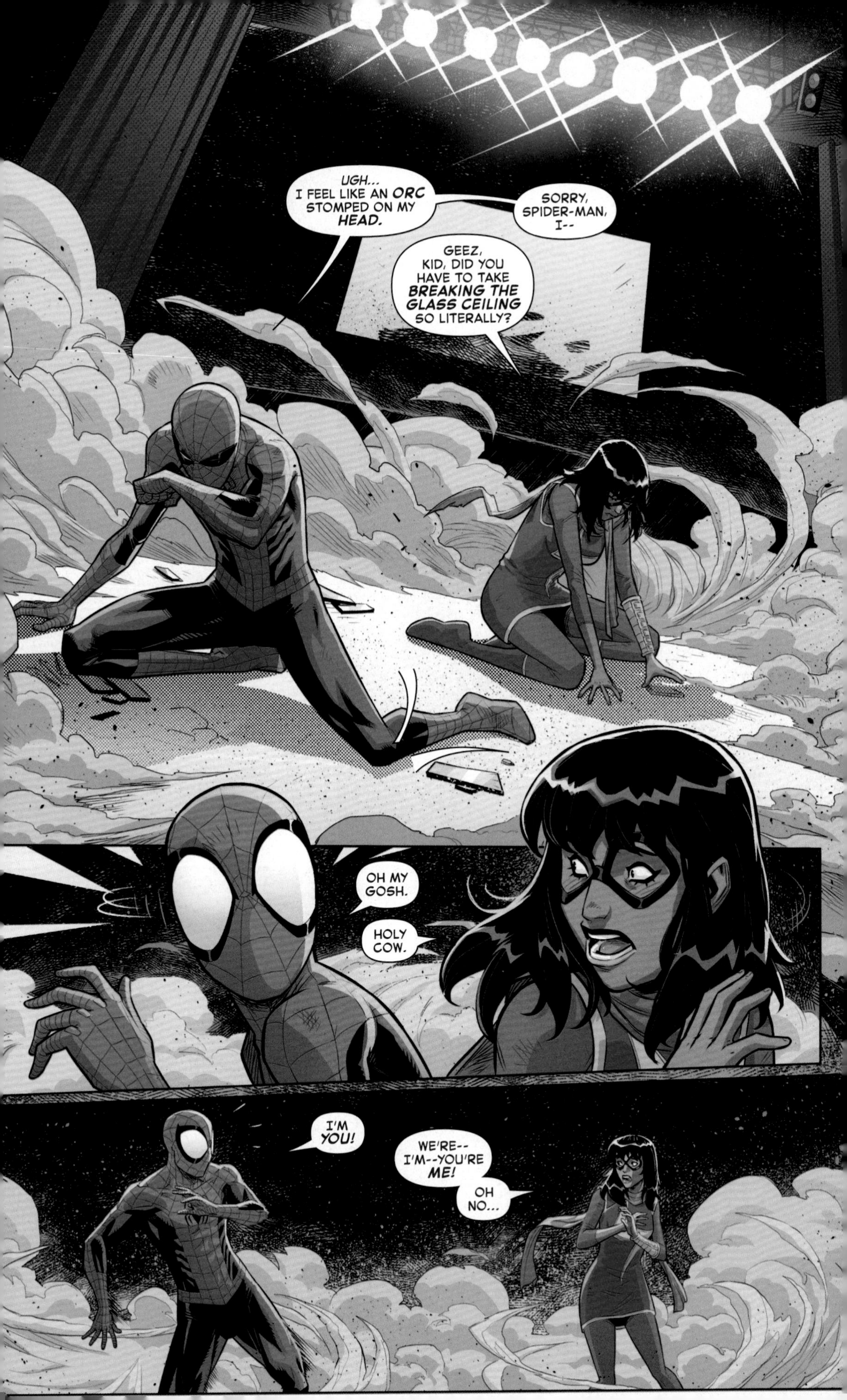
UGH... I FEEL LIKE AN ORC STOMPED ON MY HEAD.
SORRY, SPIDER-MAN, I--
GEEZ, KID, DID YOU HAVE TO TAKE BREAKING THE GLASS CEILING SO LITERALLY?
OH MY GOSH.
HOLY COW.
I'M YOU!
WE'RE--I'M--YOU'RE ME!
OH NO...

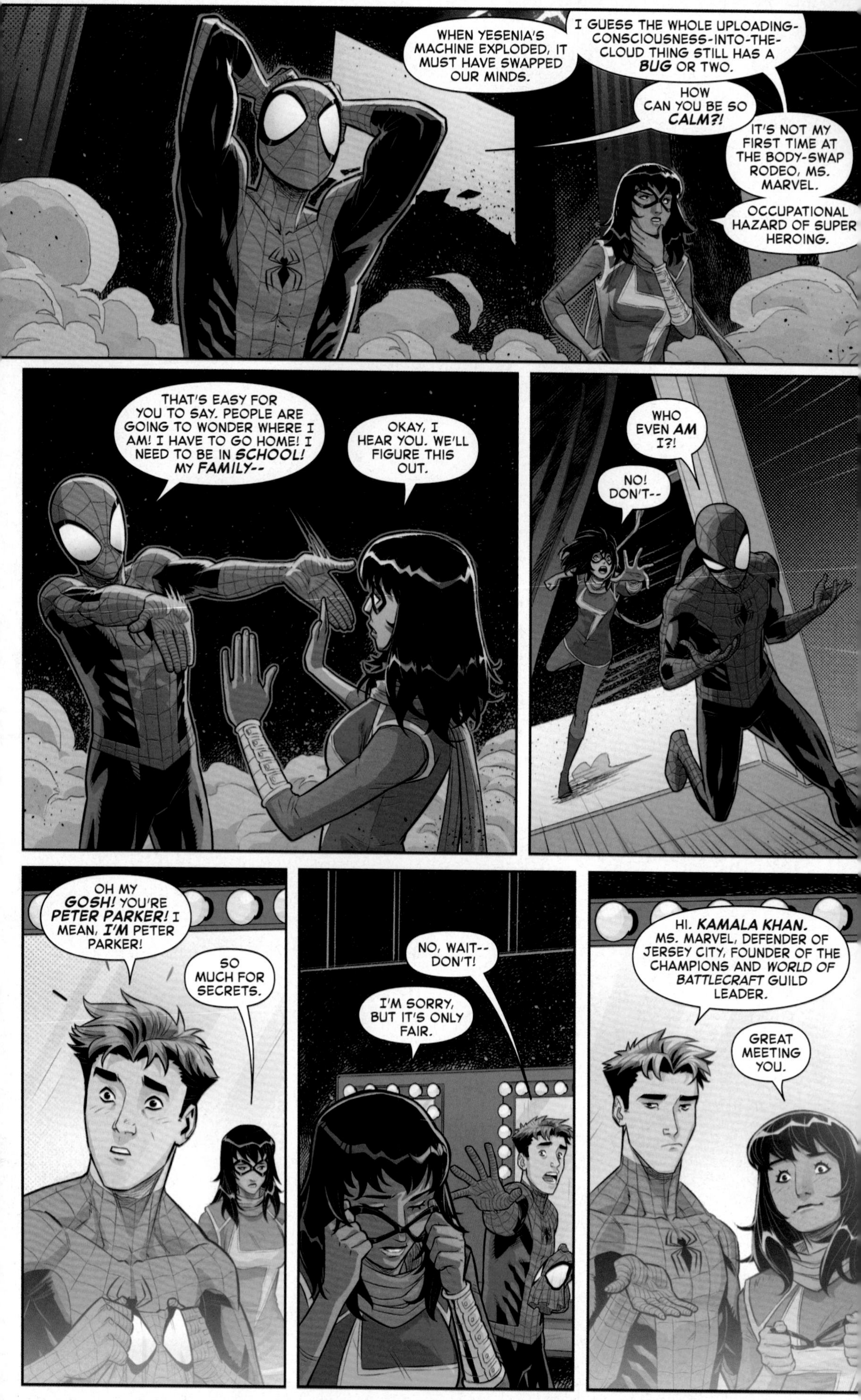

WHEN YESENIA'S MACHINE EXPLODED, IT MUST HAVE SWAPPED OUR MINDS.
I GUESS THE WHOLE UPLOADING-CONSCIOUSNESS-INTO-THE-CLOUD THING STILL HAS A BUG OR TWO.
HOW CAN YOU BE SO CALM?!
IT'S NOT MY FIRST TIME AT THE BODY-SWAP RODEO, MS. MARVEL.
OCCUPATIONAL HAZARD OF SUPER HEROING.
THAT'S EASY FOR YOU TO SAY. PEOPLE ARE GOING TO WONDER WHERE I AM! I HAVE TO GO HOME! I NEED TO BE IN SCHOOL! MY FAMILY--
OKAY, I HEAR YOU. WE'LL FIGURE THIS OUT.
WHO EVEN AM I?!
NO! DON'T--
OH MY GOSH! YOU'RE PETER PARKER! I MEAN, I'M PETER PARKER!
SO MUCH FOR SECRETS.
NO, WAIT-- DON'T!
I'M SORRY, BUT IT'S ONLY FAIR.
HI. KAMALA KHAN. MS. MARVEL, DEFENDER OF JERSEY CITY, FOUNDER OF THE CHAMPIONS AND WORLD OF BATTLECRAFT GUILD LEADER.
GREAT MEETING YOU.

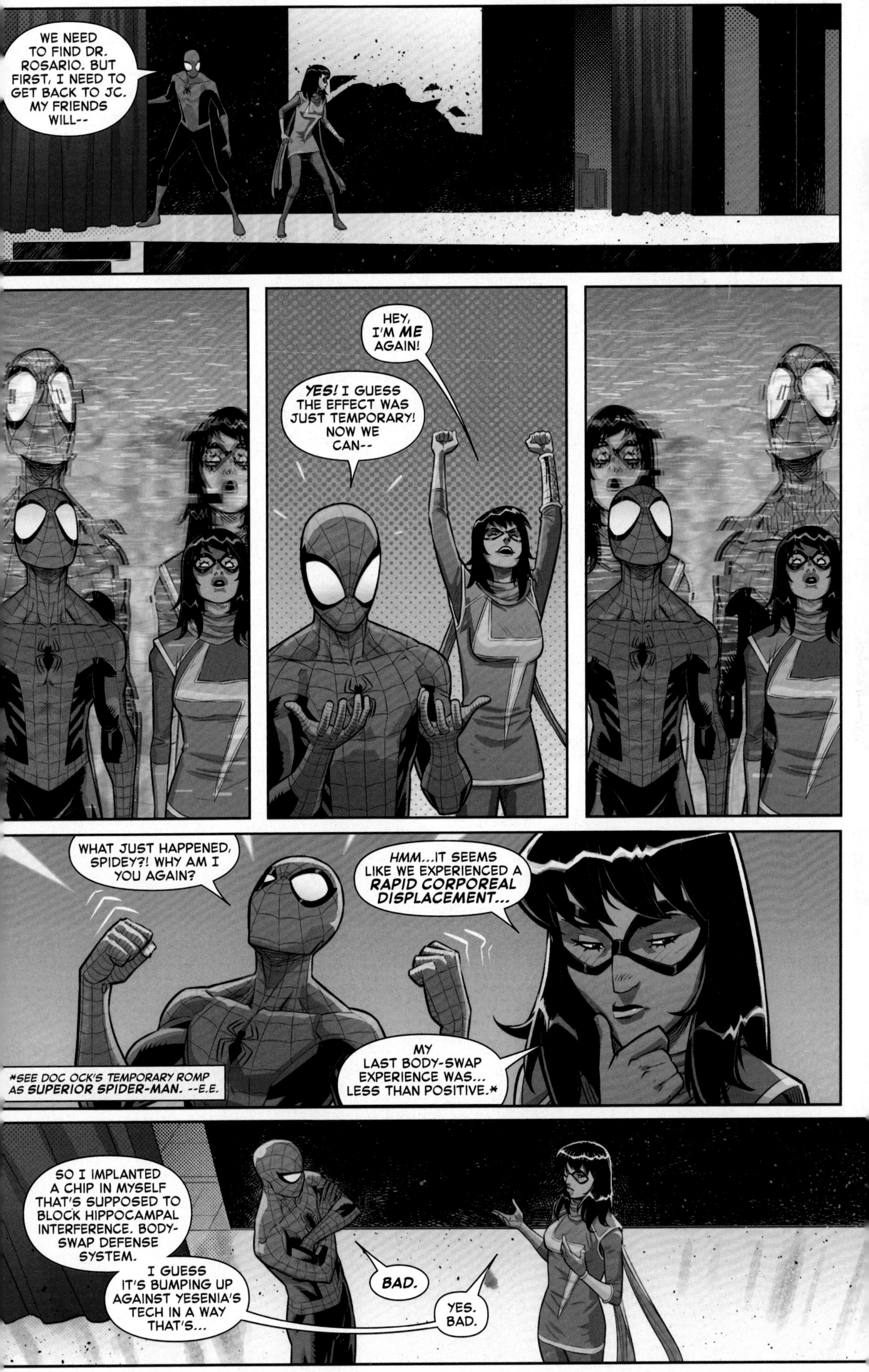

WE NEED TO FIND DR. ROSARIO. BUT FIRST, I NEED TO GET BACK TO JC. MY FRIENDS WILL--
HEY, I'M *ME* AGAIN!
YES! I GUESS THE EFFECT WAS JUST TEMPORARY! NOW WE CAN--
WHAT JUST HAPPENED, SPIDEY?! WHY AM I YOU AGAIN?
HMM...IT SEEMS LIKE WE EXPERIENCED A *RAPID CORPOREAL DISPLACEMENT*...
MY LAST BODY-SWAP EXPERIENCE WAS... LESS THAN POSITIVE.*
*SEE DOC OCK'S TEMPORARY ROMP AS *SUPERIOR SPIDER-MAN*. --E.E.
SO I IMPLANTED A CHIP IN MYSELF THAT'S SUPPOSED TO BLOCK HIPPOCAMPAL INTERFERENCE. BODY-SWAP DEFENSE SYSTEM.
I GUESS IT'S BUMPING UP AGAINST YESENIA'S TECH IN A WAY THAT'S...
BAD.
YES. BAD.

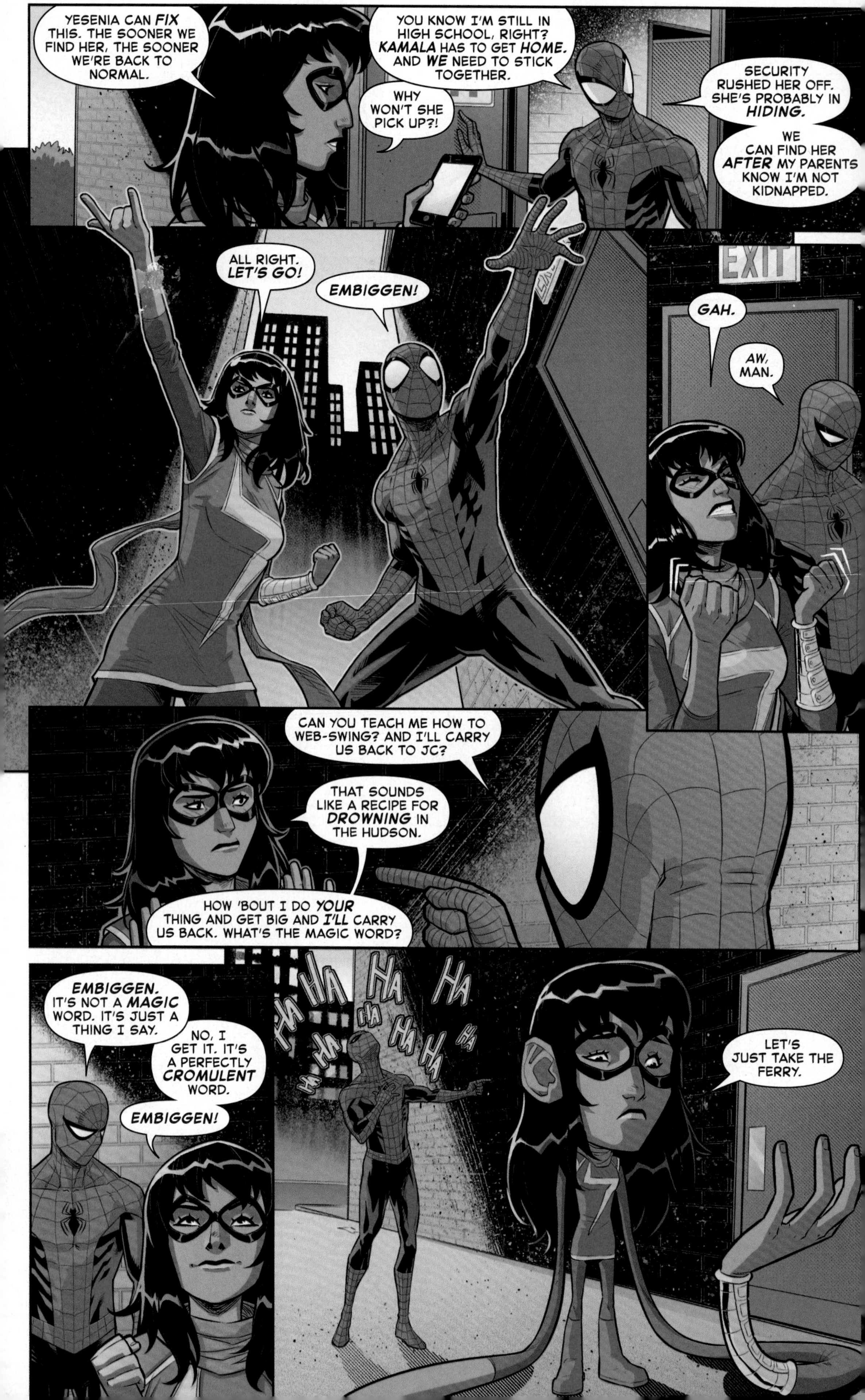
YESENIA CAN FIX THIS. THE SOONER WE FIND HER, THE SOONER WE'RE BACK TO NORMAL.
YOU KNOW I'M STILL IN HIGH SCHOOL, RIGHT? KAMALA HAS TO GET HOME. AND WE NEED TO STICK TOGETHER.
WHY WON'T SHE PICK UP?!
SECURITY RUSHED HER OFF. SHE'S PROBABLY IN HIDING.
WE CAN FIND HER AFTER MY PARENTS KNOW I'M NOT KIDNAPPED.
ALL RIGHT. LET'S GO!
EMBIGGEN!
EXIT
GAH.
AW, MAN.
CAN YOU TEACH ME HOW TO WEB-SWING? AND I'LL CARRY US BACK TO JC?
THAT SOUNDS LIKE A RECIPE FOR DROWNING IN THE HUDSON.
HOW 'BOUT I DO YOUR THING AND GET BIG AND I'LL CARRY US BACK. WHAT'S THE MAGIC WORD?
EMBIGGEN. IT'S NOT A MAGIC WORD. IT'S JUST A THING I SAY.
NO, I GET IT. IT'S A PERFECTLY CROMULENT WORD.
EMBIGGEN!
HA HA HA HA HA HA HA HA HA HA HA HA
LET'S JUST TAKE THE FERRY.

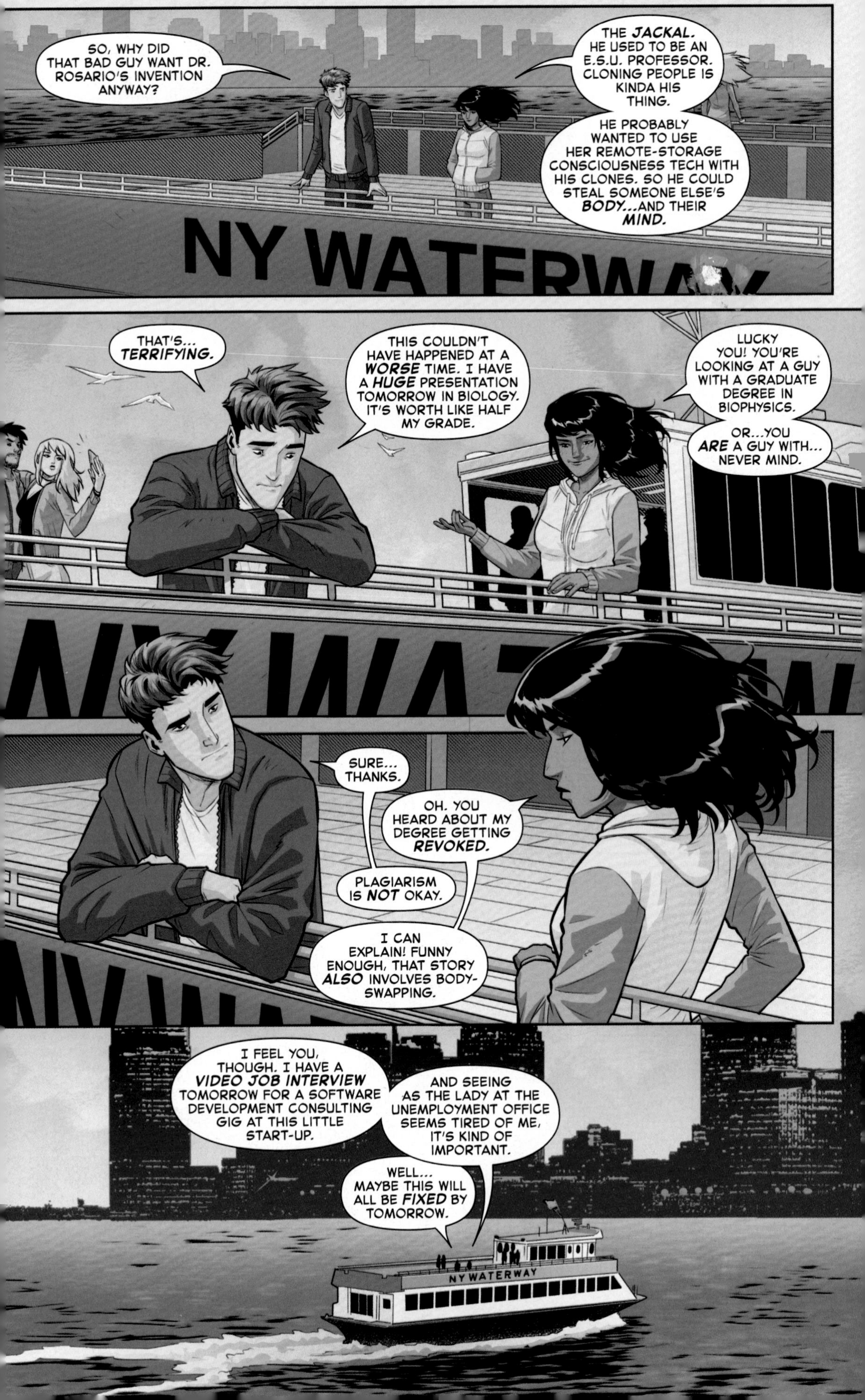
SO, WHY DID THAT BAD GUY WANT DR. ROSARIO'S INVENTION ANYWAY?
THE JACKAL. HE USED TO BE AN E.S.U. PROFESSOR. CLONING PEOPLE IS KINDA HIS THING.
HE PROBABLY WANTED TO USE HER REMOTE-STORAGE CONSCIOUSNESS TECH WITH HIS CLONES. SO HE COULD STEAL SOMEONE ELSE'S BODY...AND THEIR MIND.
NY WATERWAY
THAT'S... TERRIFYING.
THIS COULDN'T HAVE HAPPENED AT A WORSE TIME. I HAVE A HUGE PRESENTATION TOMORROW IN BIOLOGY. IT'S WORTH LIKE HALF MY GRADE.
LUCKY YOU! YOU'RE LOOKING AT A GUY WITH A GRADUATE DEGREE IN BIOPHYSICS.
OR...YOU ARE A GUY WITH... NEVER MIND.
SURE... THANKS.
OH. YOU HEARD ABOUT MY DEGREE GETTING REVOKED.
PLAGIARISM IS NOT OKAY.
I CAN EXPLAIN! FUNNY ENOUGH, THAT STORY ALSO INVOLVES BODY-SWAPPING.
I FEEL YOU, THOUGH. I HAVE A VIDEO JOB INTERVIEW TOMORROW FOR A SOFTWARE DEVELOPMENT CONSULTING GIG AT THIS LITTLE START-UP.
AND SEEING AS THE LADY AT THE UNEMPLOYMENT OFFICE SEEMS TIRED OF ME, IT'S KIND OF IMPORTANT.
WELL... MAYBE THIS WILL ALL BE FIXED BY TOMORROW.
NY WATERWAY

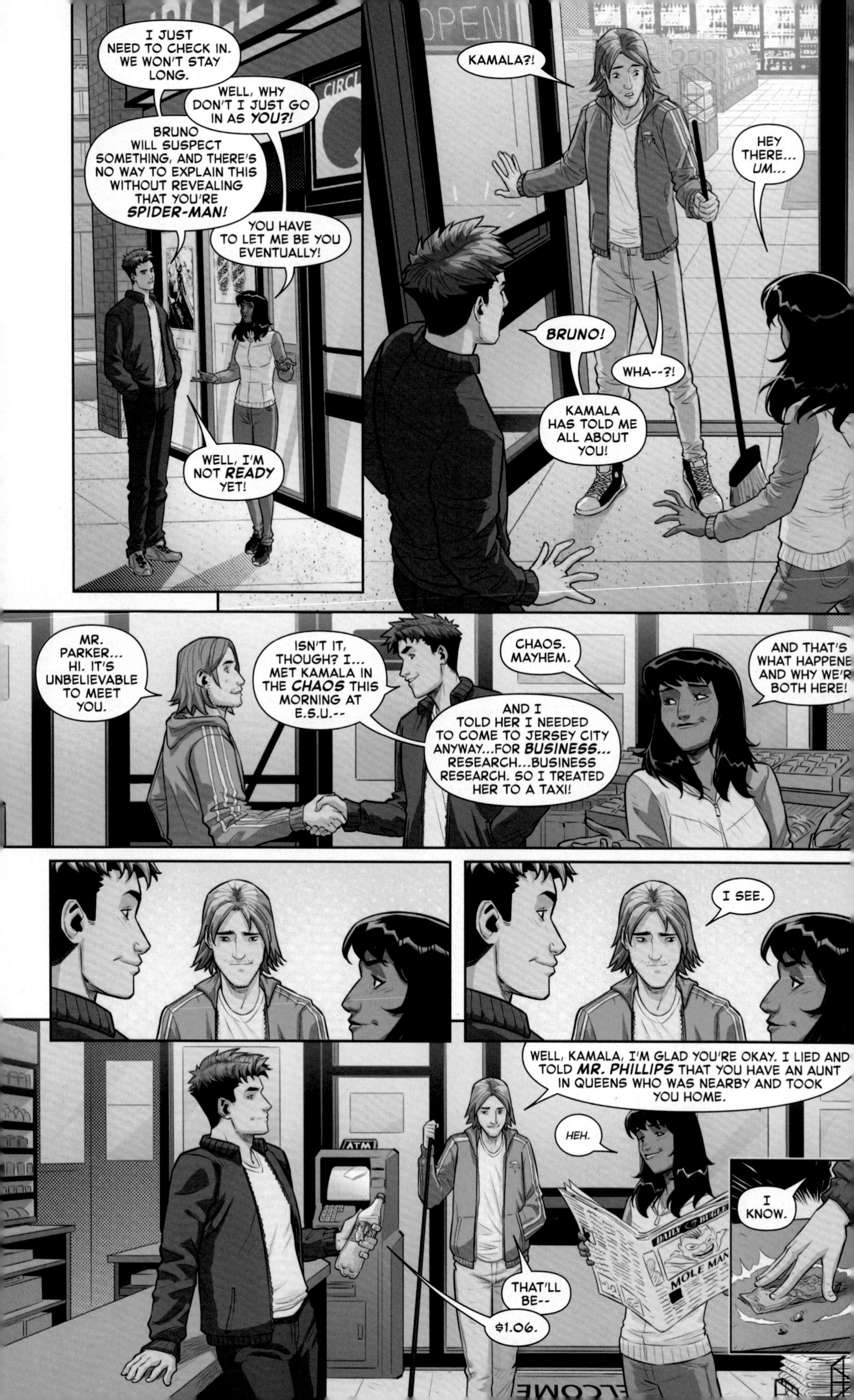
I JUST NEED TO CHECK IN. WE WON'T STAY LONG.
WELL, WHY DON'T I JUST GO IN AS YOU?!
BRUNO WILL SUSPECT SOMETHING, AND THERE'S NO WAY TO EXPLAIN THIS WITHOUT REVEALING THAT YOU'RE SPIDER-MAN!
YOU HAVE TO LET ME BE YOU EVENTUALLY!
WELL, I'M NOT READY YET!
OPEN
CIRCL
KAMALA?!
HEY THERE... UM...
BRUNO!
WHA--?!
KAMALA HAS TOLD ME ALL ABOUT YOU!
MR. PARKER... HI. IT'S UNBELIEVABLE TO MEET YOU.
ISN'T IT, THOUGH? I... MET KAMALA IN THE CHAOS THIS MORNING AT E.S.U.--
CHAOS. MAYHEM.
AND THAT'S WHAT HAPPENE AND WHY WE'R BOTH HERE!
AND I TOLD HER I NEEDED TO COME TO JERSEY CITY ANYWAY...FOR BUSINESS... RESEARCH...BUSINESS RESEARCH. SO I TREATED HER TO A TAXI!
I SEE.
WELL, KAMALA, I'M GLAD YOU'RE OKAY. I LIED AND TOLD MR. PHILLIPS THAT YOU HAVE AN AUNT IN QUEENS WHO WAS NEARBY AND TOOK YOU HOME.
HEH.
ATM
DAILY BUGLE
MOLE MAN
I KNOW.
THAT'LL BE--
$1.06.

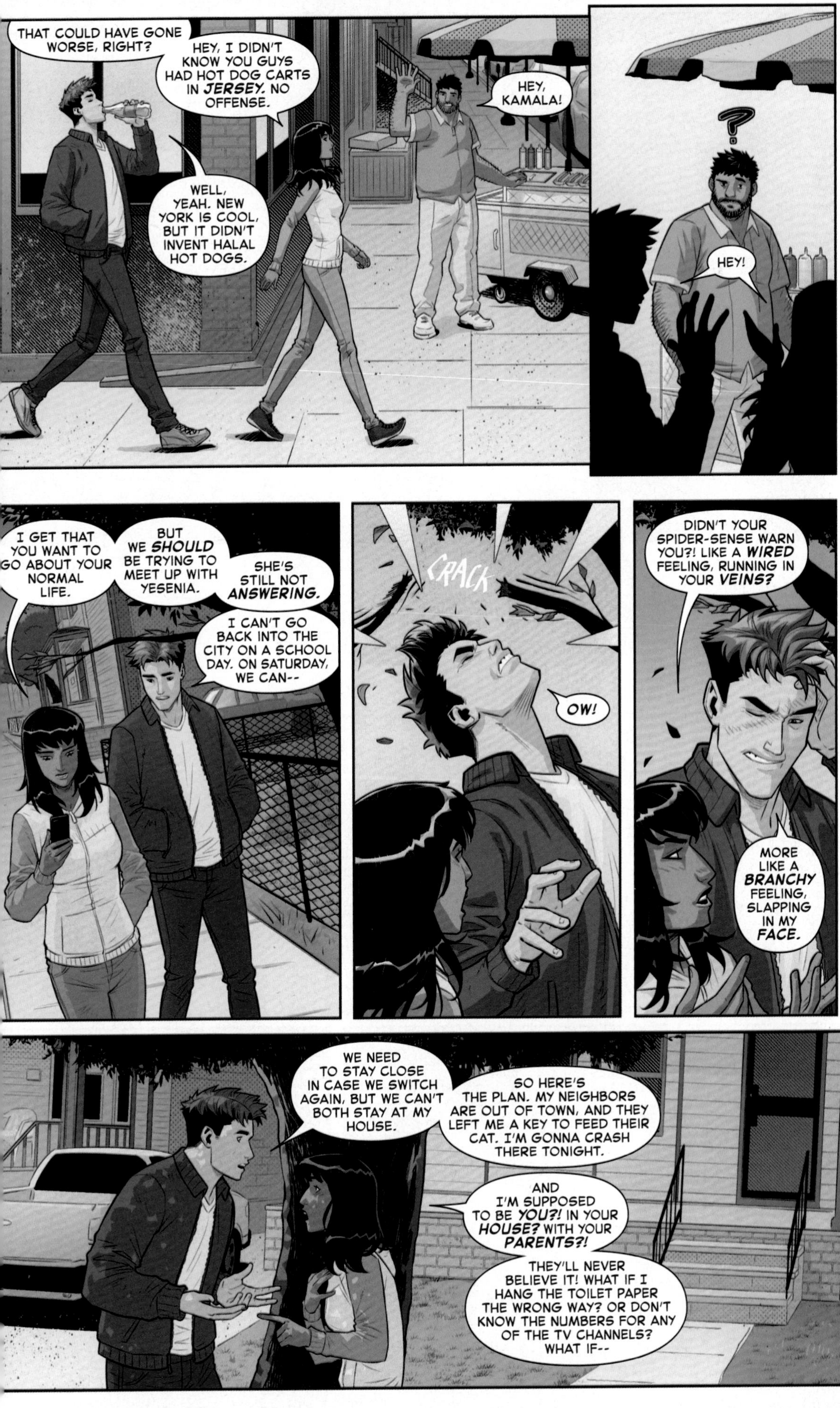
THAT COULD HAVE GONE WORSE, RIGHT?
HEY, I DIDN'T KNOW YOU GUYS HAD HOT DOG CARTS IN JERSEY. NO OFFENSE.
WELL, YEAH. NEW YORK IS COOL, BUT IT DIDN'T INVENT HALAL HOT DOGS.
HEY, KAMALA!
?
HEY!
I GET THAT YOU WANT TO GO ABOUT YOUR NORMAL LIFE.
BUT WE SHOULD BE TRYING TO MEET UP WITH YESENIA.
SHE'S STILL NOT ANSWERING.
I CAN'T GO BACK INTO THE CITY ON A SCHOOL DAY. ON SATURDAY, WE CAN--
CRACK
OW!
DIDN'T YOUR SPIDER-SENSE WARN YOU?! LIKE A WIRED FEELING, RUNNING IN YOUR VEINS?
MORE LIKE A BRANCHY FEELING, SLAPPING IN MY FACE.
WE NEED TO STAY CLOSE IN CASE WE SWITCH AGAIN, BUT WE CAN'T BOTH STAY AT MY HOUSE.
SO HERE'S THE PLAN. MY NEIGHBORS ARE OUT OF TOWN, AND THEY LEFT ME A KEY TO FEED THEIR CAT. I'M GONNA CRASH THERE TONIGHT.
AND I'M SUPPOSED TO BE YOU?! IN YOUR HOUSE? WITH YOUR PARENTS?!
THEY'LL NEVER BELIEVE IT! WHAT IF I HANG THE TOILET PAPER THE WRONG WAY? OR DON'T KNOW THE NUMBERS FOR ANY OF THE TV CHANNELS? WHAT IF--

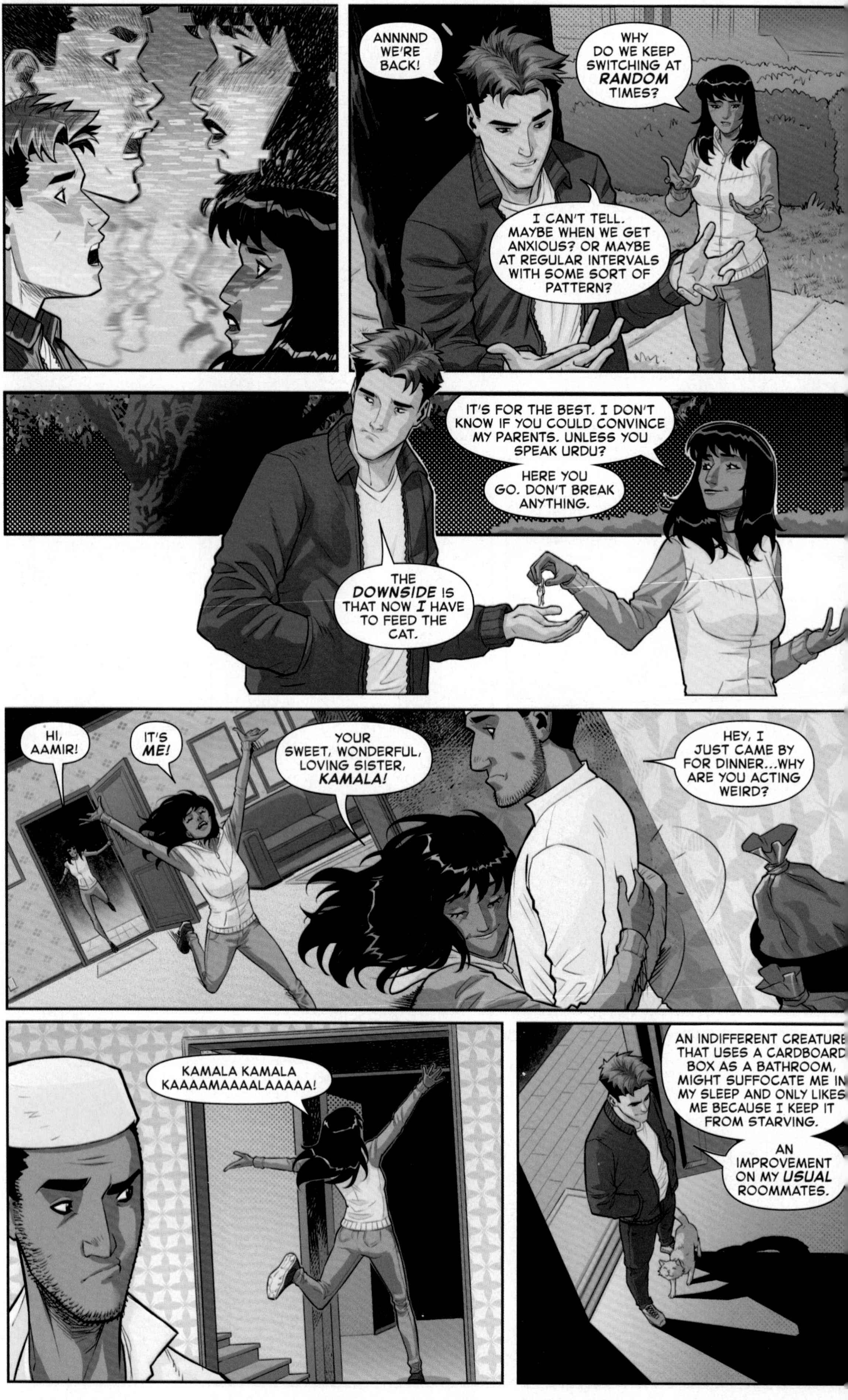
ANNNND WE'RE BACK!
WHY DO WE KEEP SWITCHING AT RANDOM TIMES?
I CAN'T TELL. MAYBE WHEN WE GET ANXIOUS? OR MAYBE AT REGULAR INTERVALS WITH SOME SORT OF PATTERN?
IT'S FOR THE BEST. I DON'T KNOW IF YOU COULD CONVINCE MY PARENTS. UNLESS YOU SPEAK URDU?
HERE YOU GO. DON'T BREAK ANYTHING.
THE DOWNSIDE IS THAT NOW I HAVE TO FEED THE CAT.
HI, AAMIR!
IT'S ME!
YOUR SWEET, WONDERFUL, LOVING SISTER, KAMALA!
HEY, I JUST CAME BY FOR DINNER...WHY ARE YOU ACTING WEIRD?
KAMALA KAMALA KAAAAMAAAALAAAAA!
AN INDIFFERENT CREATURE THAT USES A CARDBOARD BOX AS A BATHROOM, MIGHT SUFFOCATE ME IN MY SLEEP AND ONLY LIKES ME BECAUSE I KEEP IT FROM STARVING.
AN IMPROVEMENT ON MY USUAL ROOMMATES.

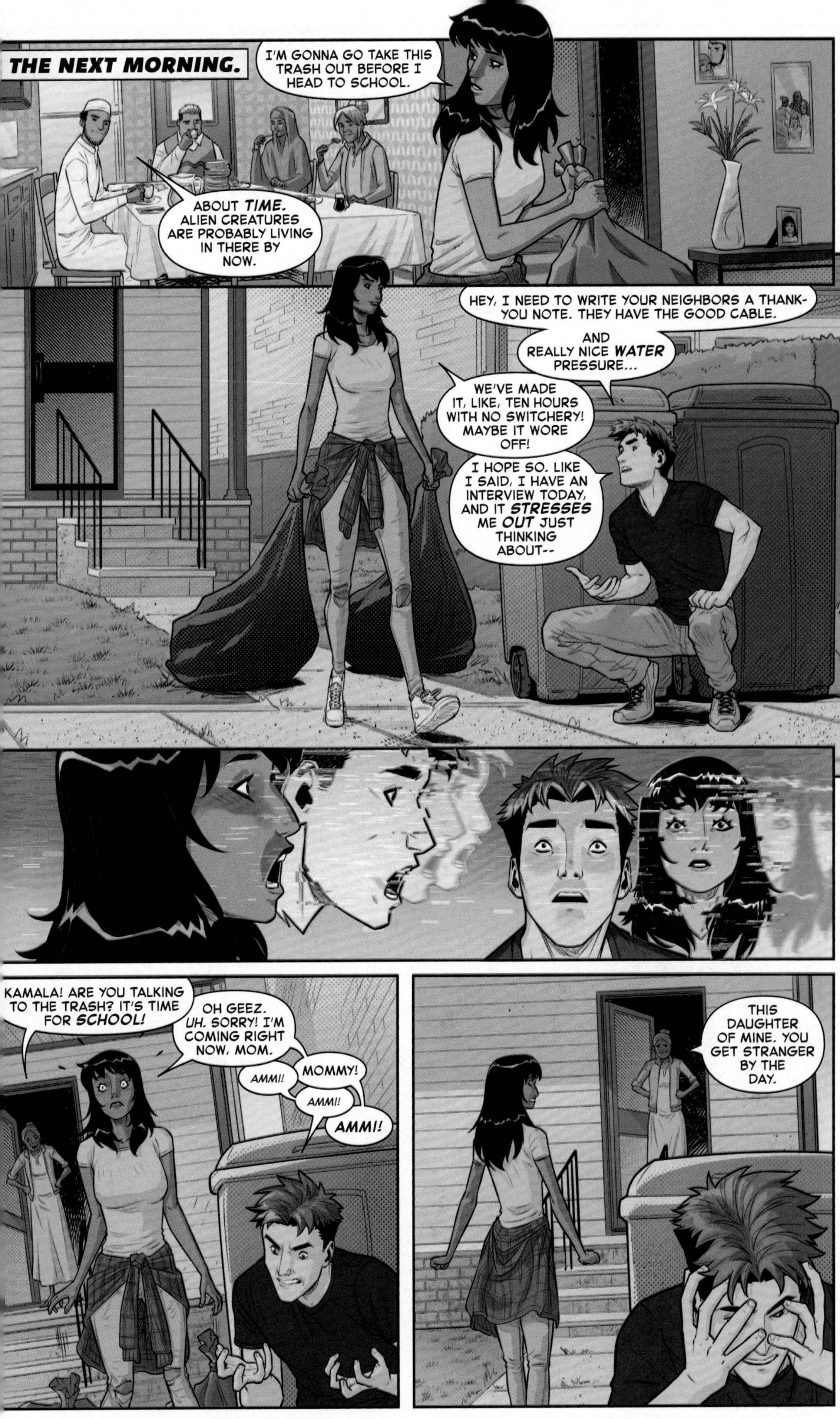
THE NEXT MORNING.
I'M GONNA GO TAKE THIS TRASH OUT BEFORE I HEAD TO SCHOOL.
ABOUT TIME. ALIEN CREATURES ARE PROBABLY LIVING IN THERE BY NOW.
HEY, I NEED TO WRITE YOUR NEIGHBORS A THANK-YOU NOTE. THEY HAVE THE GOOD CABLE.
AND REALLY NICE WATER PRESSURE...
WE'VE MADE IT, LIKE, TEN HOURS WITH NO SWITCHERY! MAYBE IT WORE OFF!
I HOPE SO. LIKE I SAID, I HAVE AN INTERVIEW TODAY, AND IT STRESSES ME OUT JUST THINKING ABOUT--
KAMALA! ARE YOU TALKING TO THE TRASH? IT'S TIME FOR SCHOOL!
OH GEEZ. UH. SORRY! I'M COMING RIGHT NOW, MOM.
MOMMY!
AMMI!
AMMI!
AMMI!
THIS DAUGHTER OF MINE. YOU GET STRANGER BY THE DAY.

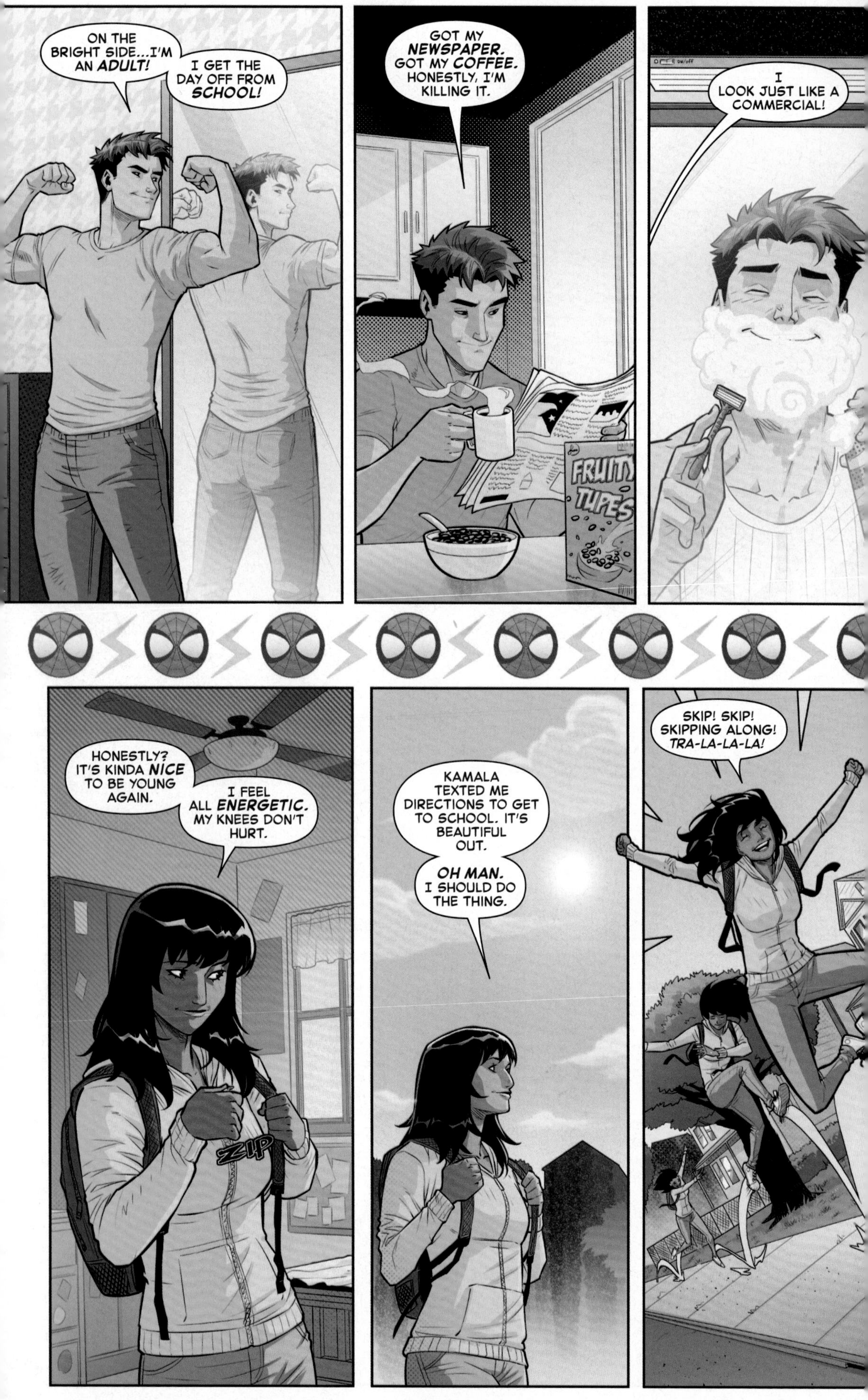
ON THE BRIGHT SIDE...I'M AN *ADULT!*
I GET THE DAY OFF FROM ***SCHOOL!***
GOT MY ***NEWSPAPER.*** GOT MY ***COFFEE.*** HONESTLY, I'M KILLING IT.
I LOOK JUST LIKE A COMMERCIAL!
HONESTLY? IT'S KINDA ***NICE*** TO BE YOUNG AGAIN.
I FEEL ALL ***ENERGETIC.*** MY KNEES DON'T HURT.
ZIP
KAMALA TEXTED ME DIRECTIONS TO GET TO SCHOOL. IT'S BEAUTIFUL OUT.
OH MAN. I SHOULD DO THE THING.
SKIP! SKIP! SKIPPING ALONG! *TRA-LA-LA-LA!*

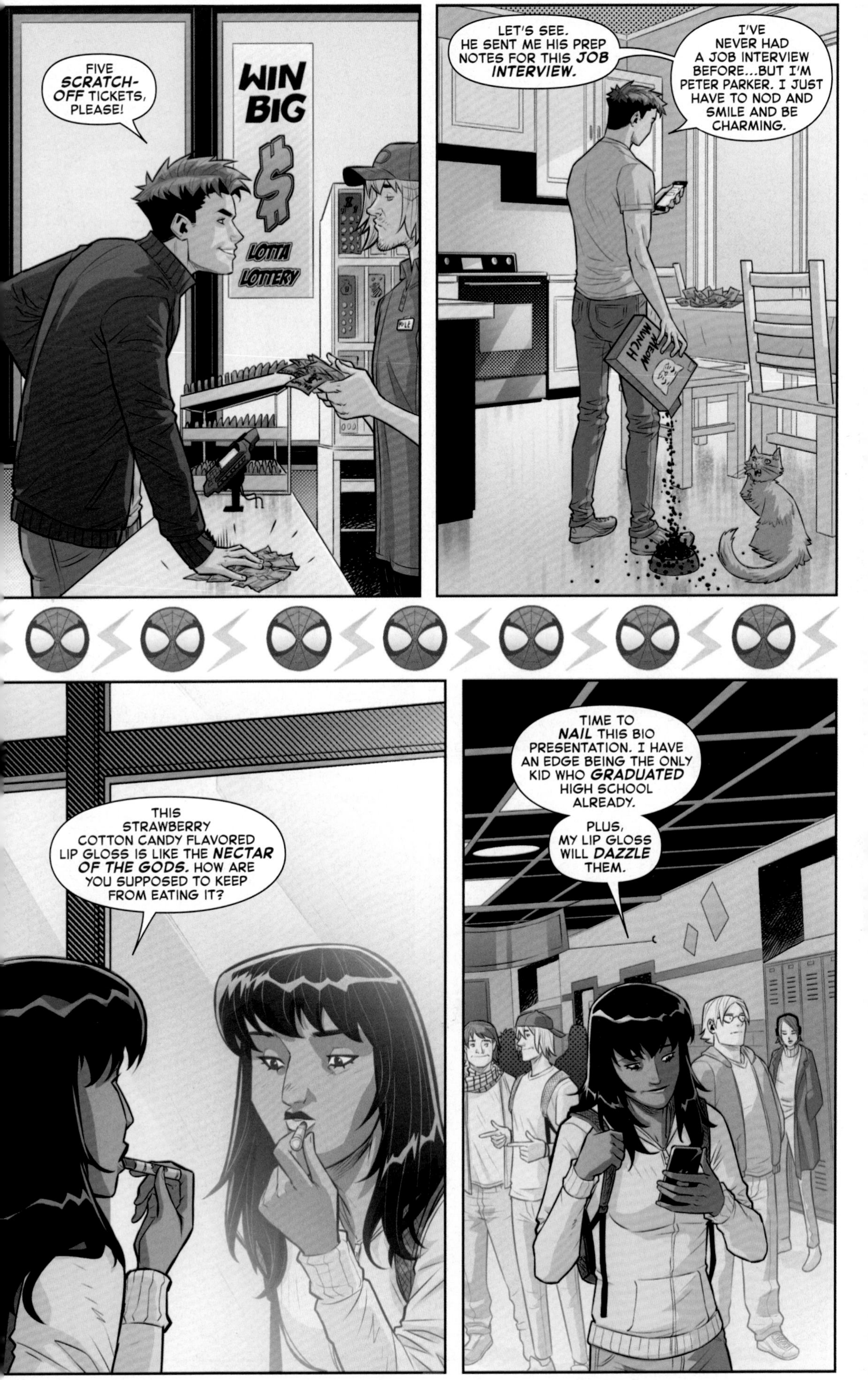
FIVE SCRATCH-OFF TICKETS, PLEASE!
WIN BIG
$
LOTTA LOTTERY
LET'S SEE. HE SENT ME HIS PREP NOTES FOR THIS JOB INTERVIEW.
I'VE NEVER HAD A JOB INTERVIEW BEFORE...BUT I'M PETER PARKER. I JUST HAVE TO NOD AND SMILE AND BE CHARMING.
MEOW MUNCH
THIS STRAWBERRY COTTON CANDY FLAVORED LIP GLOSS IS LIKE THE NECTAR OF THE GODS. HOW ARE YOU SUPPOSED TO KEEP FROM EATING IT?
TIME TO NAIL THIS BIO PRESENTATION. I HAVE AN EDGE BEING THE ONLY KID WHO GRADUATED HIGH SCHOOL ALREADY.
PLUS, MY LIP GLOSS WILL DAZZLE THEM.

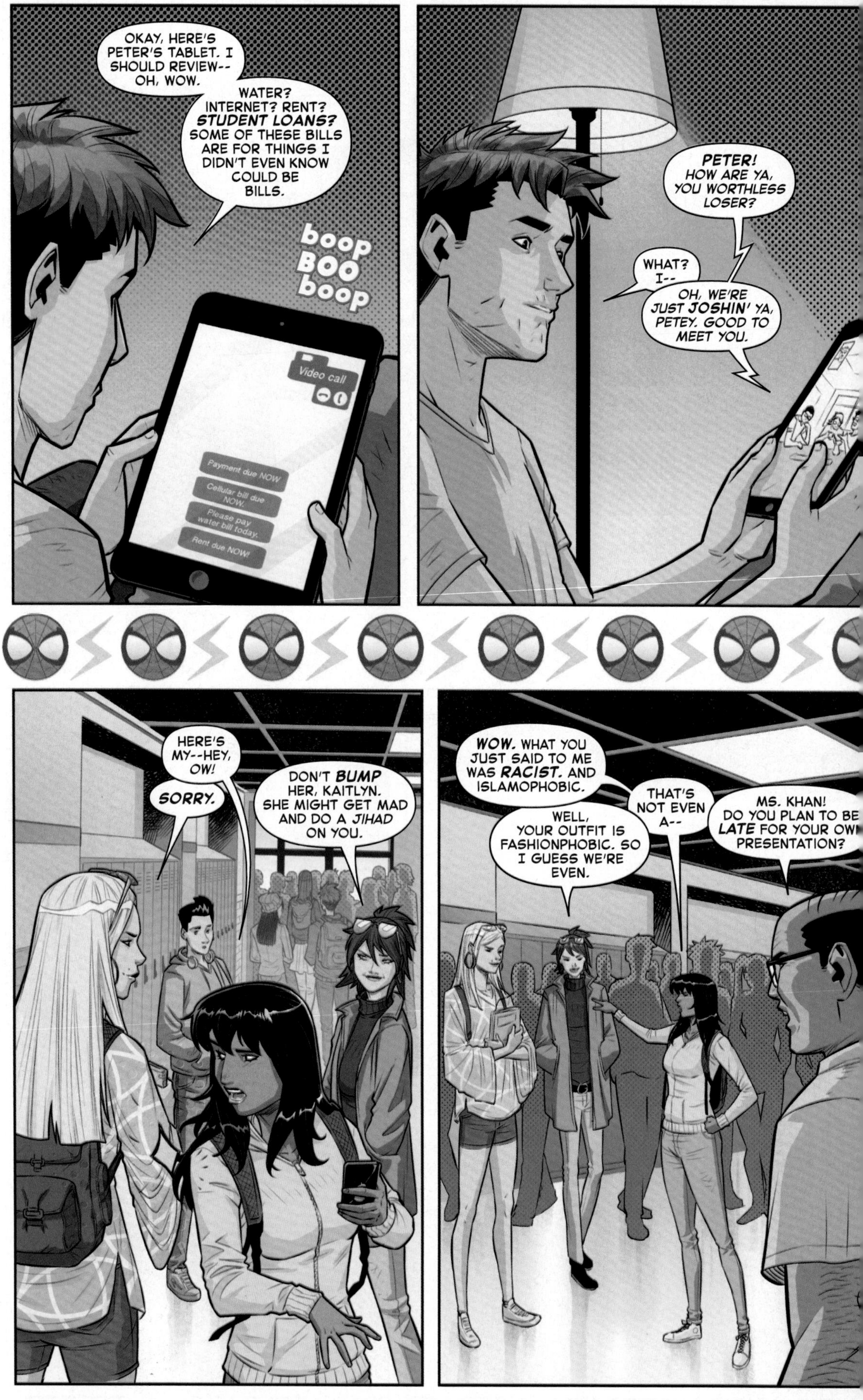
OKAY, HERE'S PETER'S TABLET. I SHOULD REVIEW-- OH, WOW.
WATER? INTERNET? RENT? STUDENT LOANS? SOME OF THESE BILLS ARE FOR THINGS I DIDN'T EVEN KNOW COULD BE BILLS.
boop BOO boop
Video call
Payment due NOW
Cellular bill due NOW.
Please pay water bill today.
Rent due NOW!
PETER! HOW ARE YA, YOU WORTHLESS LOSER?
WHAT? I--
OH, WE'RE JUST JOSHIN' YA, PETEY. GOOD TO MEET YOU.
HERE'S MY--HEY, OW!
SORRY.
DON'T BUMP HER, KAITLYN. SHE MIGHT GET MAD AND DO A JIHAD ON YOU.
WOW. WHAT YOU JUST SAID TO ME WAS RACIST. AND ISLAMOPHOBIC.
WELL, YOUR OUTFIT IS FASHIONPHOBIC. SO I GUESS WE'RE EVEN.
THAT'S NOT EVEN A--
MS. KHAN! DO YOU PLAN TO BE LATE FOR YOUR OW PRESENTATION?

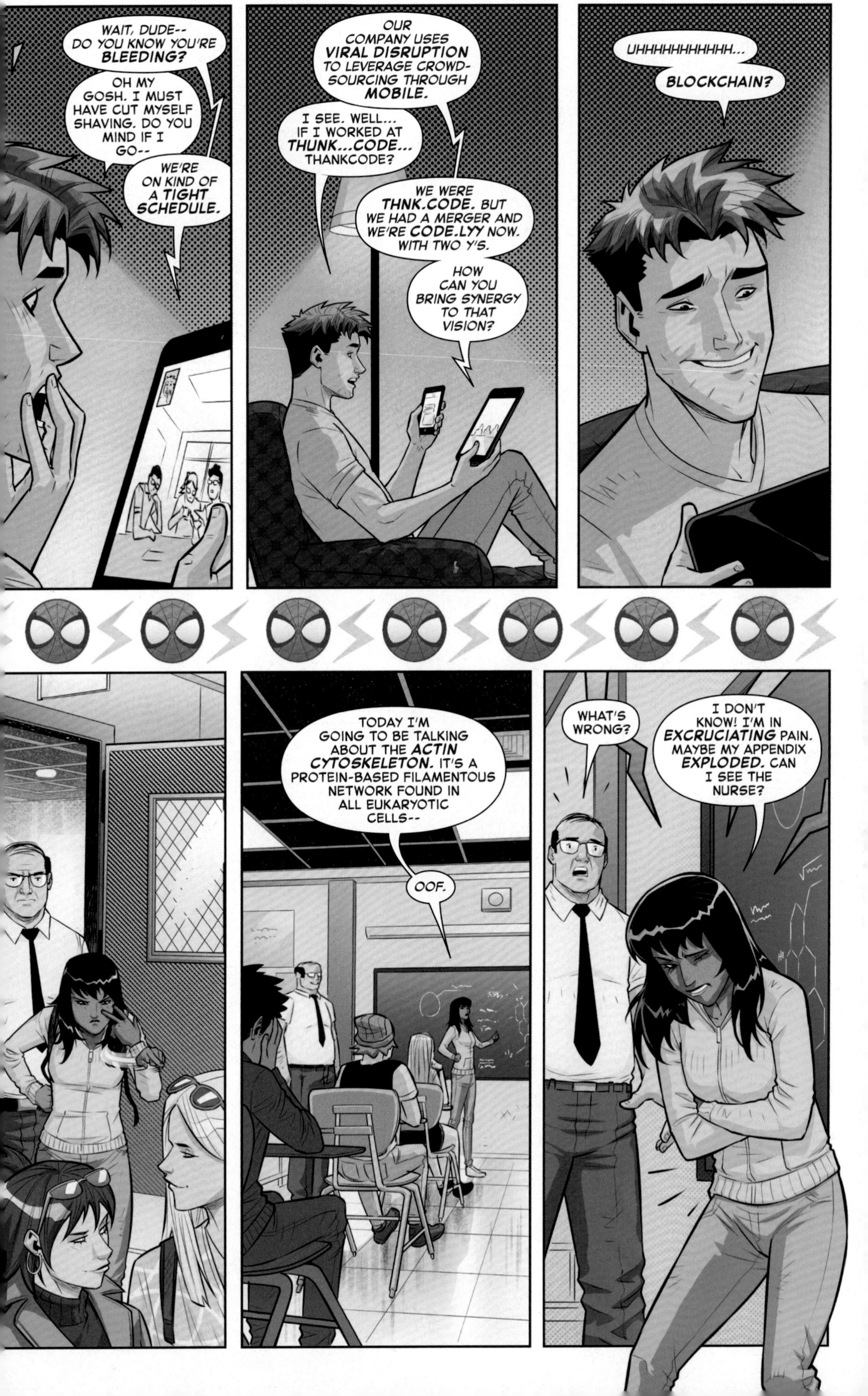
WAIT, DUDE-- DO YOU KNOW YOU'RE BLEEDING?
OH MY GOSH. I MUST HAVE CUT MYSELF SHAVING. DO YOU MIND IF I GO--
WE'RE ON KIND OF A TIGHT SCHEDULE.
OUR COMPANY USES VIRAL DISRUPTION TO LEVERAGE CROWD-SOURCING THROUGH MOBILE.
I SEE. WELL... IF I WORKED AT THUNK...CODE... THANKCODE?
WE WERE THNK.CODE. BUT WE HAD A MERGER AND WE'RE CODE.LYY NOW. WITH TWO Y'S.
HOW CAN YOU BRING SYNERGY TO THAT VISION?
UHHHHHHHHHHH...
BLOCKCHAIN?
TODAY I'M GOING TO BE TALKING ABOUT THE ACTIN CYTOSKELETON. IT'S A PROTEIN-BASED FILAMENTOUS NETWORK FOUND IN ALL EUKARYOTIC CELLS--
OOF.
WHAT'S WRONG?
I DON'T KNOW! I'M IN EXCRUCIATING PAIN. MAYBE MY APPENDIX EXPLODED. CAN I SEE THE NURSE?

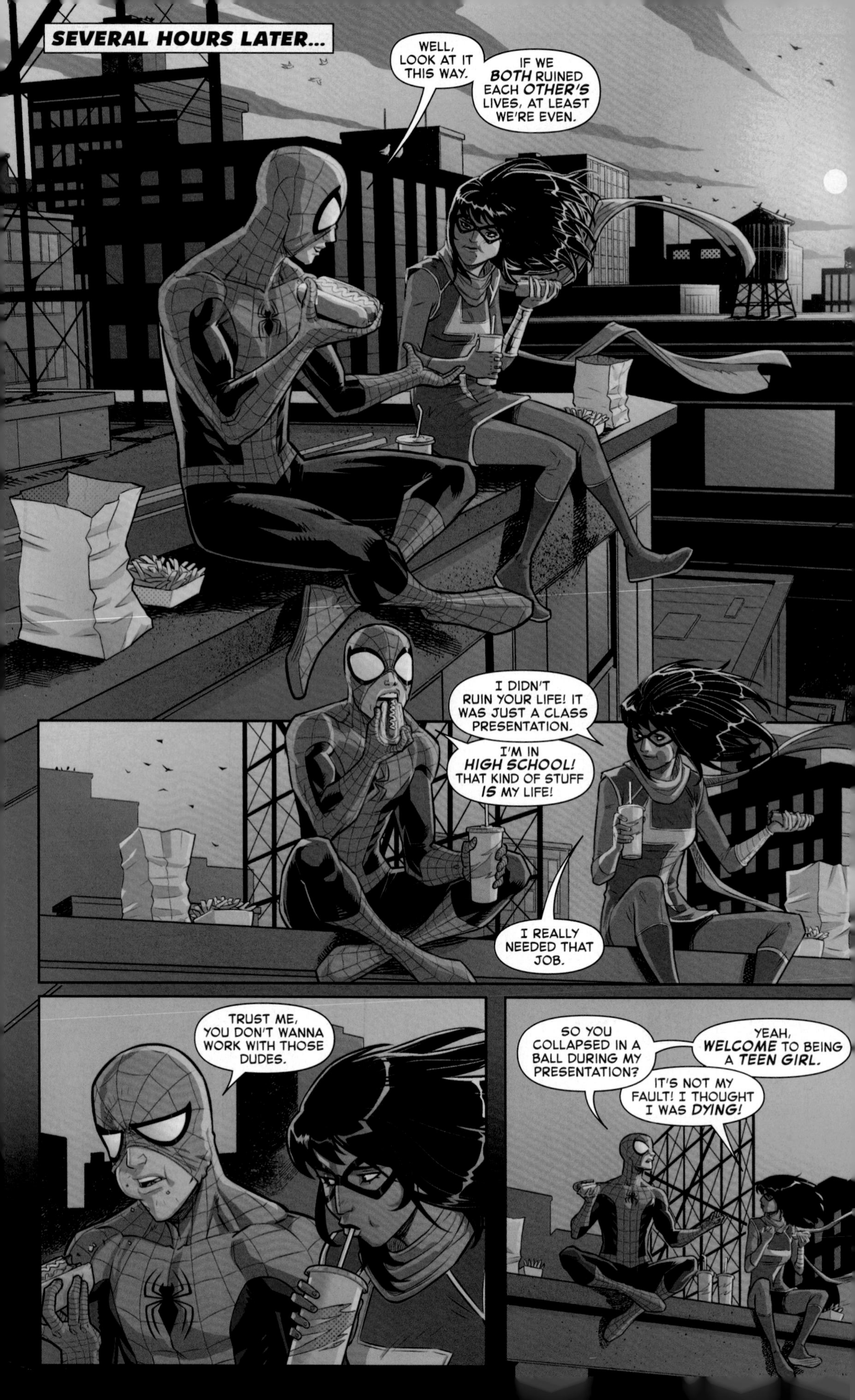
SEVERAL HOURS LATER...
WELL, LOOK AT IT THIS WAY.
IF WE BOTH RUINED EACH OTHER'S LIVES, AT LEAST WE'RE EVEN.
I DIDN'T RUIN YOUR LIFE! IT WAS JUST A CLASS PRESENTATION.
I'M IN HIGH SCHOOL! THAT KIND OF STUFF IS MY LIFE!
I REALLY NEEDED THAT JOB.
TRUST ME, YOU DON'T WANNA WORK WITH THOSE DUDES.
SO YOU COLLAPSED IN A BALL DURING MY PRESENTATION?
YEAH, WELCOME TO BEING A TEEN GIRL.
IT'S NOT MY FAULT! I THOUGHT I WAS DYING!

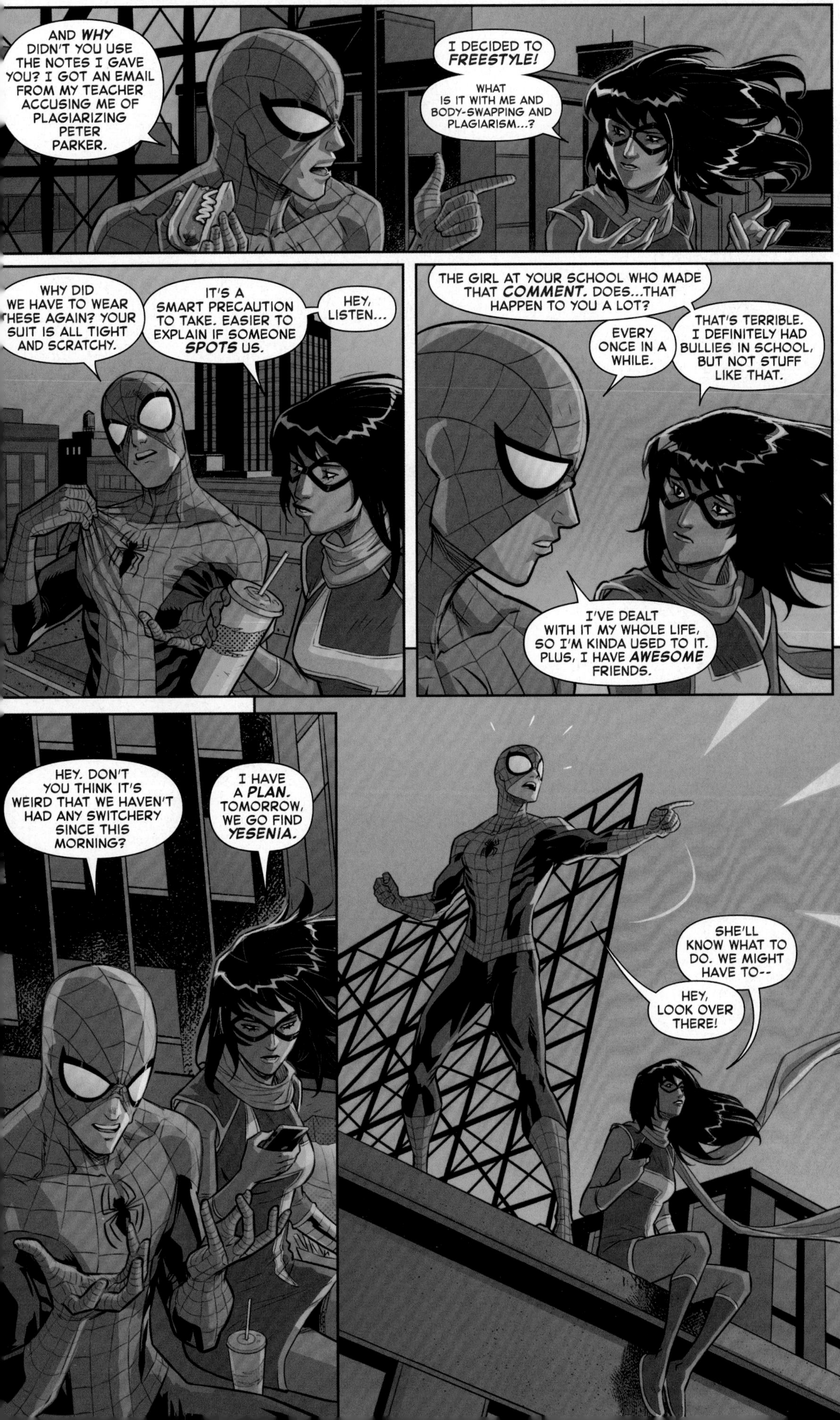
AND WHY DIDN'T YOU USE THE NOTES I GAVE YOU? I GOT AN EMAIL FROM MY TEACHER ACCUSING ME OF PLAGIARIZING PETER PARKER.
I DECIDED TO FREESTYLE!
WHAT IS IT WITH ME AND BODY-SWAPPING AND PLAGIARISM...?
WHY DID WE HAVE TO WEAR THESE AGAIN? YOUR SUIT IS ALL TIGHT AND SCRATCHY.
IT'S A SMART PRECAUTION TO TAKE. EASIER TO EXPLAIN IF SOMEONE SPOTS US.
HEY, LISTEN...
THE GIRL AT YOUR SCHOOL WHO MADE THAT COMMENT. DOES...THAT HAPPEN TO YOU A LOT?
EVERY ONCE IN A WHILE.
THAT'S TERRIBLE. I DEFINITELY HAD BULLIES IN SCHOOL, BUT NOT STUFF LIKE THAT.
I'VE DEALT WITH IT MY WHOLE LIFE, SO I'M KINDA USED TO IT. PLUS, I HAVE AWESOME FRIENDS.
HEY. DON'T YOU THINK IT'S WEIRD THAT WE HAVEN'T HAD ANY SWITCHERY SINCE THIS MORNING?
I HAVE A PLAN. TOMORROW, WE GO FIND YESENIA.
SHE'LL KNOW WHAT TO DO. WE MIGHT HAVE TO--
HEY, LOOK OVER THERE!

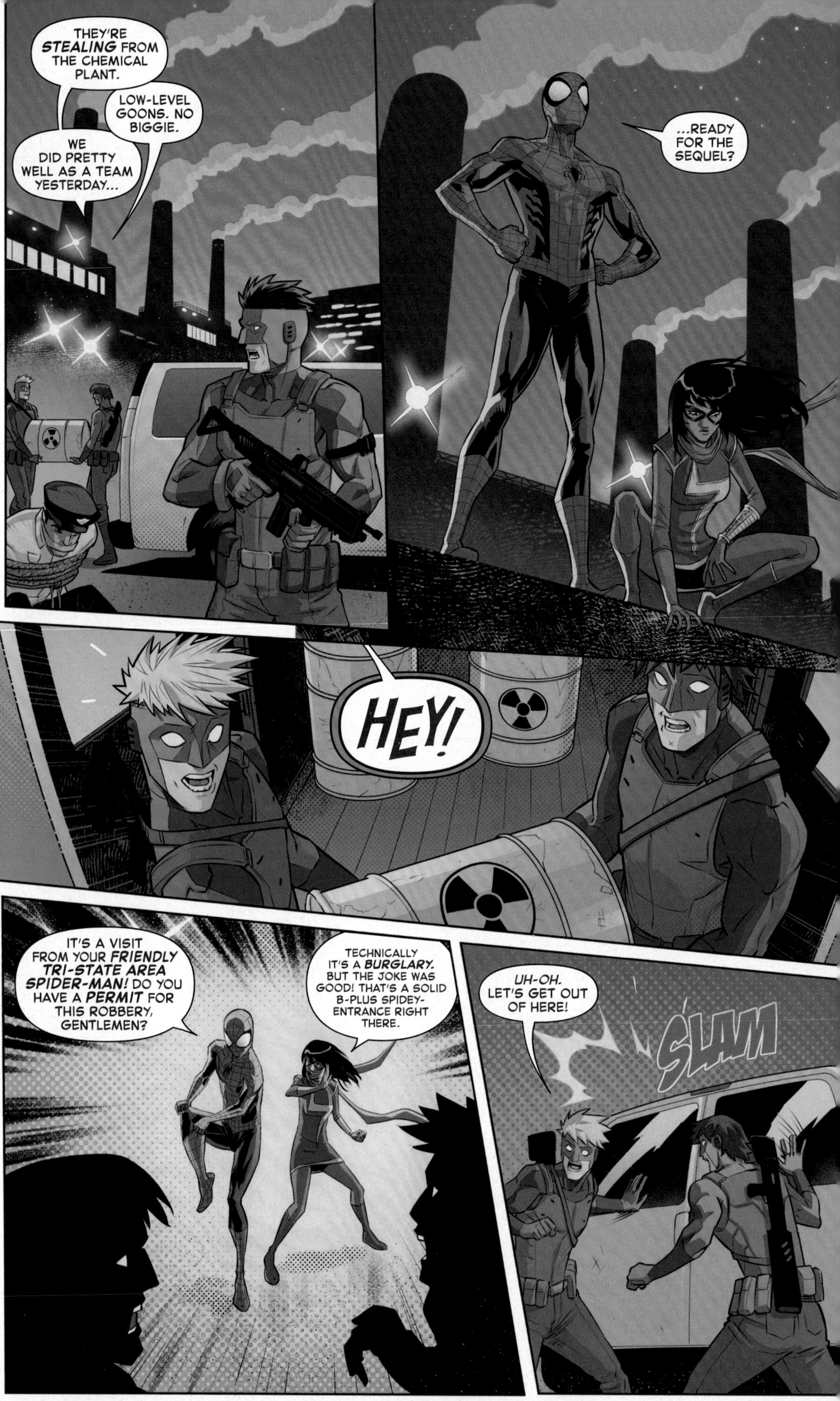
THEY'RE STEALING FROM THE CHEMICAL PLANT.
LOW-LEVEL GOONS. NO BIGGIE.
WE DID PRETTY WELL AS A TEAM YESTERDAY...
...READY FOR THE SEQUEL?
HEY!
IT'S A VISIT FROM YOUR FRIENDLY TRI-STATE AREA SPIDER-MAN! DO YOU HAVE A PERMIT FOR THIS ROBBERY, GENTLEMEN?
TECHNICALLY IT'S A BURGLARY. BUT THE JOKE WAS GOOD! THAT'S A SOLID B-PLUS SPIDEY-ENTRANCE RIGHT THERE.
UH-OH. LET'S GET OUT OF HERE!
SLAM

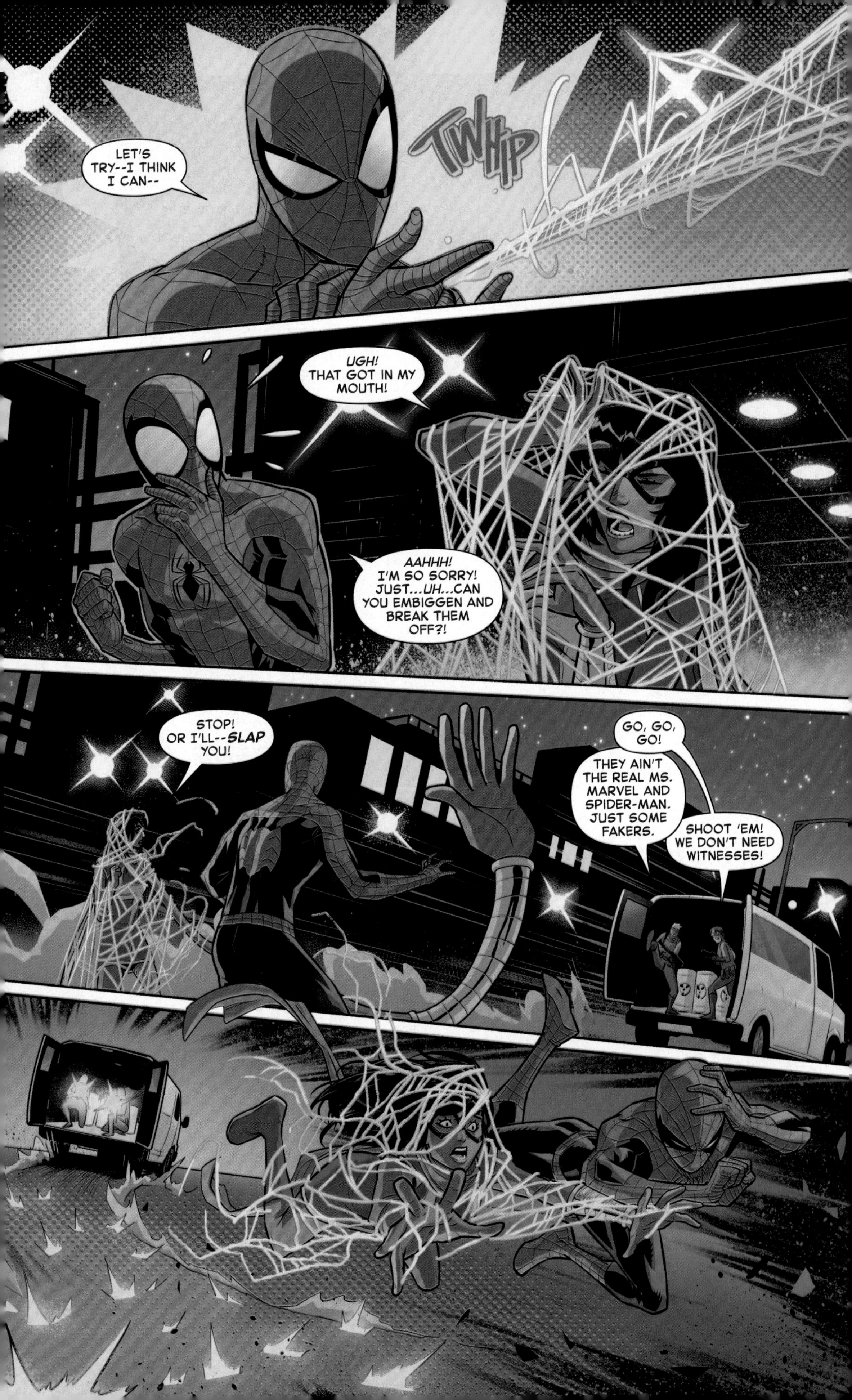
LET'S TRY--I THINK I CAN--
TWHIP
UGH! THAT GOT IN MY MOUTH!
AAHHH! I'M SO SORRY! JUST...UH...CAN YOU EMBIGGEN AND BREAK THEM OFF?!
STOP! OR I'LL--SLAP YOU!
GO, GO, GO!
THEY AIN'T THE REAL MS. MARVEL AND SPIDER-MAN. JUST SOME FAKERS.
SHOOT 'EM! WE DON'T NEED WITNESSES!

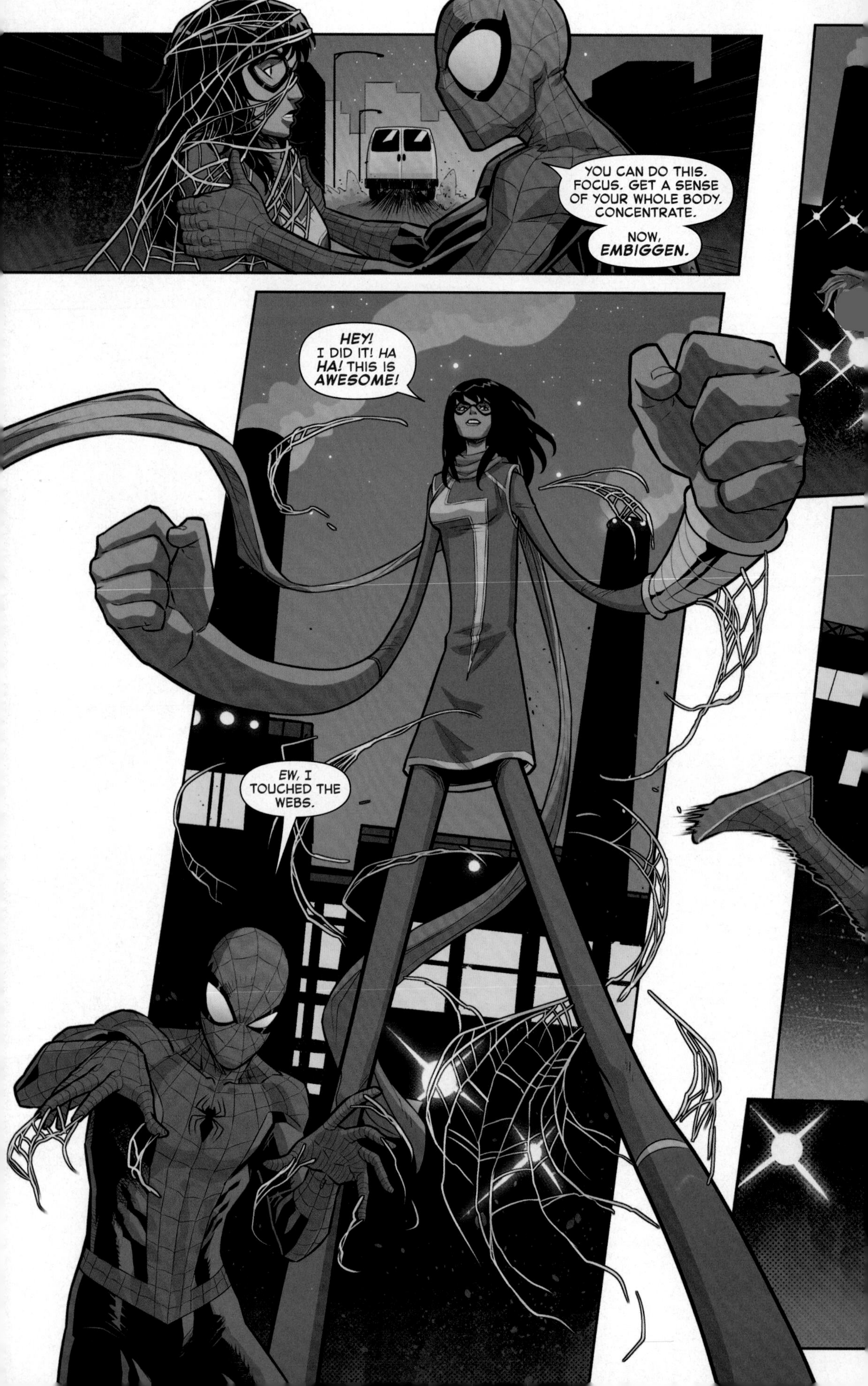
YOU CAN DO THIS. FOCUS. GET A SENSE OF YOUR WHOLE BODY. CONCENTRATE.
NOW, EMBIGGEN.
HEY! I DID IT! HA HA! THIS IS AWESOME!
EW, I TOUCHED THE WEBS.

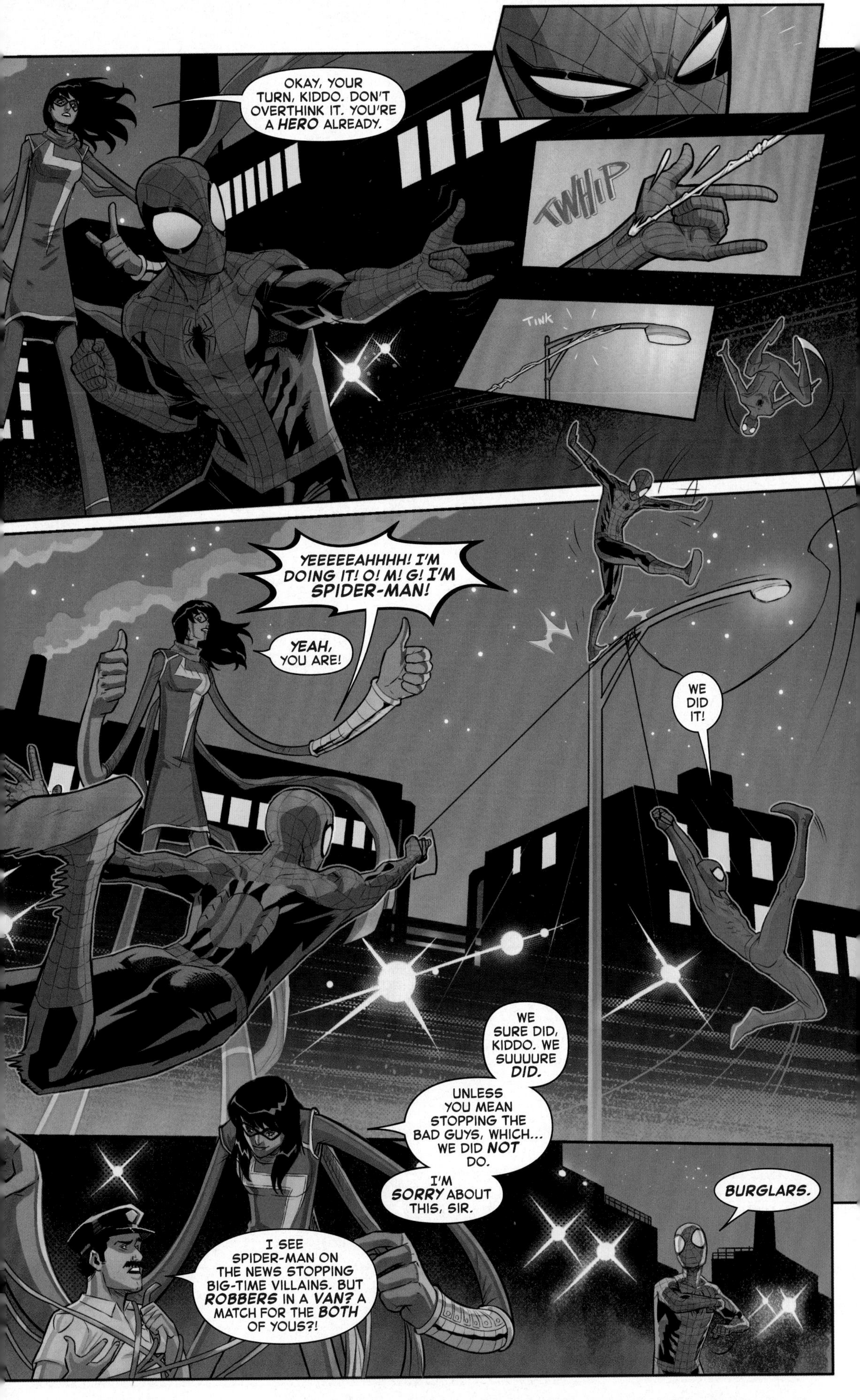

OKAY, YOUR TURN, KIDDO. DON'T OVERTHINK IT. YOU'RE A *HERO* ALREADY.
TWHIP
TINK
YEEEEEAHHHH! I'M DOING IT! O! M! G! I'M SPIDER-MAN!
YEAH, YOU ARE!
WE DID IT!
WE SURE DID, KIDDO. WE SUUUURE *DID.*
UNLESS YOU MEAN STOPPING THE BAD GUYS, WHICH... WE DID *NOT* DO.
I'M *SORRY* ABOUT THIS, SIR.
BURGLARS.
I SEE SPIDER-MAN ON THE NEWS STOPPING BIG-TIME VILLAINS. BUT *ROBBERS* IN A *VAN?* A MATCH FOR THE *BOTH* OF YOUS?!

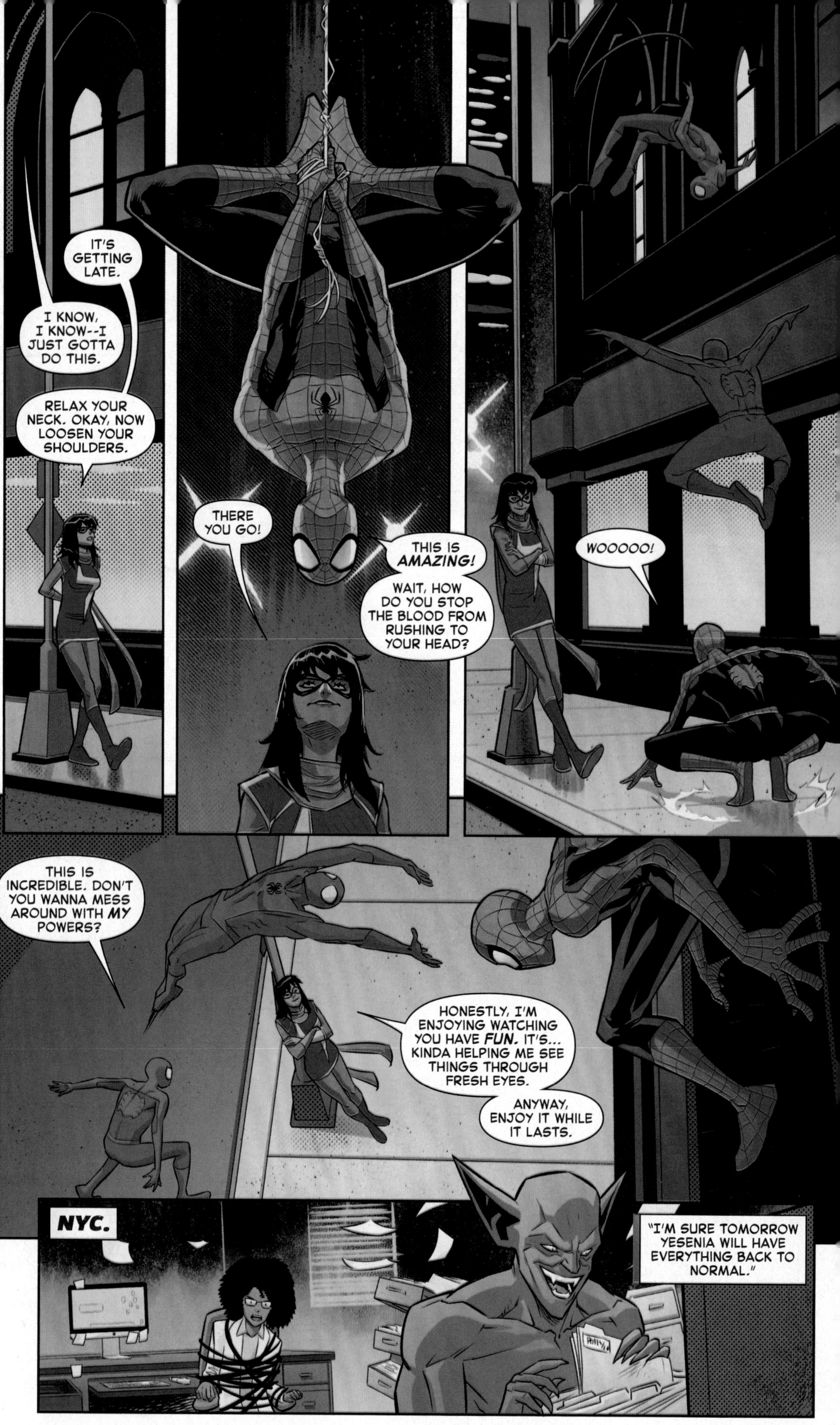
IT'S GETTING LATE.
I KNOW, I KNOW--I JUST GOTTA DO THIS.
RELAX YOUR NECK. OKAY, NOW LOOSEN YOUR SHOULDERS.
THERE YOU GO!
THIS IS AMAZING!
WAIT, HOW DO YOU STOP THE BLOOD FROM RUSHING TO YOUR HEAD?
WOOOOO!
THIS IS INCREDIBLE. DON'T YOU WANNA MESS AROUND WITH MY POWERS?
HONESTLY, I'M ENJOYING WATCHING YOU HAVE FUN. IT'S... KINDA HELPING ME SEE THINGS THROUGH FRESH EYES.
ANYWAY, ENJOY IT WHILE IT LASTS.
NYC.
"I'M SURE TOMORROW YESENIA WILL HAVE EVERYTHING BACK TO NORMAL."

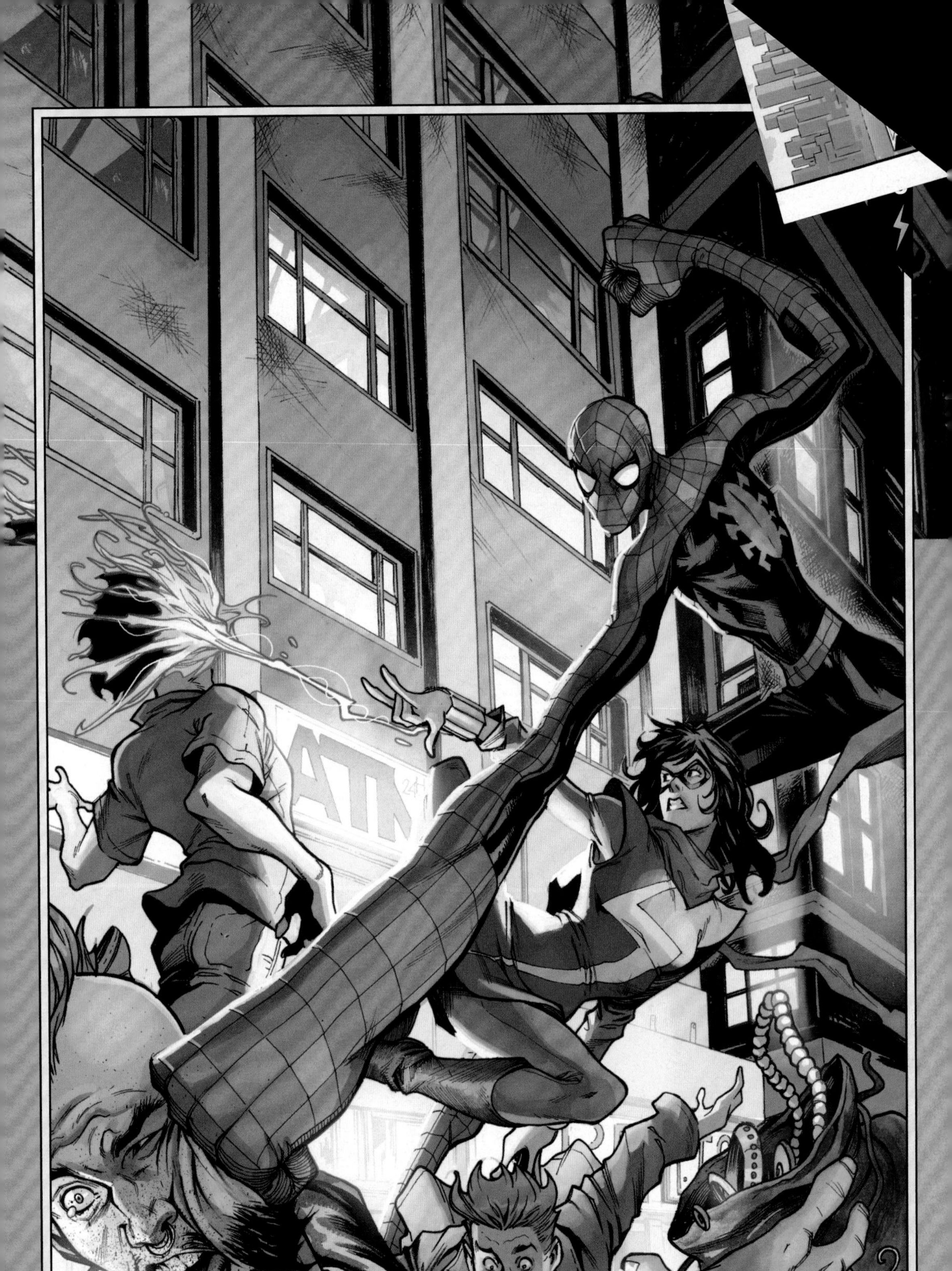

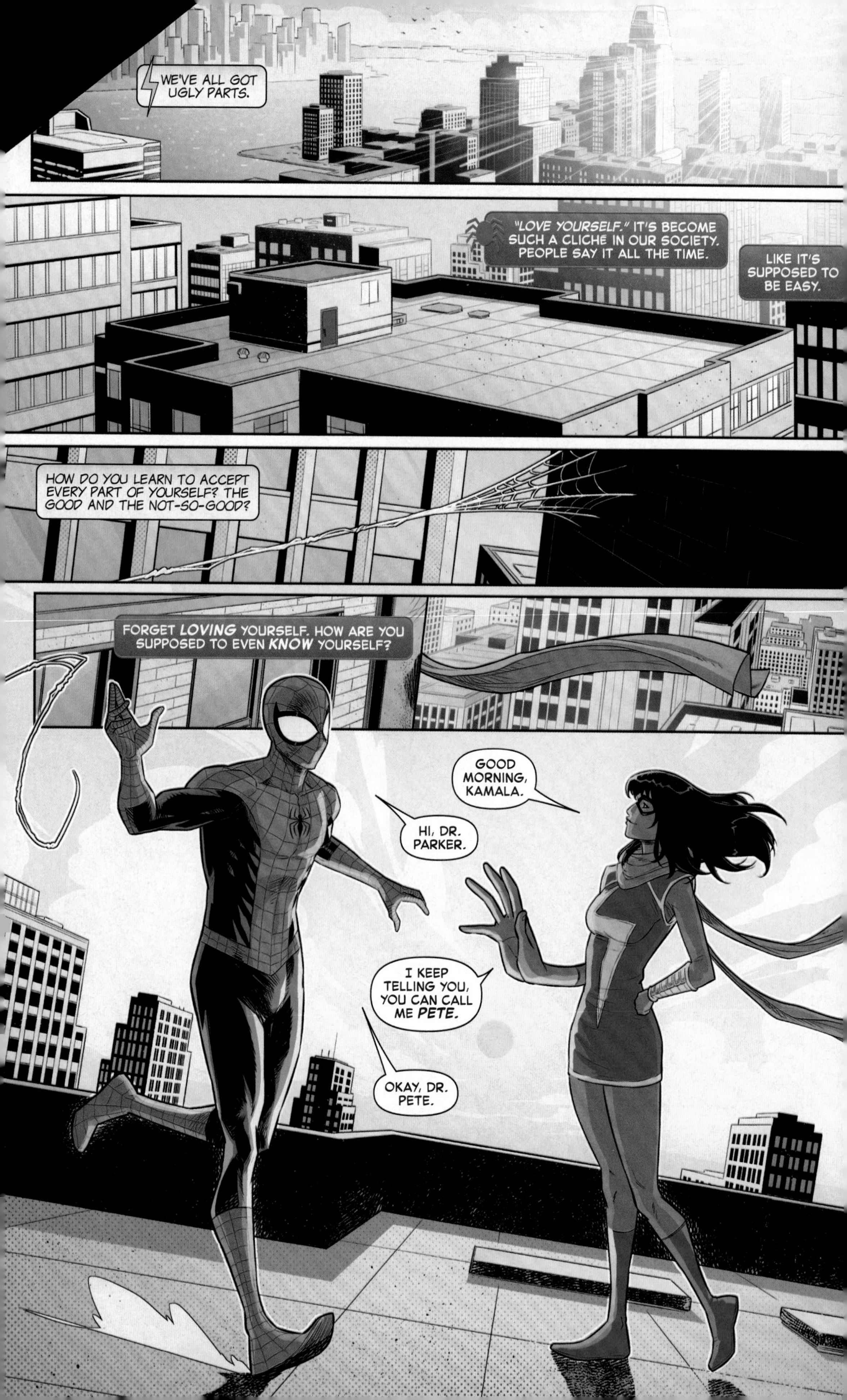
WE'VE ALL GOT UGLY PARTS.
"LOVE YOURSELF." IT'S BECOME SUCH A CLICHE IN OUR SOCIETY. PEOPLE SAY IT ALL THE TIME.
LIKE IT'S SUPPOSED TO BE EASY.
HOW DO YOU LEARN TO ACCEPT EVERY PART OF YOURSELF? THE GOOD AND THE NOT-SO-GOOD?
FORGET LOVING YOURSELF. HOW ARE YOU SUPPOSED TO EVEN KNOW YOURSELF?
GOOD MORNING, KAMALA.
HI, DR. PARKER.
I KEEP TELLING YOU, YOU CAN CALL ME PETE.
OKAY, DR. PETE.

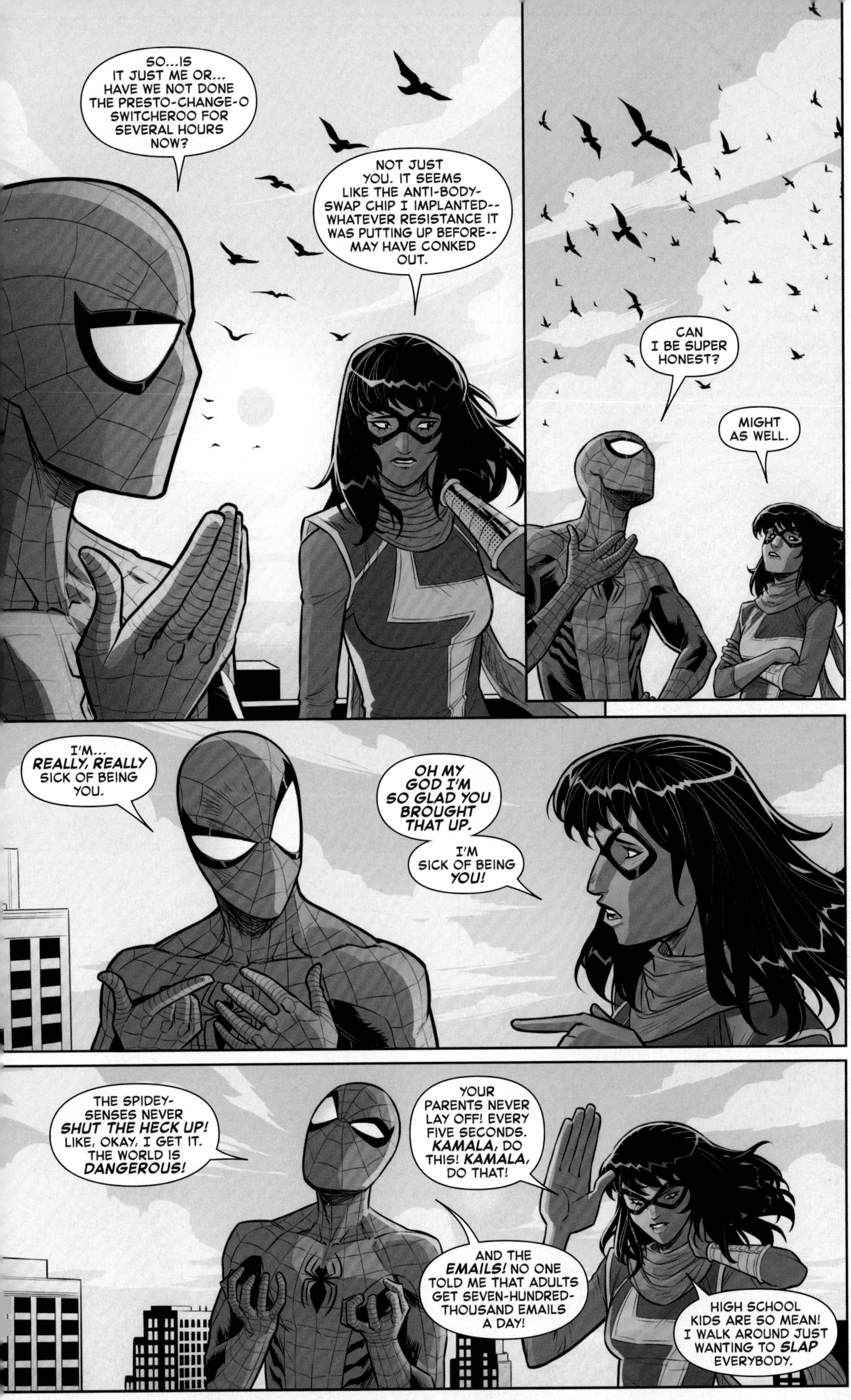
SO...IS IT JUST ME OR... HAVE WE NOT DONE THE PRESTO-CHANGE-O SWITCHEROO FOR SEVERAL HOURS NOW?
NOT JUST YOU. IT SEEMS LIKE THE ANTI-BODY-SWAP CHIP I IMPLANTED--WHATEVER RESISTANCE IT WAS PUTTING UP BEFORE--MAY HAVE CONKED OUT.
CAN I BE SUPER HONEST?
MIGHT AS WELL.
I'M... REALLY, REALLY SICK OF BEING YOU.
OH MY GOD I'M SO GLAD YOU BROUGHT THAT UP.
I'M SICK OF BEING YOU!
THE SPIDEY-SENSES NEVER SHUT THE HECK UP! LIKE, OKAY, I GET IT. THE WORLD IS DANGEROUS!
YOUR PARENTS NEVER LAY OFF! EVERY FIVE SECONDS. KAMALA, DO THIS! KAMALA, DO THAT!
AND THE EMAILS! NO ONE TOLD ME THAT ADULTS GET SEVEN-HUNDRED-THOUSAND EMAILS A DAY!
HIGH SCHOOL KIDS ARE SO MEAN! I WALK AROUND JUST WANTING TO SLAP EVERYBODY.

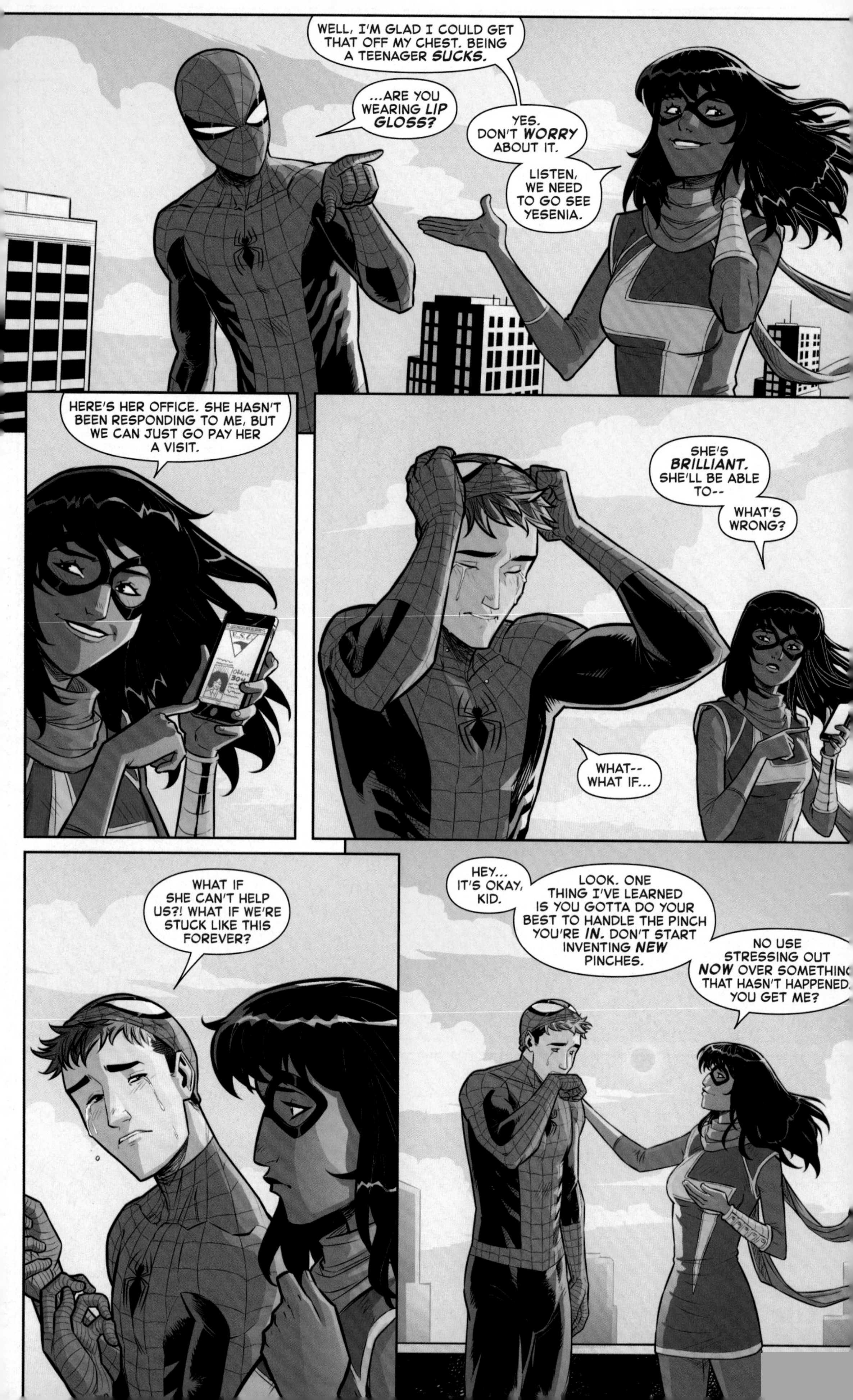
WELL, I'M GLAD I COULD GET THAT OFF MY CHEST. BEING A TEENAGER SUCKS.
...ARE YOU WEARING LIP GLOSS?
YES. DON'T WORRY ABOUT IT.
LISTEN, WE NEED TO GO SEE YESENIA.
HERE'S HER OFFICE. SHE HASN'T BEEN RESPONDING TO ME, BUT WE CAN JUST GO PAY HER A VISIT.
SHE'S BRILLIANT. SHE'LL BE ABLE TO--
WHAT'S WRONG?
WHAT-- WHAT IF...
WHAT IF SHE CAN'T HELP US?! WHAT IF WE'RE STUCK LIKE THIS FOREVER?
HEY... IT'S OKAY, KID.
LOOK. ONE THING I'VE LEARNED IS YOU GOTTA DO YOUR BEST TO HANDLE THE PINCH YOU'RE IN. DON'T START INVENTING NEW PINCHES.
NO USE STRESSING OUT NOW OVER SOMETHING THAT HASN'T HAPPENED. YOU GET ME?

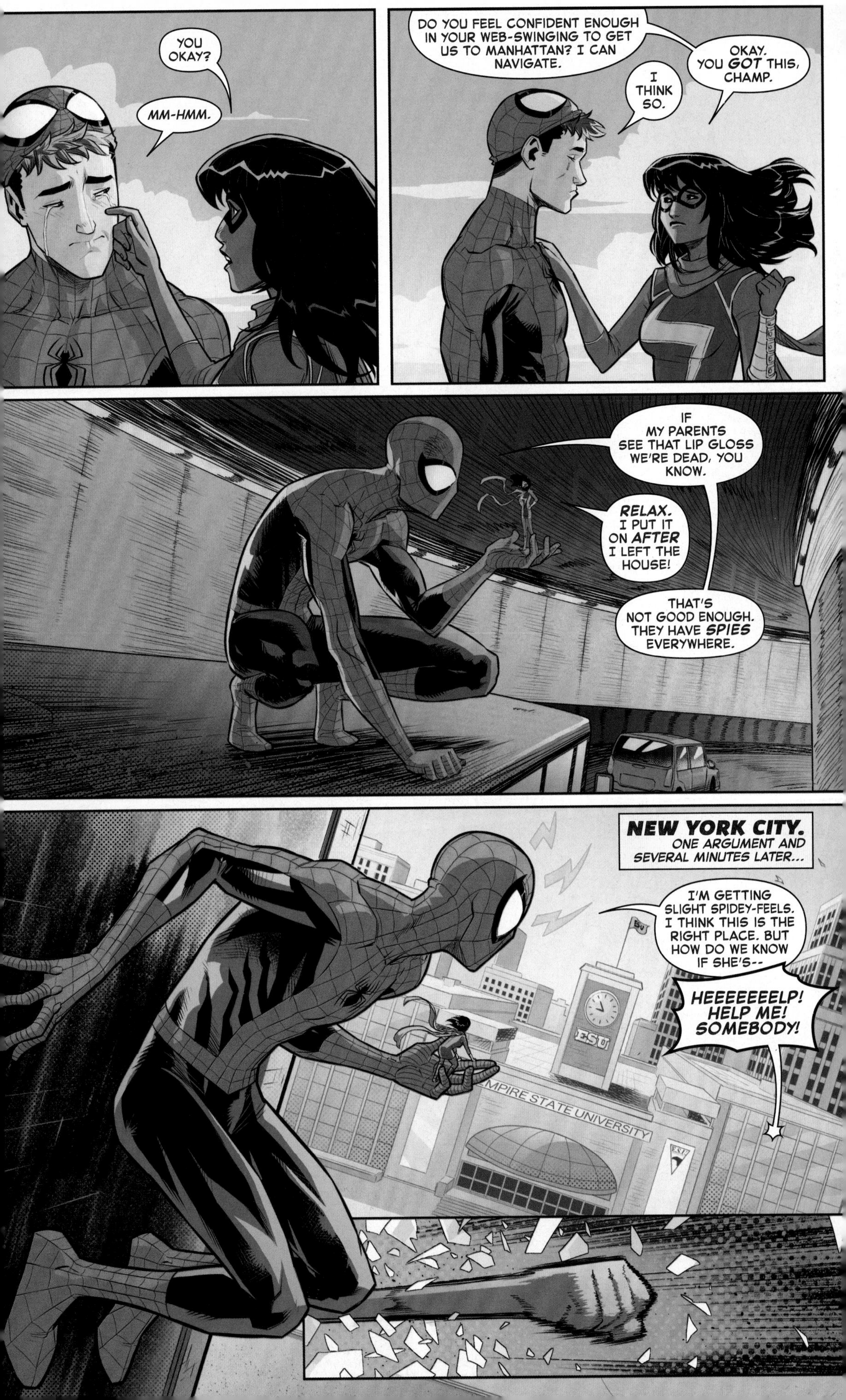
YOU OKAY?
MM-HMM.
DO YOU FEEL CONFIDENT ENOUGH IN YOUR WEB-SWINGING TO GET US TO MANHATTAN? I CAN NAVIGATE.
I THINK SO.
OKAY. YOU GOT THIS, CHAMP.
IF MY PARENTS SEE THAT LIP GLOSS WE'RE DEAD, YOU KNOW.
RELAX. I PUT IT ON AFTER I LEFT THE HOUSE!
THAT'S NOT GOOD ENOUGH. THEY HAVE SPIES EVERYWHERE.
NEW YORK CITY. ONE ARGUMENT AND SEVERAL MINUTES LATER...
I'M GETTING SLIGHT SPIDEY-FEELS. I THINK THIS IS THE RIGHT PLACE. BUT HOW DO WE KNOW IF SHE'S--
HEEEEEEELP! HELP ME! SOMEBODY!
ESU
EMPIRE STATE UNIVERSITY

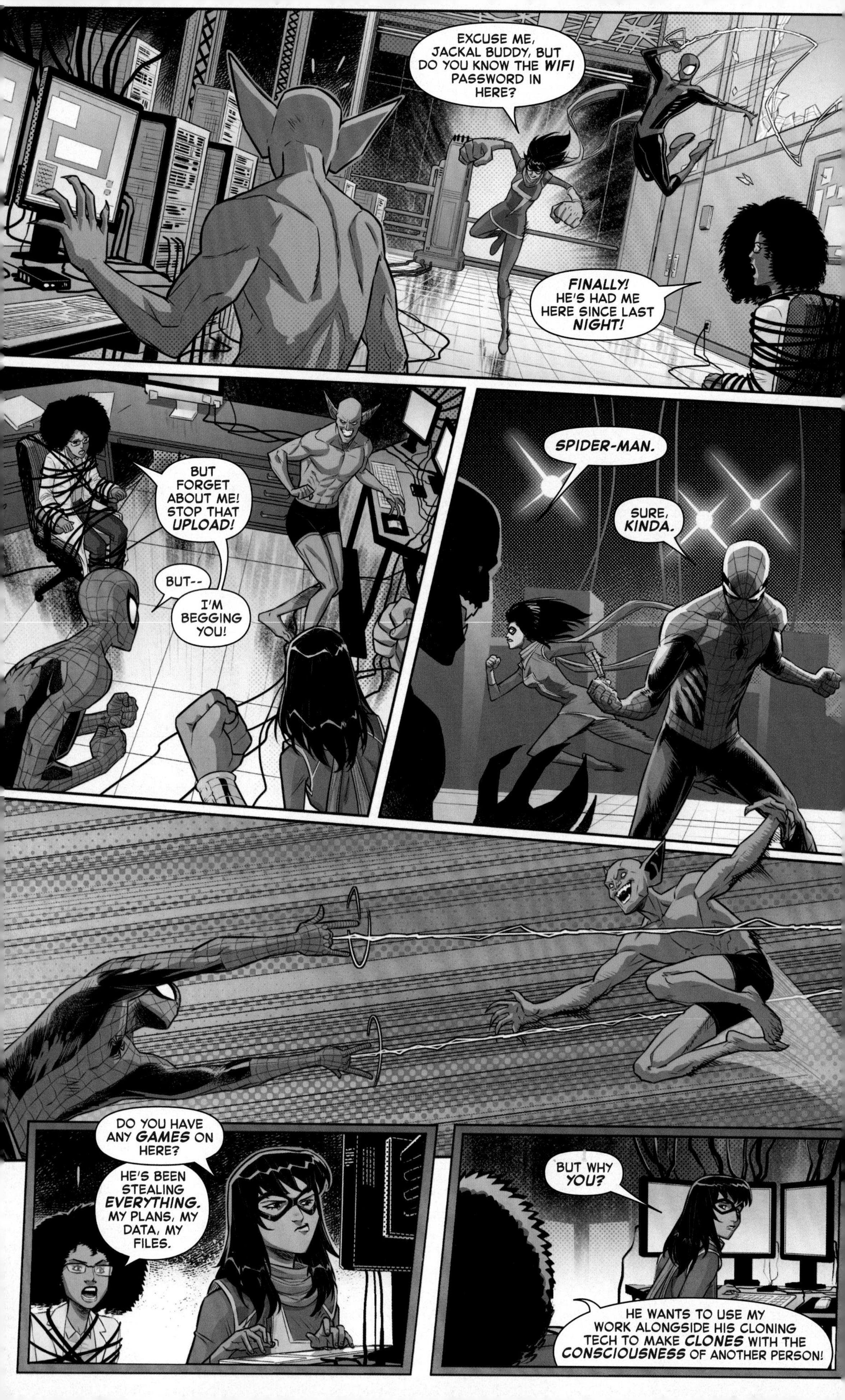
EXCUSE ME, JACKAL BUDDY, BUT DO YOU KNOW THE WIFI PASSWORD IN HERE?
FINALLY! HE'S HAD ME HERE SINCE LAST NIGHT!
BUT FORGET ABOUT ME! STOP THAT UPLOAD!
BUT--
I'M BEGGING YOU!
SPIDER-MAN.
SURE, KINDA.
DO YOU HAVE ANY GAMES ON HERE?
HE'S BEEN STEALING EVERYTHING. MY PLANS, MY DATA, MY FILES.
BUT WHY YOU?
HE WANTS TO USE MY WORK ALONGSIDE HIS CLONING TECH TO MAKE CLONES WITH THE CONSCIOUSNESS OF ANOTHER PERSON!

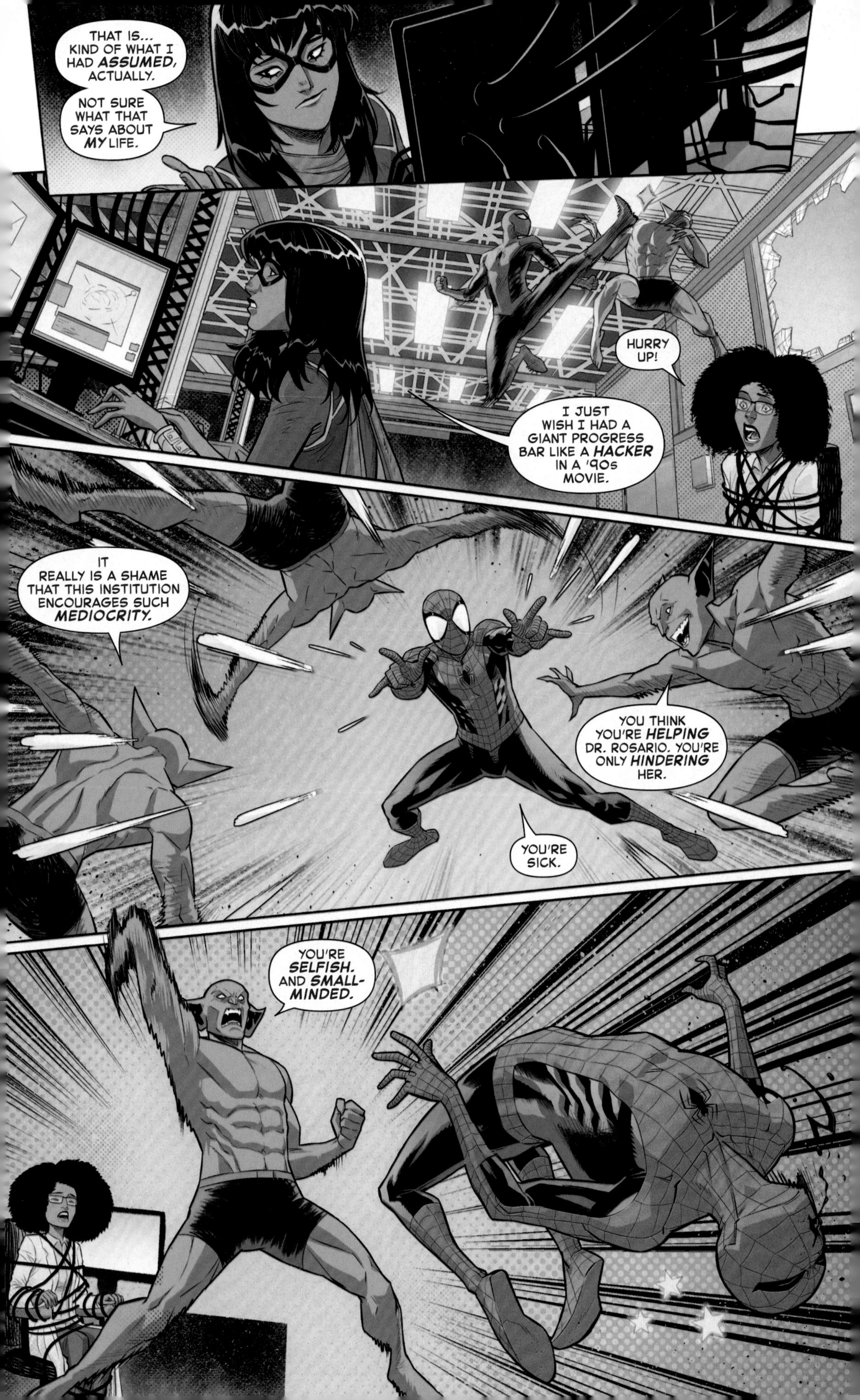
THAT IS... KIND OF WHAT I HAD ASSUMED, ACTUALLY.
NOT SURE WHAT THAT SAYS ABOUT MY LIFE.
HURRY UP!
I JUST WISH I HAD A GIANT PROGRESS BAR LIKE A HACKER IN A '90s MOVIE.
IT REALLY IS A SHAME THAT THIS INSTITUTION ENCOURAGES SUCH MEDIOCRITY.
YOU THINK YOU'RE HELPING DR. ROSARIO. YOU'RE ONLY HINDERING HER.
YOU'RE SICK.
YOU'RE SELFISH. AND SMALL-MINDED.

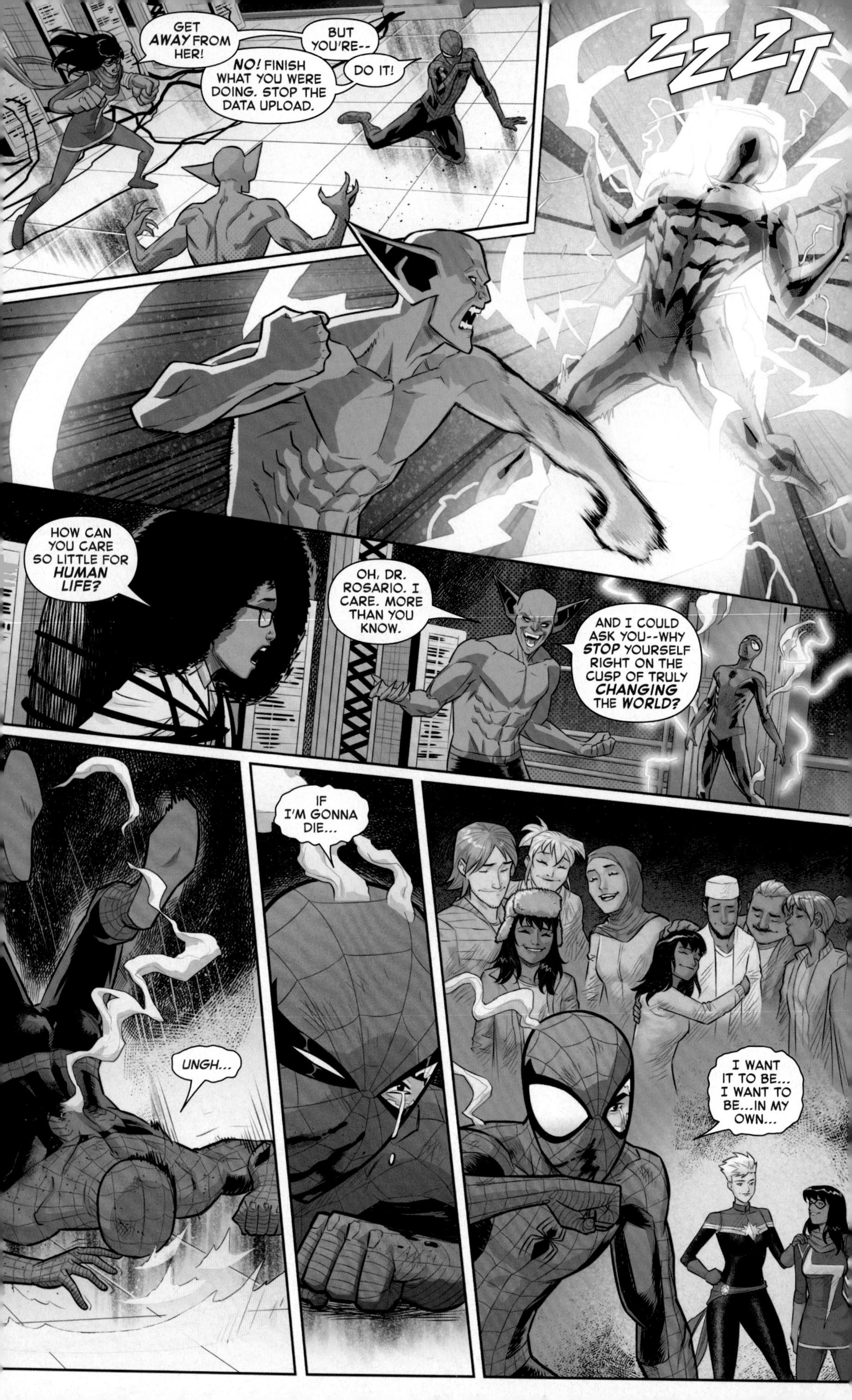
GET AWAY FROM HER!
BUT YOU'RE--
NO! FINISH WHAT YOU WERE DOING. STOP THE DATA UPLOAD.
DO IT!
ZZZT
HOW CAN YOU CARE SO LITTLE FOR HUMAN LIFE?
OH, DR. ROSARIO. I CARE. MORE THAN YOU KNOW.
AND I COULD ASK YOU--WHY STOP YOURSELF RIGHT ON THE CUSP OF TRULY CHANGING THE WORLD?
UNGH...
IF I'M GONNA DIE...
I WANT IT TO BE... I WANT TO BE...IN MY OWN...

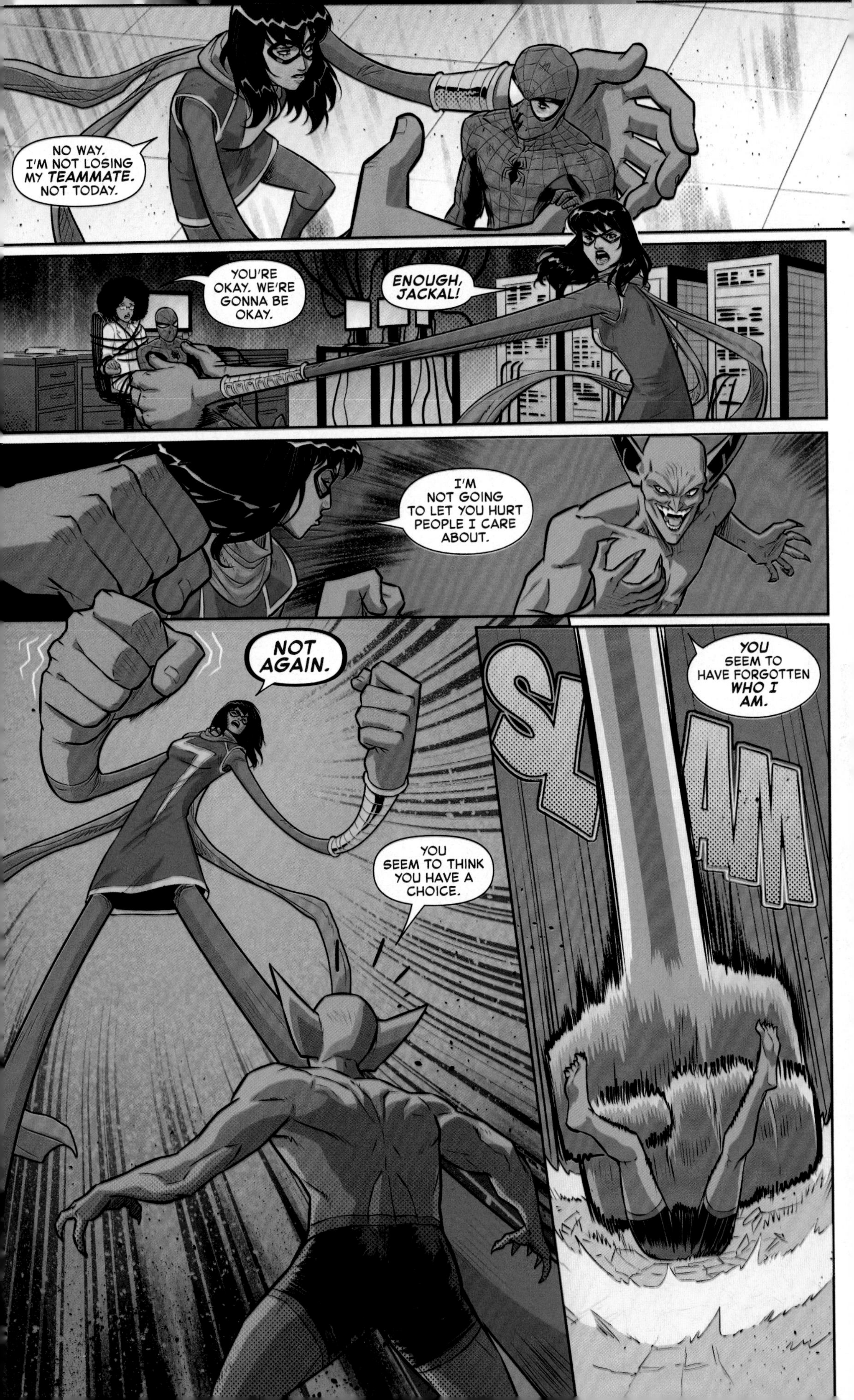
NO WAY. I'M NOT LOSING MY *TEAMMATE.* NOT TODAY.
YOU'RE OKAY. WE'RE GONNA BE OKAY.
ENOUGH, JACKAL!
I'M NOT GOING TO LET YOU HURT PEOPLE I CARE ABOUT.
NOT AGAIN.
YOU SEEM TO THINK YOU HAVE A CHOICE.
SLAM
YOU SEEM TO HAVE FORGOTTEN *WHO I AM.*

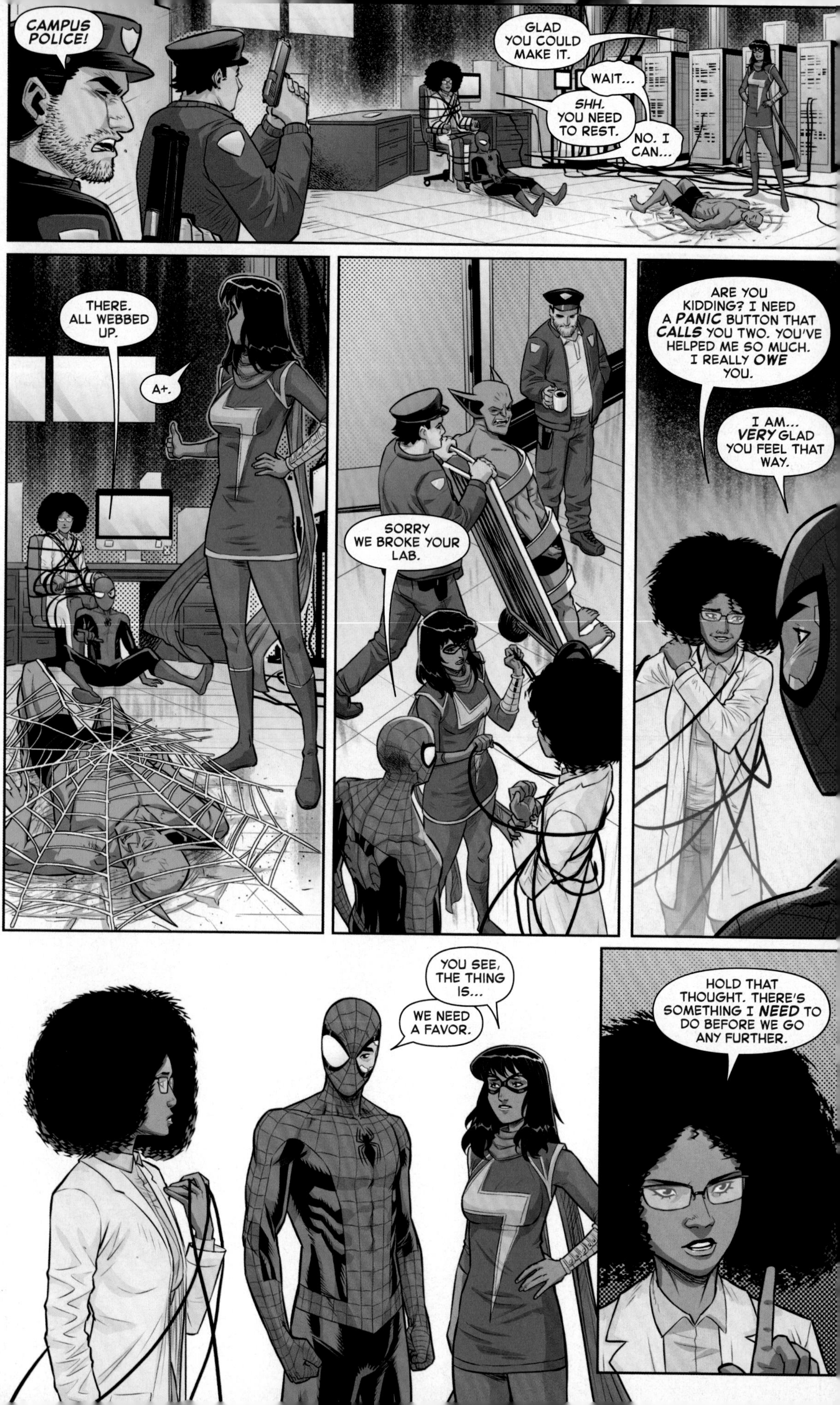
CAMPUS POLICE!
GLAD YOU COULD MAKE IT.
WAIT...
SHH. YOU NEED TO REST.
NO. I CAN...
THERE. ALL WEBBED UP.
A+.
SORRY WE BROKE YOUR LAB.
ARE YOU KIDDING? I NEED A PANIC BUTTON THAT CALLS YOU TWO. YOU'VE HELPED ME SO MUCH. I REALLY OWE YOU.
I AM... VERY GLAD YOU FEEL THAT WAY.
YOU SEE, THE THING IS...
WE NEED A FAVOR.
HOLD THAT THOUGHT. THERE'S SOMETHING I NEED TO DO BEFORE WE GO ANY FURTHER.

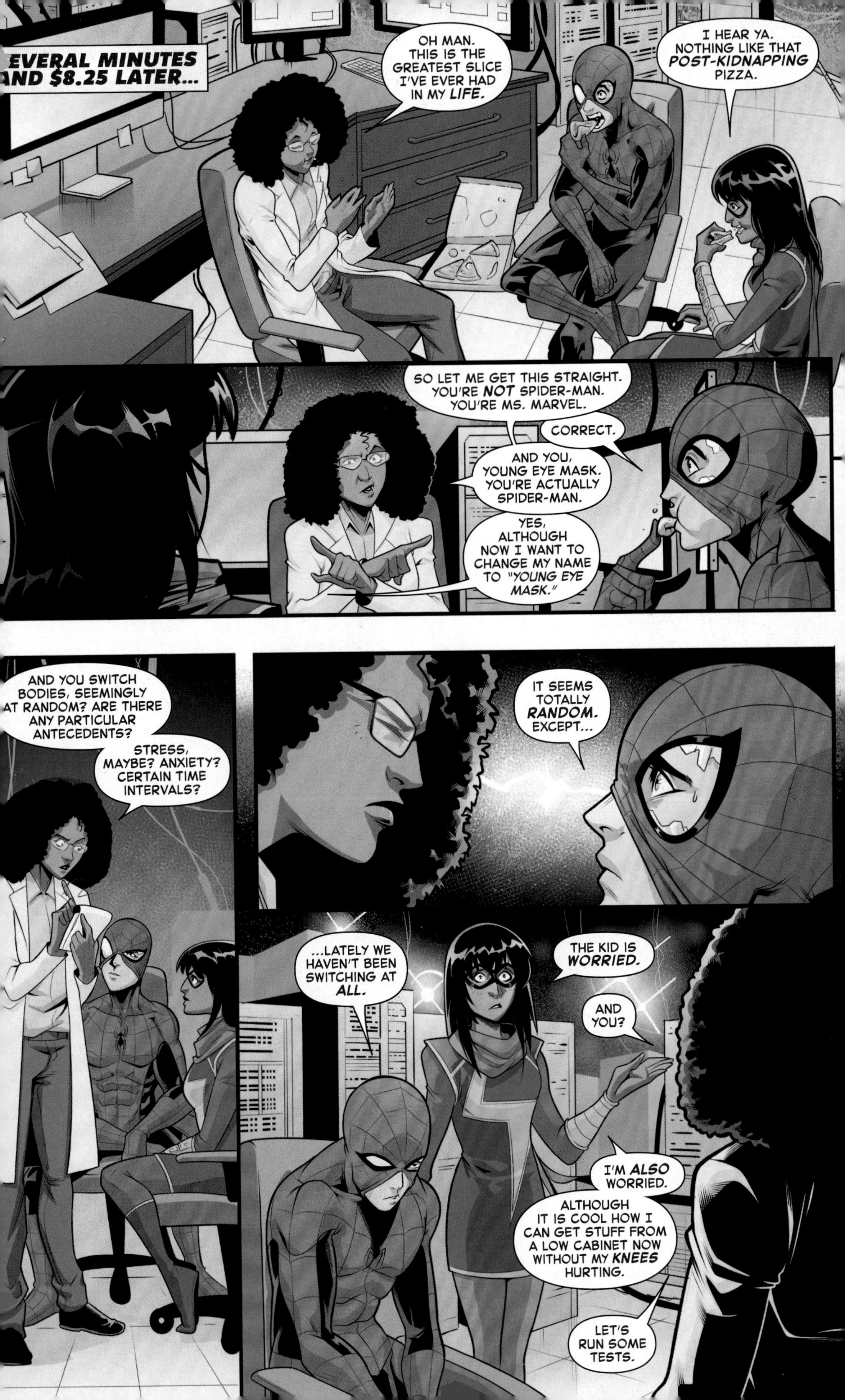
EVERAL MINUTES AND $8.25 LATER...
OH MAN. THIS IS THE GREATEST SLICE I'VE EVER HAD IN MY LIFE.
I HEAR YA. NOTHING LIKE THAT POST-KIDNAPPING PIZZA.
SO LET ME GET THIS STRAIGHT. YOU'RE NOT SPIDER-MAN. YOU'RE MS. MARVEL.
CORRECT.
AND YOU, YOUNG EYE MASK. YOU'RE ACTUALLY SPIDER-MAN.
YES, ALTHOUGH NOW I WANT TO CHANGE MY NAME TO "YOUNG EYE MASK."
AND YOU SWITCH BODIES, SEEMINGLY AT RANDOM? ARE THERE ANY PARTICULAR ANTECEDENTS?
STRESS, MAYBE? ANXIETY? CERTAIN TIME INTERVALS?
IT SEEMS TOTALLY RANDOM. EXCEPT...
...LATELY WE HAVEN'T BEEN SWITCHING AT ALL.
THE KID IS WORRIED.
AND YOU?
I'M ALSO WORRIED.
ALTHOUGH IT IS COOL HOW I CAN GET STUFF FROM A LOW CABINET NOW WITHOUT MY KNEES HURTING.
LET'S RUN SOME TESTS.

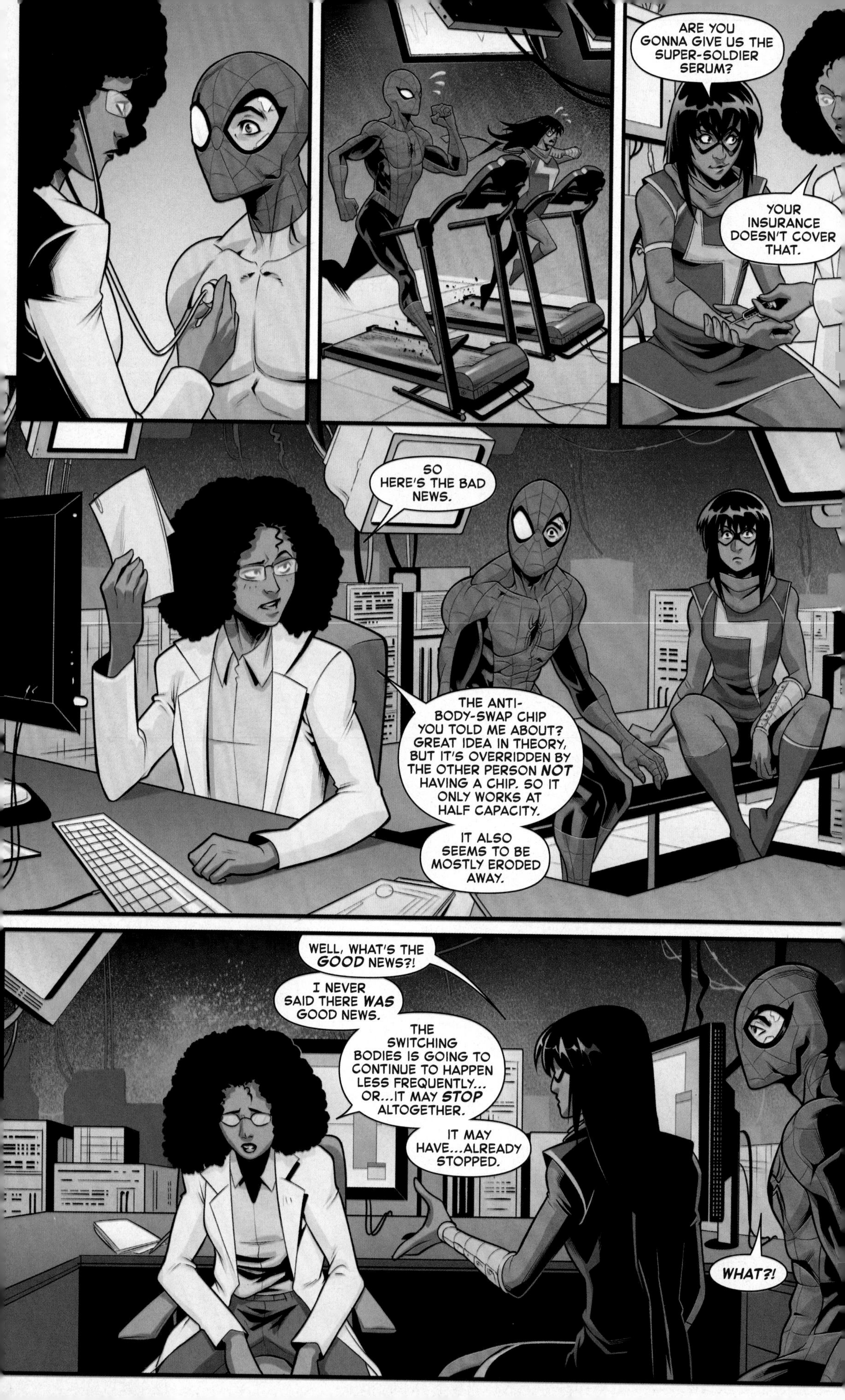
ARE YOU GONNA GIVE US THE SUPER-SOLDIER SERUM?
YOUR INSURANCE DOESN'T COVER THAT.
SO HERE'S THE BAD NEWS.
THE ANTI-BODY-SWAP CHIP YOU TOLD ME ABOUT? GREAT IDEA IN THEORY, BUT IT'S OVERRIDDEN BY THE OTHER PERSON NOT HAVING A CHIP. SO IT ONLY WORKS AT HALF CAPACITY.
IT ALSO SEEMS TO BE MOSTLY ERODED AWAY.
WELL, WHAT'S THE GOOD NEWS?!
I NEVER SAID THERE WAS GOOD NEWS.
THE SWITCHING BODIES IS GOING TO CONTINUE TO HAPPEN LESS FREQUENTLY... OR...IT MAY STOP ALTOGETHER.
IT MAY HAVE...ALREADY STOPPED.
WHAT?!

SO WE'RE JUST GONNA BE TRAPPED LIKE THIS? *FOREVER?* CAN'T YOU *DO* SOMETHING?

I'M...SO, SO SORRY. IF I HAD POLLY, I COULD, MAYBE. BUT THE MACHINE IS DESTROYED.

MY...MY LIFE. I WANT TO BE *ME* AGAIN.

WAIT! I HAVE AN IDEA.

A *PROFESSOR* HERE AT ESU-- CURT CONNORS. HE DISCOVERED A WAY TO *SEPARATE* PARTS OF YOUR PERSONALITY.

USING THE ISOTOPE GENOME ACCELERATOR! I SAW HIM PRESENT A PAPER ON THAT. HOW DO YOU KNOW ABOUT IT?

I'VE HAD BAD BODY-SWAP EXPERIENCES *AND* BAD SPLIT-INTO-TWO-PEOPLE EXPERIENCES.*

*SEE *AMAZING SPIDER-MAN* #2. --E.E.

WE MIGHT BE ABLE TO MODIFY ITS SETTINGS TO SWITCH OURSELVES BACK!

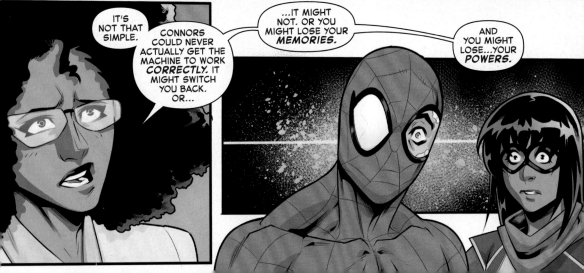

IT'S NOT THAT SIMPLE. CONNORS COULD NEVER ACTUALLY GET THE MACHINE TO WORK *CORRECTLY.* IT MIGHT SWITCH YOU BACK. OR...

...IT MIGHT NOT. OR YOU MIGHT LOSE YOUR *MEMORIES.*

AND YOU MIGHT LOSE...YOUR *POWERS.*

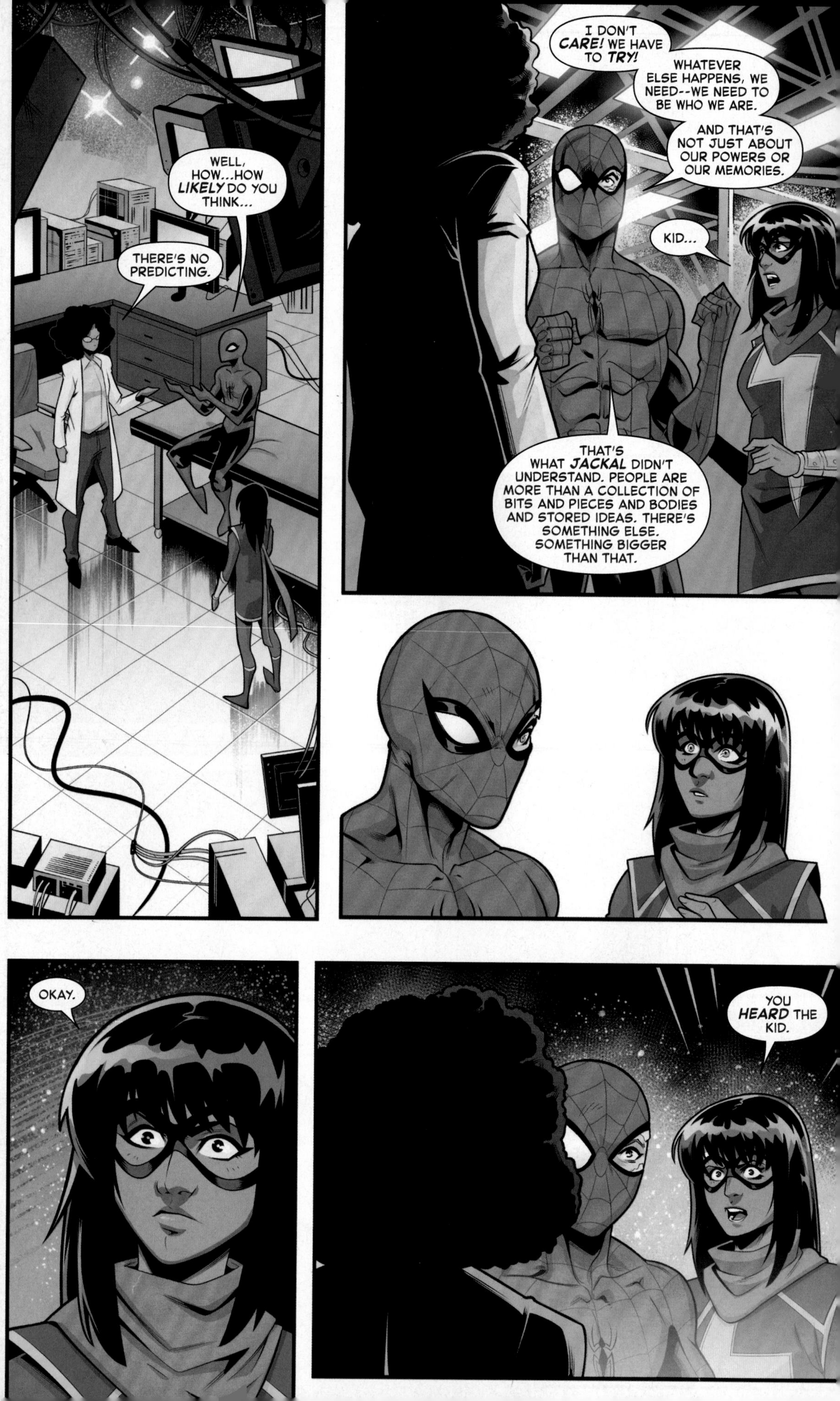
WELL, HOW...HOW LIKELY DO YOU THINK...
THERE'S NO PREDICTING.
I DON'T CARE! WE HAVE TO TRY!
WHATEVER ELSE HAPPENS, WE NEED--WE NEED TO BE WHO WE ARE.
AND THAT'S NOT JUST ABOUT OUR POWERS OR OUR MEMORIES.
KID...
THAT'S WHAT JACKAL DIDN'T UNDERSTAND. PEOPLE ARE MORE THAN A COLLECTION OF BITS AND PIECES AND BODIES AND STORED IDEAS. THERE'S SOMETHING ELSE. SOMETHING BIGGER THAN THAT.
OKAY.
YOU HEARD THE KID.

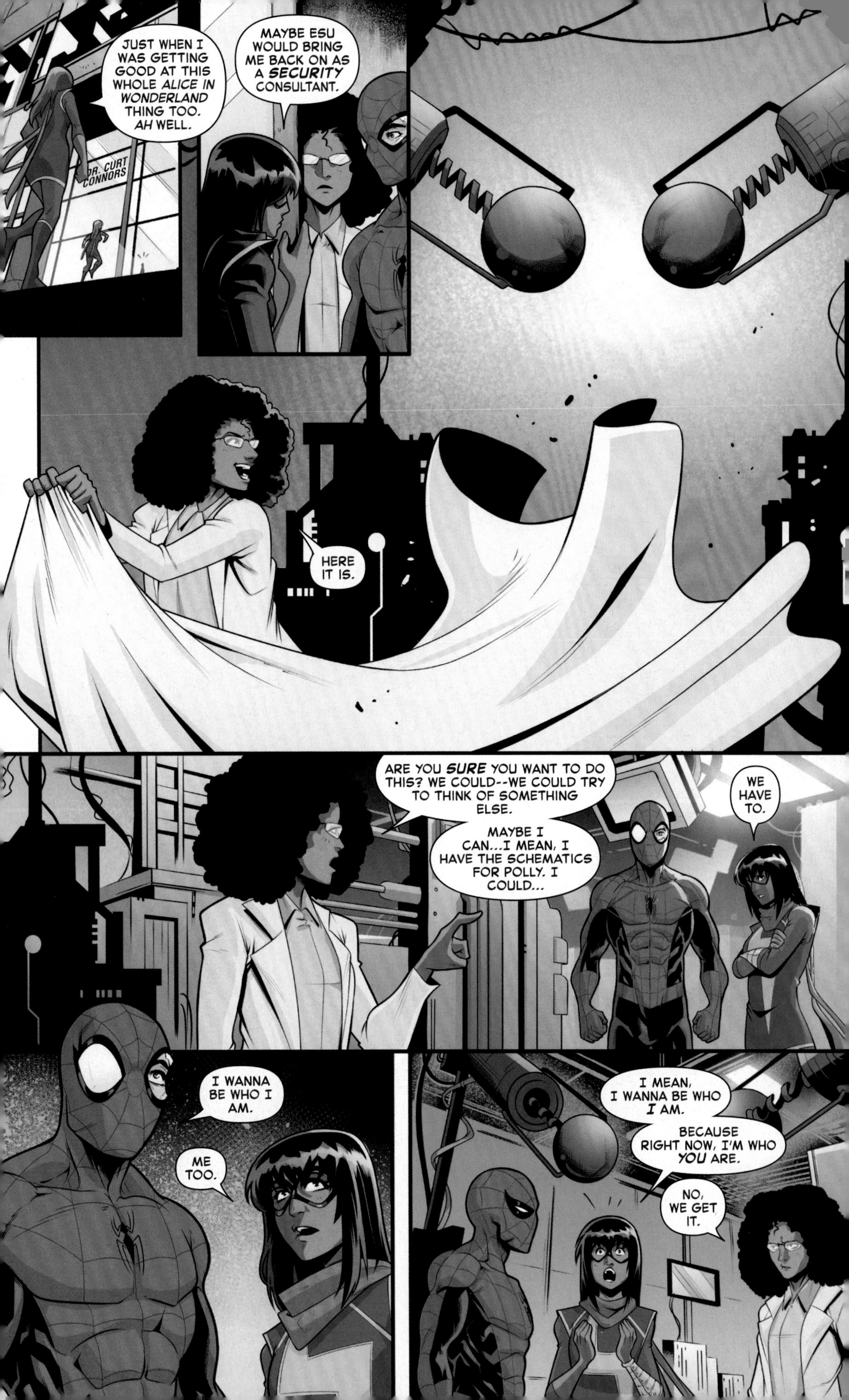
JUST WHEN I WAS GETTING GOOD AT THIS WHOLE ALICE IN WONDERLAND THING TOO. AH WELL.
DR. CURT CONNORS
MAYBE ESU WOULD BRING ME BACK ON AS A SECURITY CONSULTANT.
HERE IT IS.
ARE YOU SURE YOU WANT TO DO THIS? WE COULD--WE COULD TRY TO THINK OF SOMETHING ELSE.
MAYBE I CAN...I MEAN, I HAVE THE SCHEMATICS FOR POLLY. I COULD...
WE HAVE TO.
I WANNA BE WHO I AM.
ME TOO.
I MEAN, I WANNA BE WHO I AM.
BECAUSE RIGHT NOW, I'M WHO YOU ARE.
NO, WE GET IT.

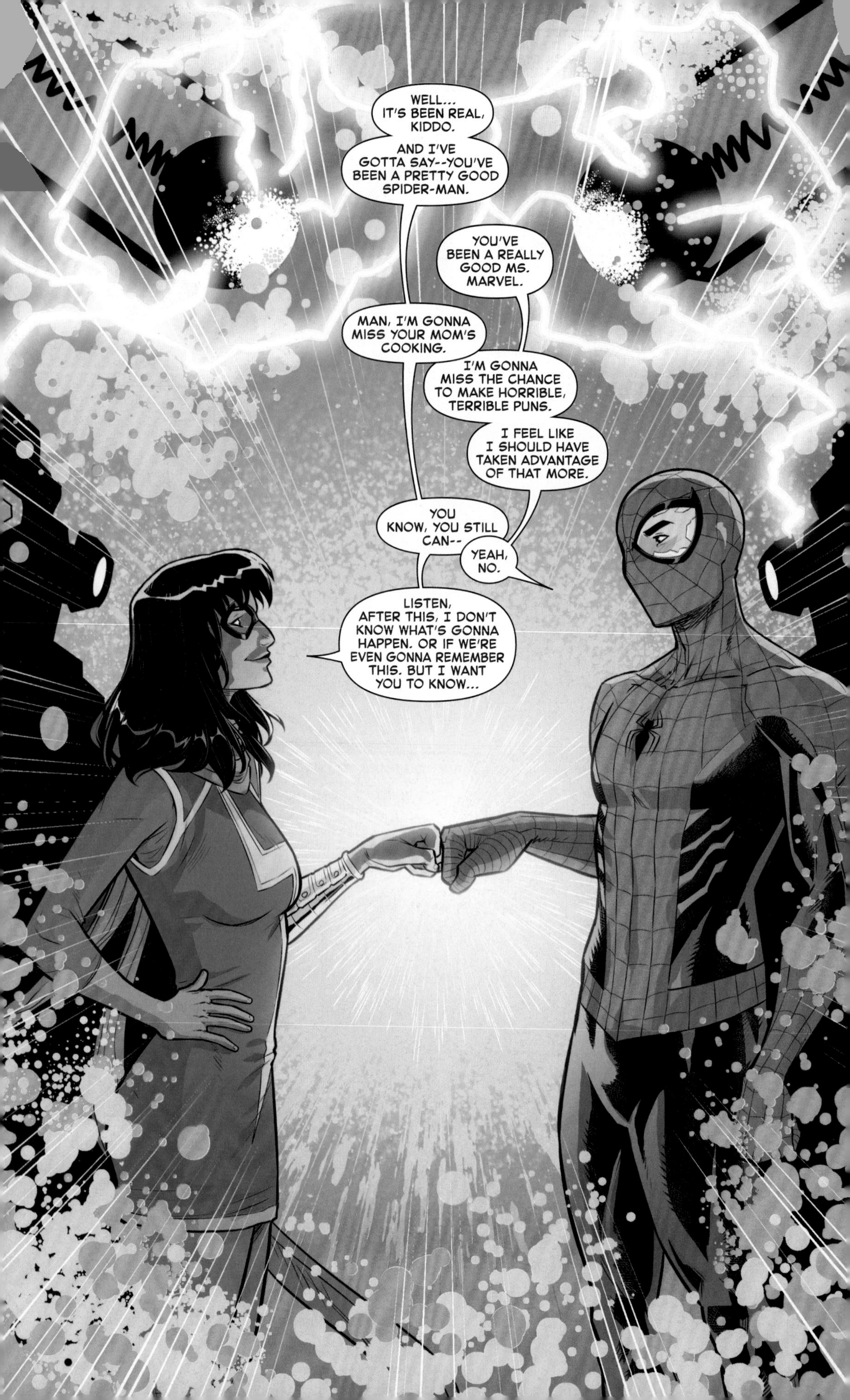
WELL... IT'S BEEN REAL, KIDDO.
AND I'VE GOTTA SAY--YOU'VE BEEN A PRETTY GOOD SPIDER-MAN.
YOU'VE BEEN A REALLY GOOD MS. MARVEL.
MAN, I'M GONNA MISS YOUR MOM'S COOKING.
I'M GONNA MISS THE CHANCE TO MAKE HORRIBLE, TERRIBLE PUNS.
I FEEL LIKE I SHOULD HAVE TAKEN ADVANTAGE OF THAT MORE.
YOU KNOW, YOU STILL CAN--
YEAH, NO.
LISTEN, AFTER THIS, I DON'T KNOW WHAT'S GONNA HAPPEN. OR IF WE'RE EVEN GONNA REMEMBER THIS. BUT I WANT YOU TO KNOW...

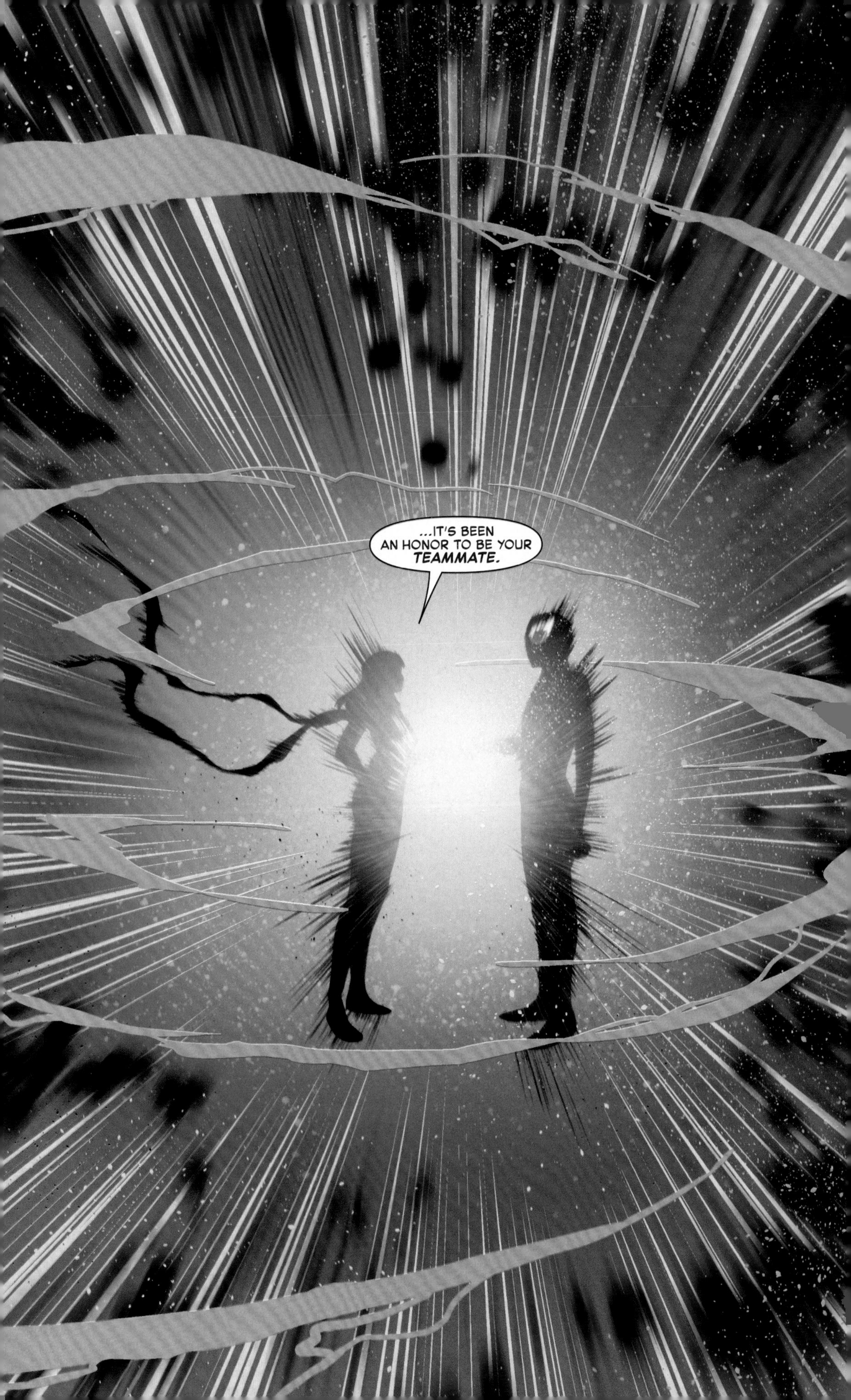
...IT'S BEEN AN HONOR TO BE YOUR TEAMMATE.

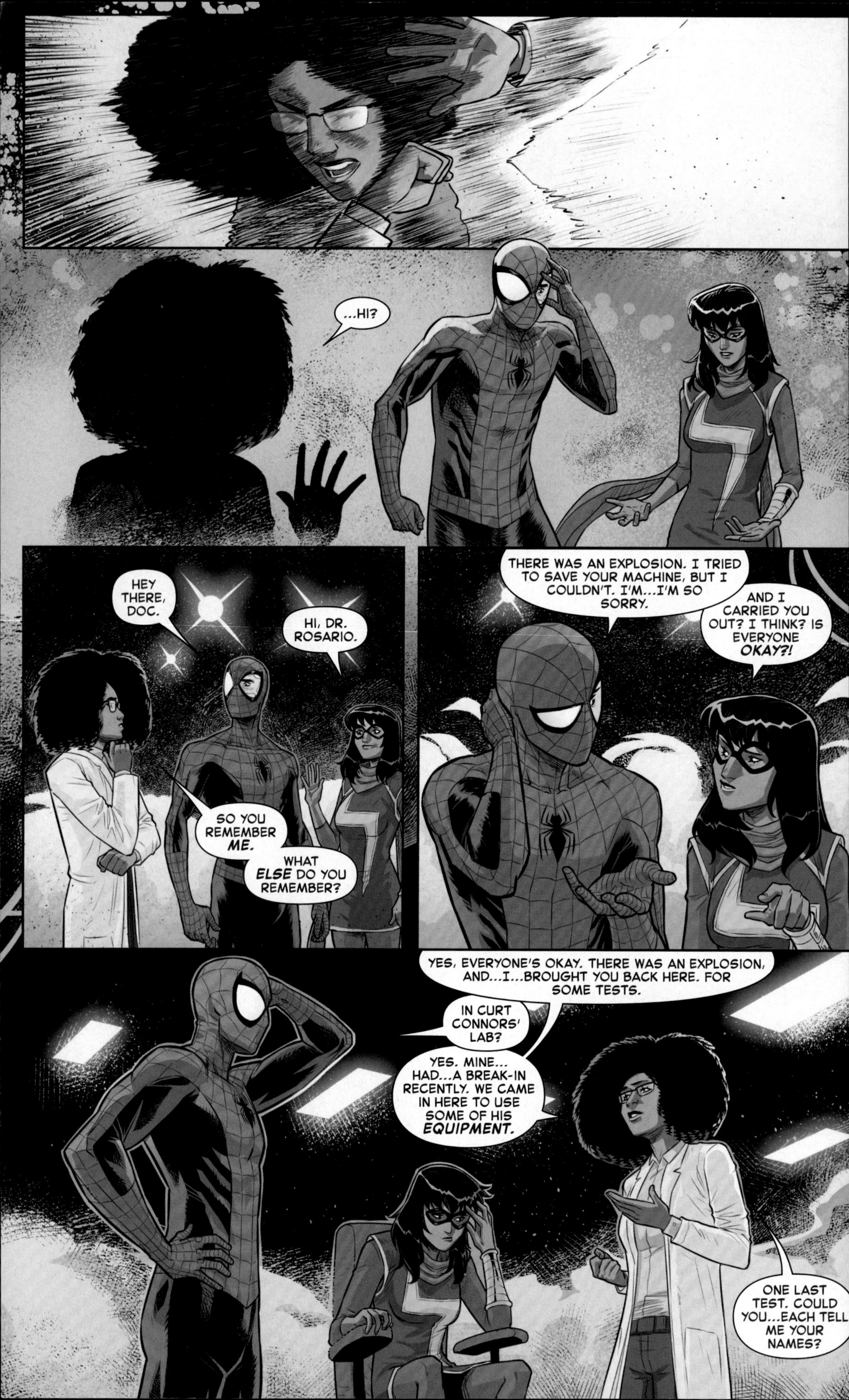
...HI?
HEY THERE, DOC.
HI, DR. ROSARIO.
SO YOU REMEMBER ME.
WHAT ELSE DO YOU REMEMBER?
THERE WAS AN EXPLOSION. I TRIED TO SAVE YOUR MACHINE, BUT I COULDN'T. I'M...I'M SO SORRY.
AND I CARRIED YOU OUT? I THINK? IS EVERYONE OKAY?!
YES, EVERYONE'S OKAY. THERE WAS AN EXPLOSION, AND...I...BROUGHT YOU BACK HERE. FOR SOME TESTS.
IN CURT CONNORS' LAB?
YES. MINE... HAD...A BREAK-IN RECENTLY. WE CAME IN HERE TO USE SOME OF HIS EQUIPMENT.
ONE LAST TEST. COULD YOU...EACH TELL ME YOUR NAMES?

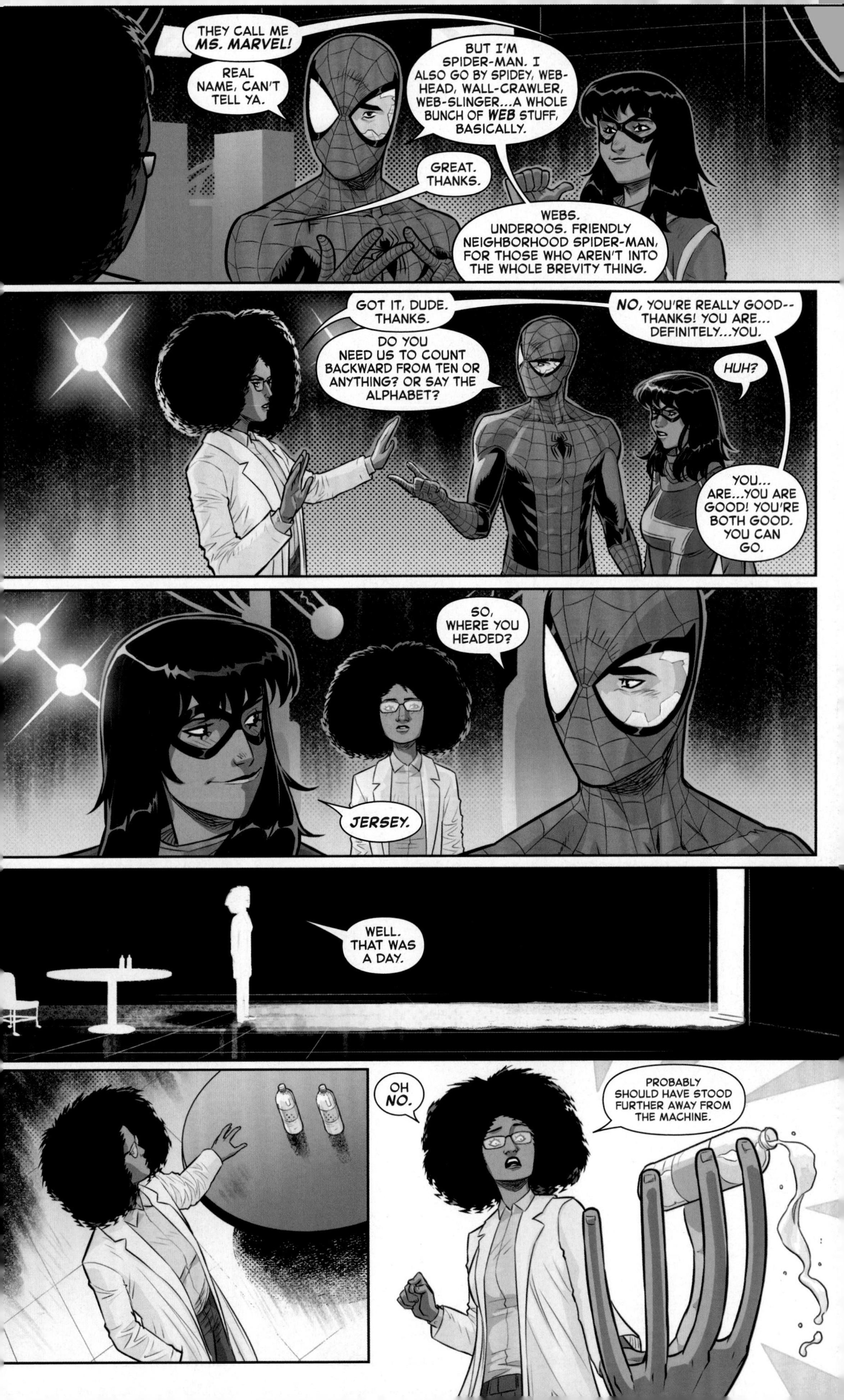
THEY CALL ME MS. MARVEL!
REAL NAME, CAN'T TELL YA.
BUT I'M SPIDER-MAN. I ALSO GO BY SPIDEY, WEB-HEAD, WALL-CRAWLER, WEB-SLINGER...A WHOLE BUNCH OF WEB STUFF, BASICALLY.
GREAT. THANKS.
WEBS. UNDEROOS. FRIENDLY NEIGHBORHOOD SPIDER-MAN, FOR THOSE WHO AREN'T INTO THE WHOLE BREVITY THING.
GOT IT, DUDE. THANKS.
DO YOU NEED US TO COUNT BACKWARD FROM TEN OR ANYTHING? OR SAY THE ALPHABET?
NO, YOU'RE REALLY GOOD--THANKS! YOU ARE... DEFINITELY...YOU.
HUH?
YOU... ARE...YOU ARE GOOD! YOU'RE BOTH GOOD. YOU CAN GO.
SO, WHERE YOU HEADED?
JERSEY.
WELL. THAT WAS A DAY.
OH NO.
PROBABLY SHOULD HAVE STOOD FURTHER AWAY FROM THE MACHINE.

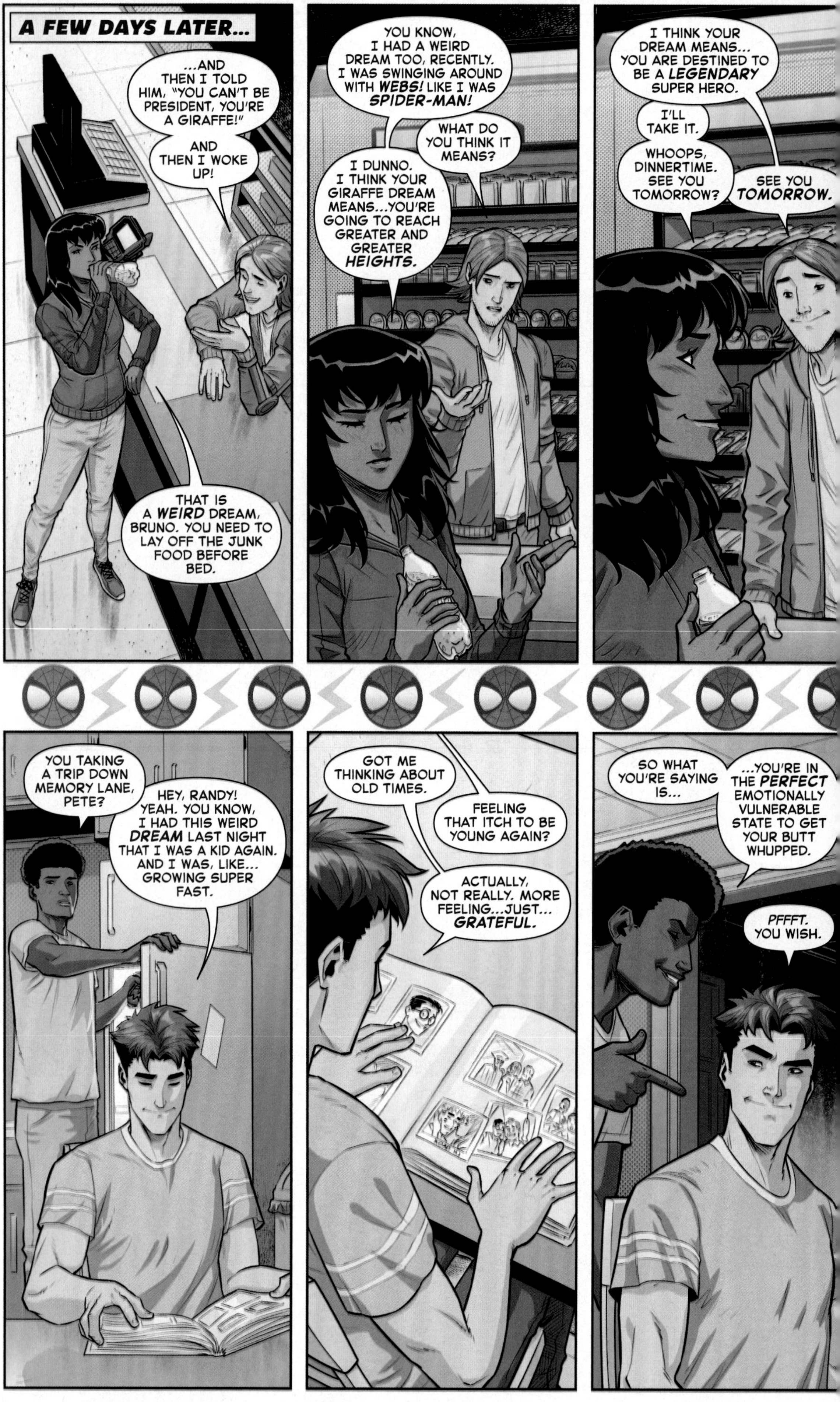
A FEW DAYS LATER...
...AND THEN I TOLD HIM, "YOU CAN'T BE PRESIDENT, YOU'RE A GIRAFFE!"
AND THEN I WOKE UP!
THAT IS A WEIRD DREAM, BRUNO. YOU NEED TO LAY OFF THE JUNK FOOD BEFORE BED.
YOU KNOW, I HAD A WEIRD DREAM TOO, RECENTLY. I WAS SWINGING AROUND WITH WEBS! LIKE I WAS SPIDER-MAN!
WHAT DO YOU THINK IT MEANS?
I DUNNO. I THINK YOUR GIRAFFE DREAM MEANS...YOU'RE GOING TO REACH GREATER AND GREATER HEIGHTS.
I THINK YOUR DREAM MEANS... YOU ARE DESTINED TO BE A LEGENDARY SUPER HERO.
I'LL TAKE IT.
WHOOPS, DINNERTIME. SEE YOU TOMORROW?
SEE YOU TOMORROW.
YOU TAKING A TRIP DOWN MEMORY LANE, PETE?
HEY, RANDY! YEAH. YOU KNOW, I HAD THIS WEIRD DREAM LAST NIGHT THAT I WAS A KID AGAIN. AND I WAS, LIKE... GROWING SUPER FAST.
GOT ME THINKING ABOUT OLD TIMES.
FEELING THAT ITCH TO BE YOUNG AGAIN?
ACTUALLY, NOT REALLY. MORE FEELING...JUST... GRATEFUL.
SO WHAT YOU'RE SAYING IS...
...YOU'RE IN THE PERFECT EMOTIONALLY VULNERABLE STATE TO GET YOUR BUTT WHUPPED.
PFFFT. YOU WISH.

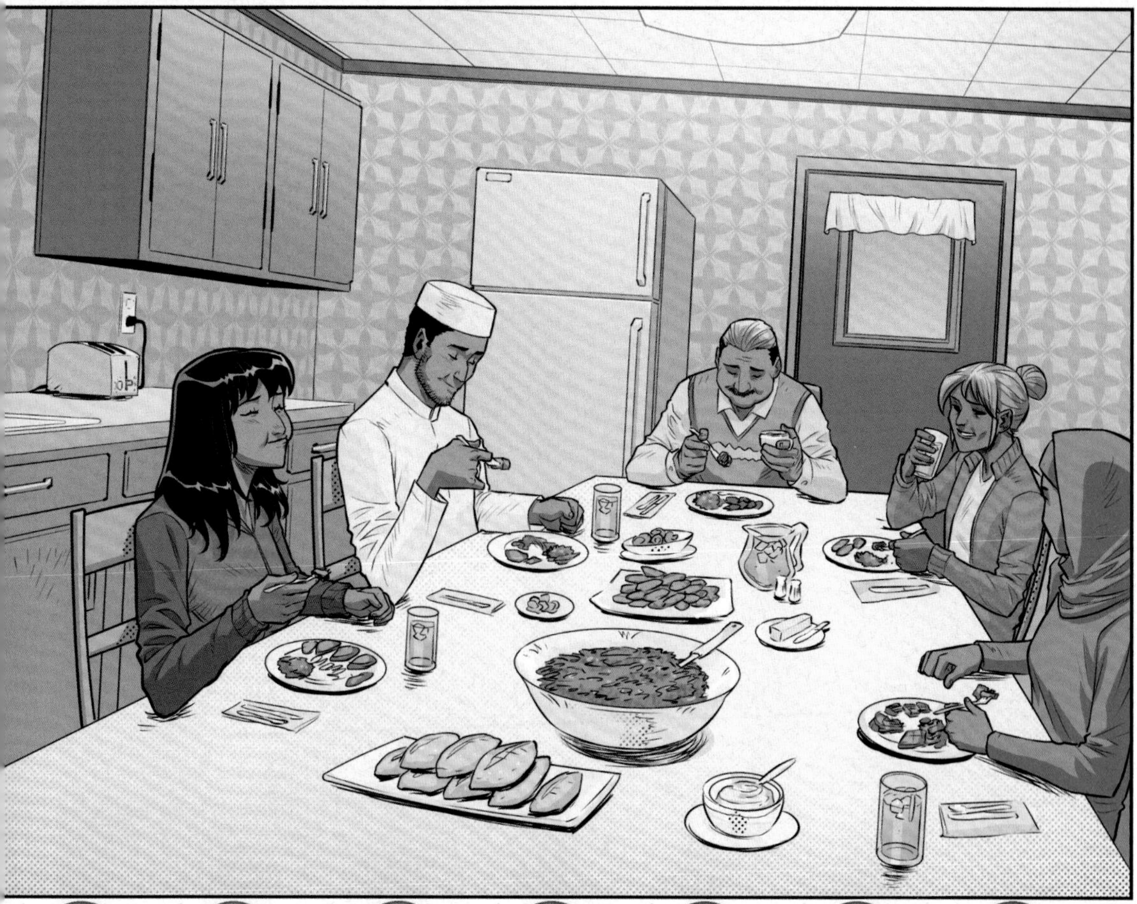

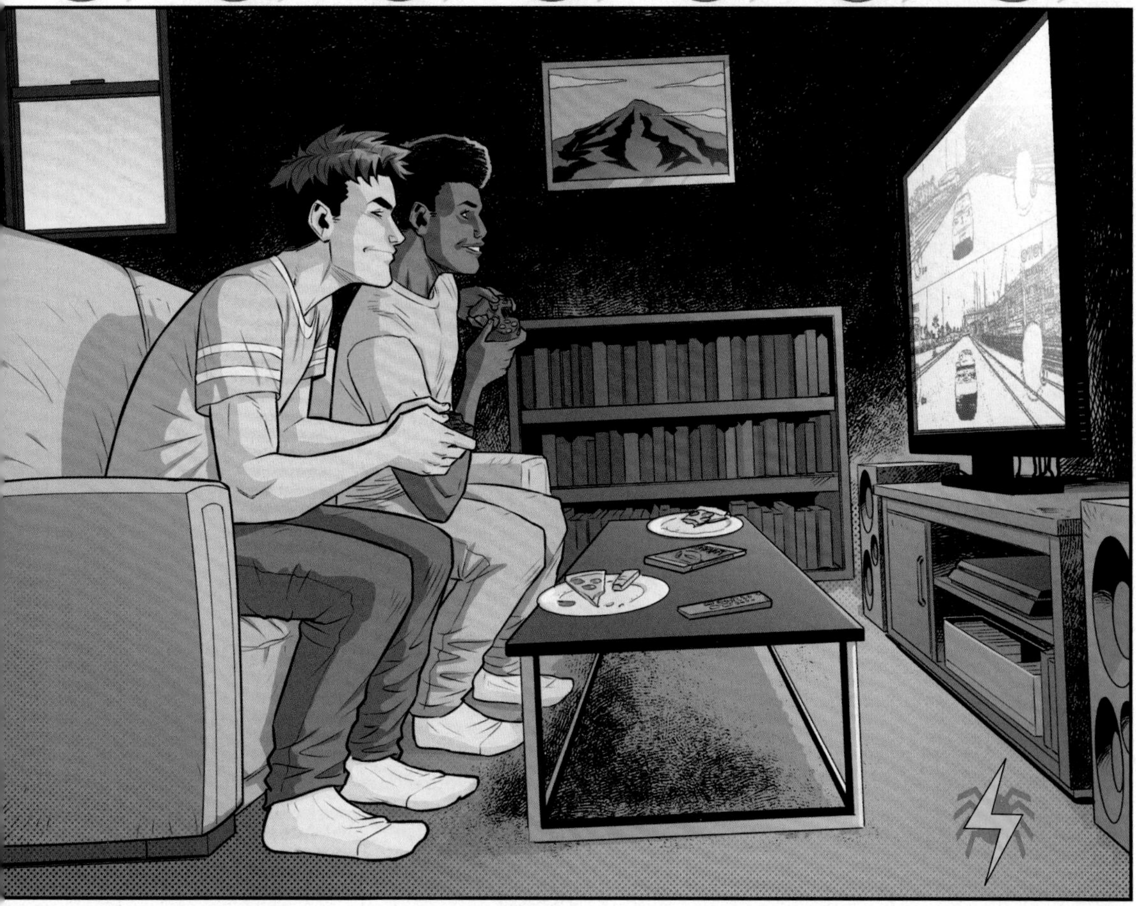

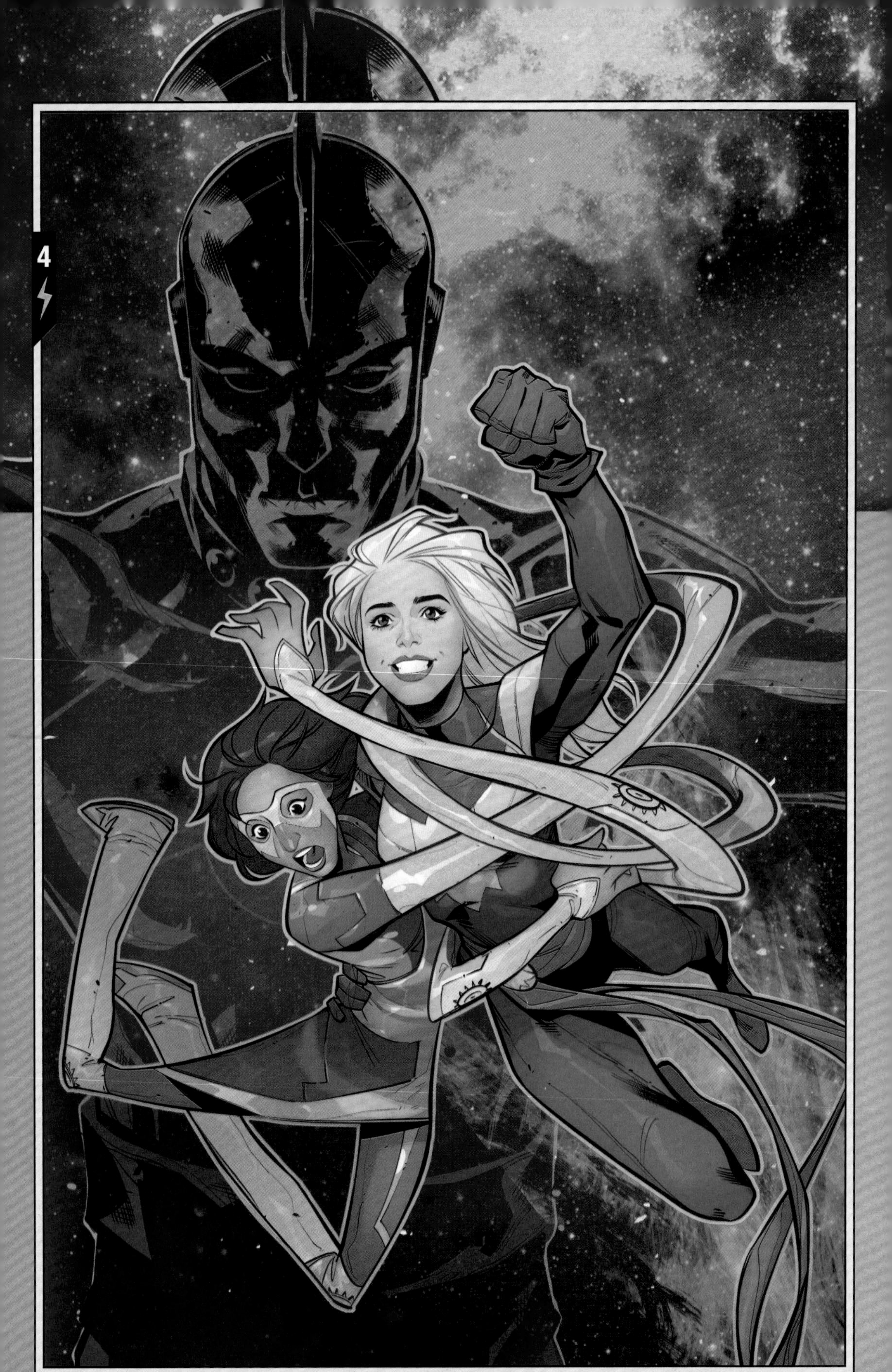
4

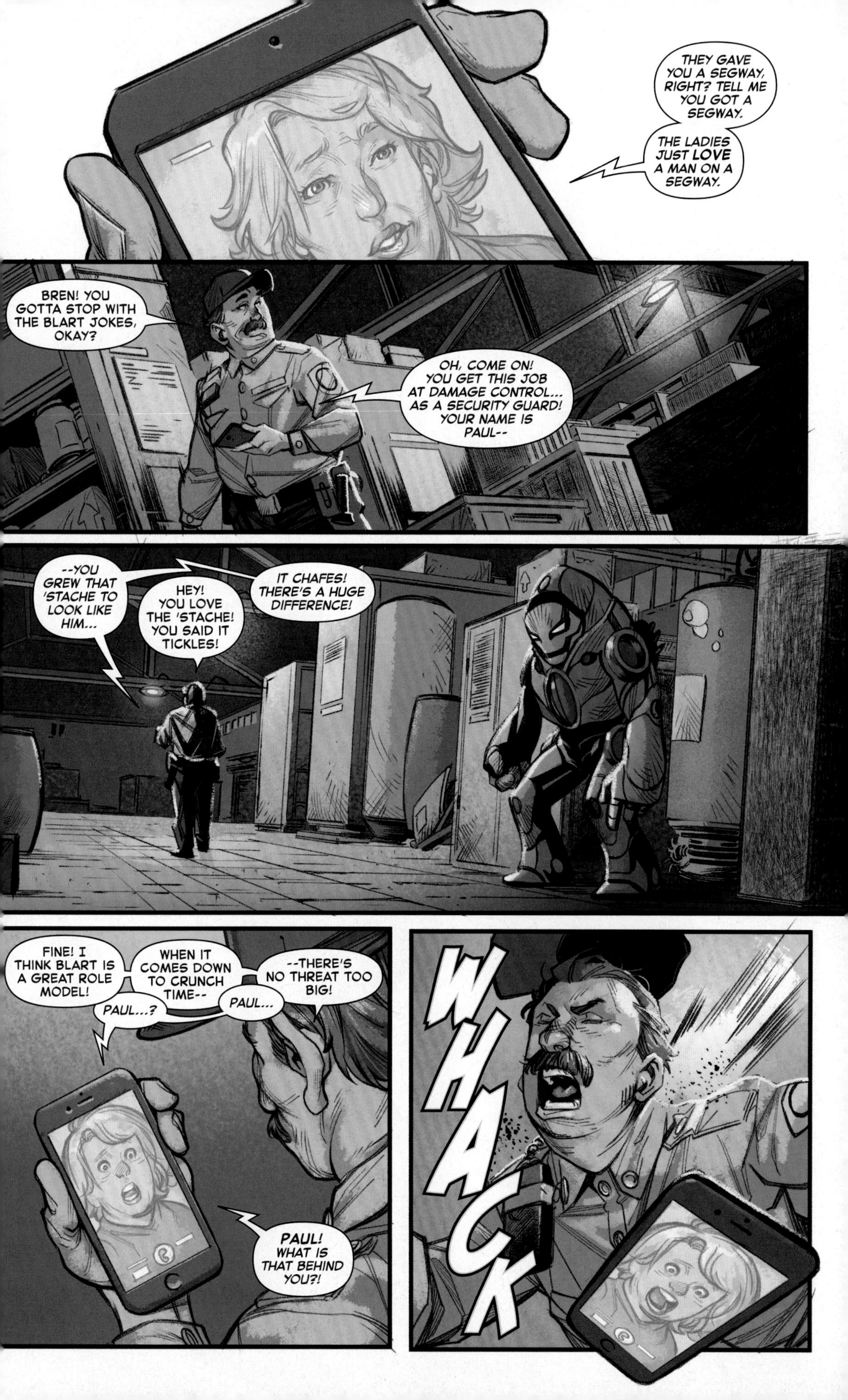
THEY GAVE YOU A SEGWAY, RIGHT? TELL ME YOU GOT A SEGWAY.
THE LADIES JUST LOVE A MAN ON A SEGWAY.
BREN! YOU GOTTA STOP WITH THE BLART JOKES, OKAY?
OH, COME ON! YOU GET THIS JOB AT DAMAGE CONTROL... AS A SECURITY GUARD! YOUR NAME IS PAUL--
--YOU GREW THAT 'STACHE TO LOOK LIKE HIM...
HEY! YOU LOVE THE 'STACHE! YOU SAID IT TICKLES!
IT CHAFES! THERE'S A HUGE DIFFERENCE!
FINE! I THINK BLART IS A GREAT ROLE MODEL!
WHEN IT COMES DOWN TO CRUNCH TIME--
--THERE'S NO THREAT TOO BIG!
PAUL...?
PAUL...
PAUL! WHAT IS THAT BEHIND YOU?!
WHACK

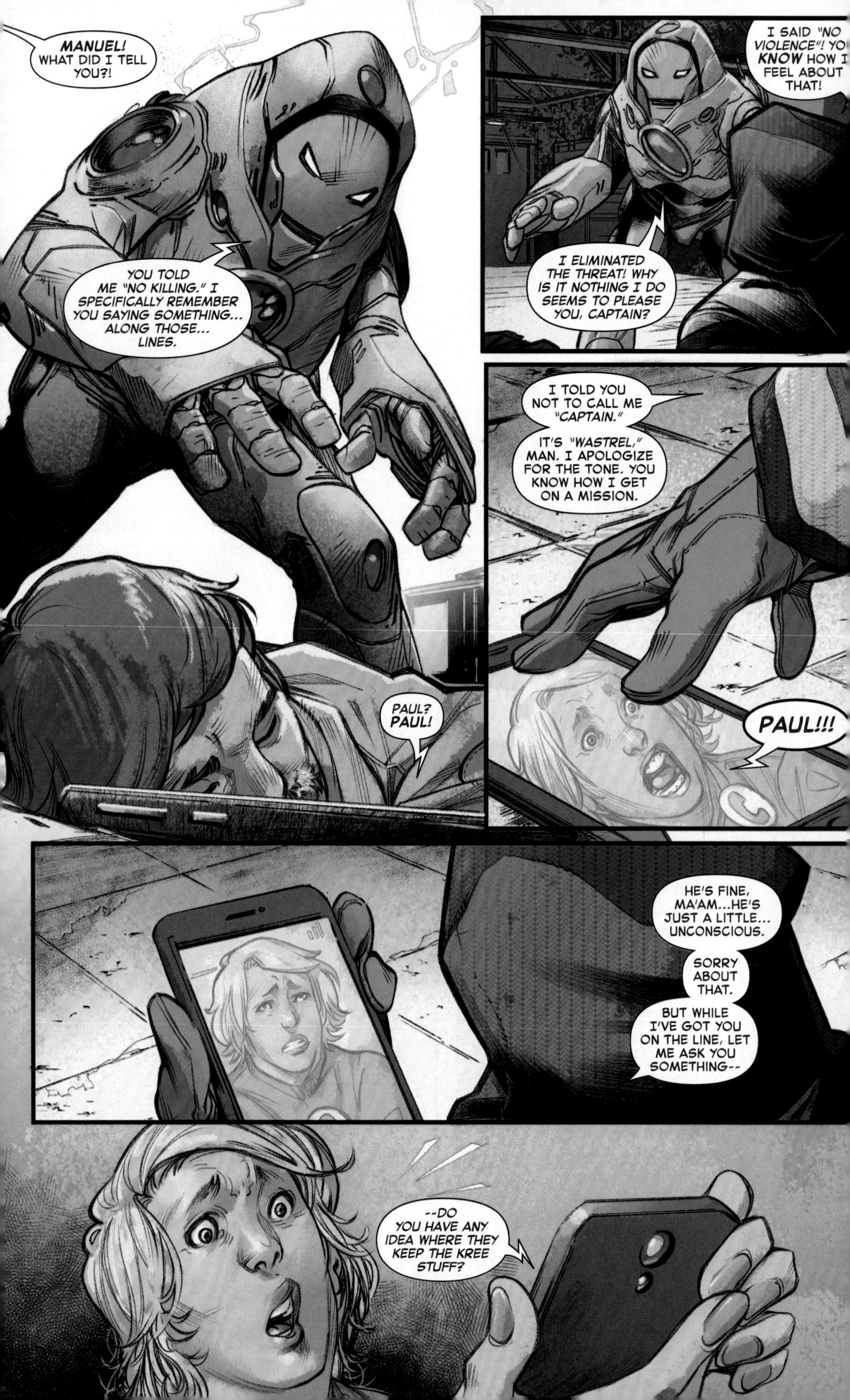

MANUEL! WHAT DID I TELL YOU?!
YOU TOLD ME "NO KILLING." I SPECIFICALLY REMEMBER YOU SAYING SOMETHING... ALONG THOSE... LINES.
I SAID "NO VIOLENCE"! YOU KNOW HOW I FEEL ABOUT THAT!
I ELIMINATED THE THREAT! WHY IS IT NOTHING I DO SEEMS TO PLEASE YOU, CAPTAIN?
PAUL? PAUL!
I TOLD YOU NOT TO CALL ME "CAPTAIN."
IT'S "WASTREL," MAN. I APOLOGIZE FOR THE TONE. YOU KNOW HOW I GET ON A MISSION.
PAUL!!!
HE'S FINE, MA'AM...HE'S JUST A LITTLE... UNCONSCIOUS.
SORRY ABOUT THAT.
BUT WHILE I'VE GOT YOU ON THE LINE, LET ME ASK YOU SOMETHING--
--DO YOU HAVE ANY IDEA WHERE THEY KEEP THE KREE STUFF?

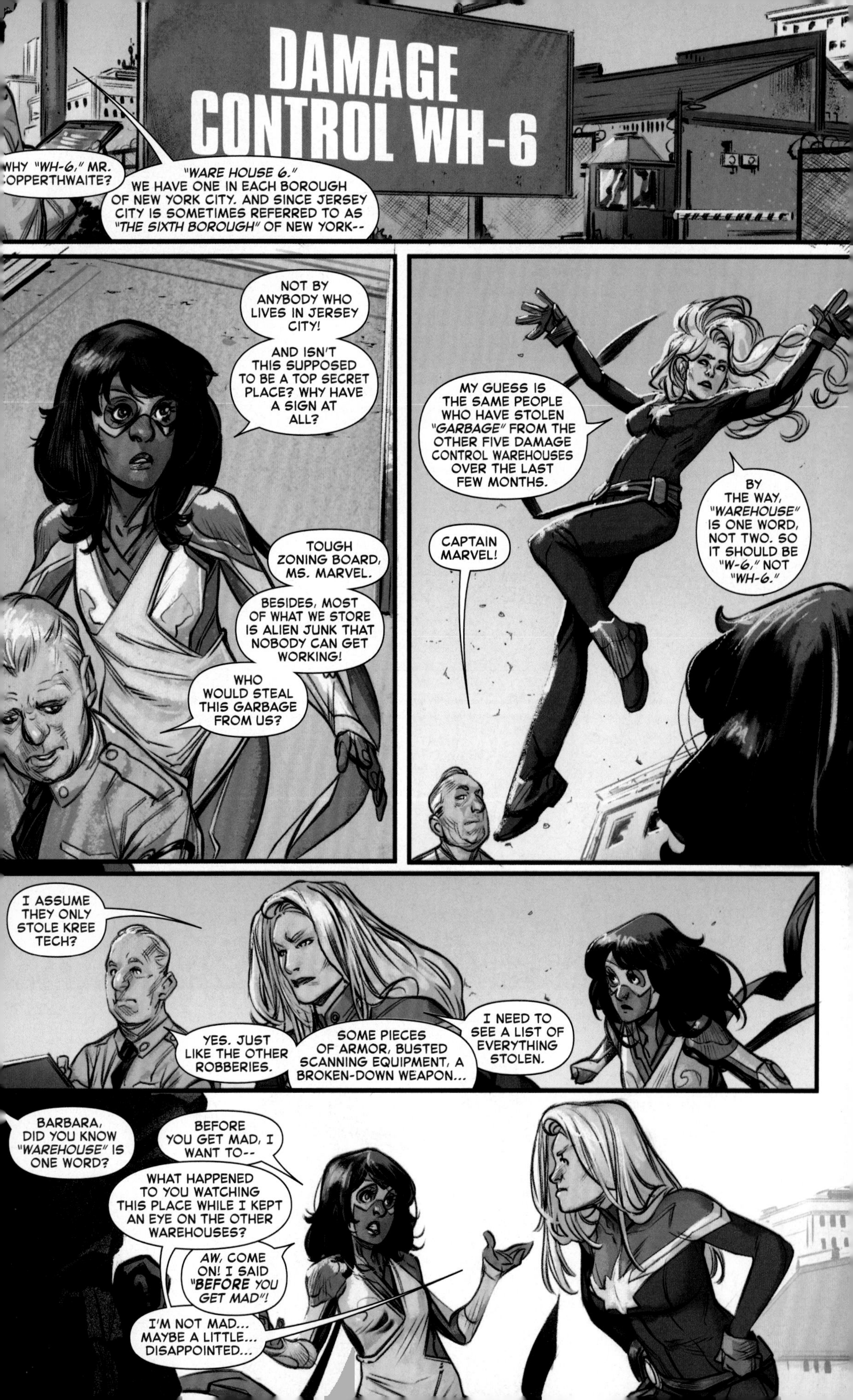
DAMAGE CONTROL WH-6
WHY "WH-6," MR. COPPERTHWAITE?
"WARE HOUSE 6." WE HAVE ONE IN EACH BOROUGH OF NEW YORK CITY. AND SINCE JERSEY CITY IS SOMETIMES REFERRED TO AS "THE SIXTH BOROUGH" OF NEW YORK--
NOT BY ANYBODY WHO LIVES IN JERSEY CITY!
AND ISN'T THIS SUPPOSED TO BE A TOP SECRET PLACE? WHY HAVE A SIGN AT ALL?
TOUGH ZONING BOARD, MS. MARVEL.
BESIDES, MOST OF WHAT WE STORE IS ALIEN JUNK THAT NOBODY CAN GET WORKING!
WHO WOULD STEAL THIS GARBAGE FROM US?
MY GUESS IS THE SAME PEOPLE WHO HAVE STOLEN "GARBAGE" FROM THE OTHER FIVE DAMAGE CONTROL WAREHOUSES OVER THE LAST FEW MONTHS.
CAPTAIN MARVEL!
BY THE WAY, "WAREHOUSE" IS ONE WORD, NOT TWO. SO IT SHOULD BE "W-6," NOT "WH-6."
I ASSUME THEY ONLY STOLE KREE TECH?
YES. JUST LIKE THE OTHER ROBBERIES.
SOME PIECES OF ARMOR, BUSTED SCANNING EQUIPMENT, A BROKEN-DOWN WEAPON...
I NEED TO SEE A LIST OF EVERYTHING STOLEN.
BARBARA, DID YOU KNOW "WAREHOUSE" IS ONE WORD?
BEFORE YOU GET MAD, I WANT TO--
WHAT HAPPENED TO YOU WATCHING THIS PLACE WHILE I KEPT AN EYE ON THE OTHER WAREHOUSES?
AW, COME ON! I SAID "BEFORE YOU GET MAD"!
I'M NOT MAD... MAYBE A LITTLE... DISAPPOINTED...

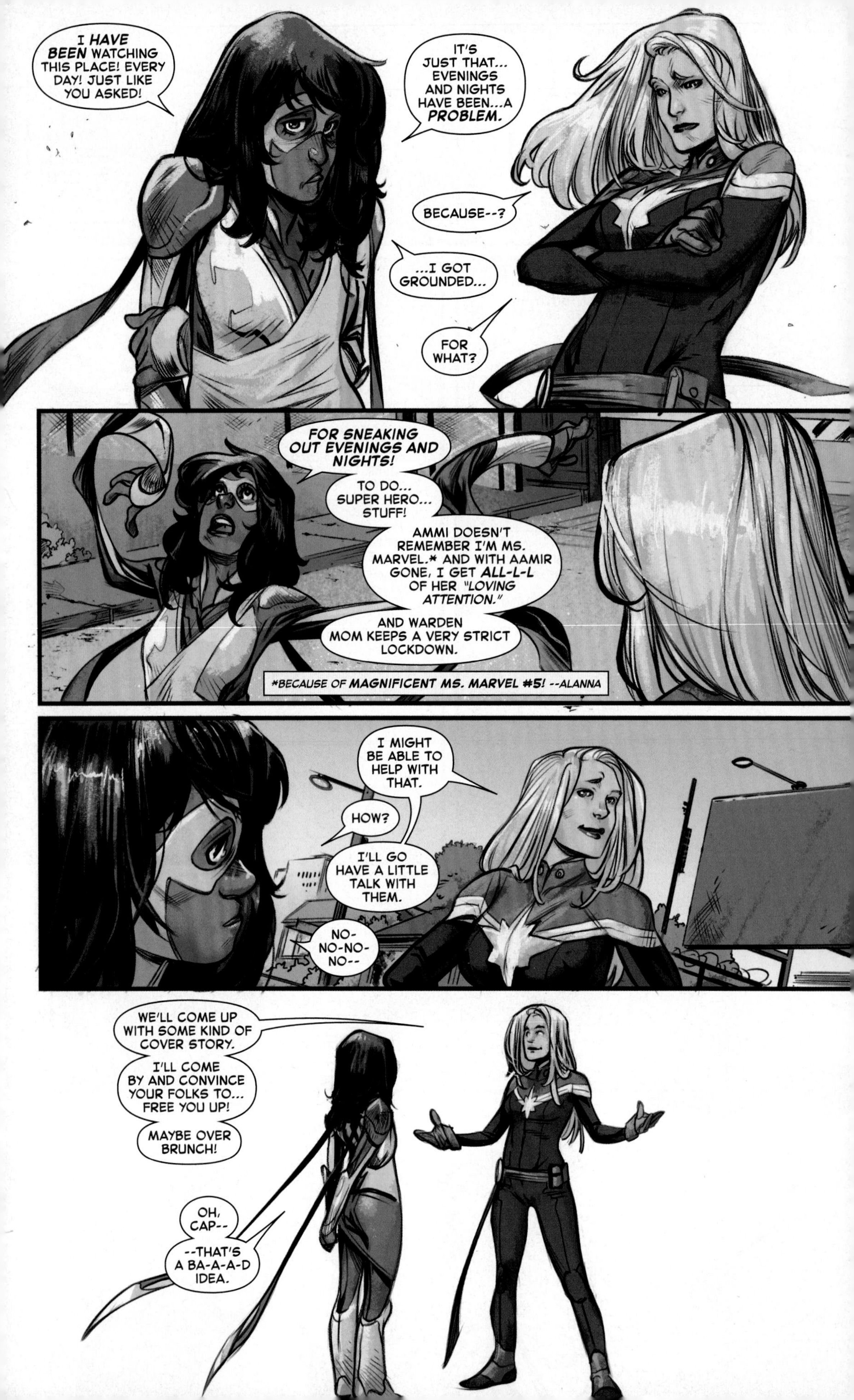
I HAVE BEEN WATCHING THIS PLACE! EVERY DAY! JUST LIKE YOU ASKED!
IT'S JUST THAT... EVENINGS AND NIGHTS HAVE BEEN...A PROBLEM.
BECAUSE--?
...I GOT GROUNDED...
FOR WHAT?
FOR SNEAKING OUT EVENINGS AND NIGHTS!
TO DO... SUPER HERO... STUFF!
AMMI DOESN'T REMEMBER I'M MS. MARVEL.* AND WITH AAMIR GONE, I GET ALL-L-L OF HER "LOVING ATTENTION."
AND WARDEN MOM KEEPS A VERY STRICT LOCKDOWN.
*BECAUSE OF MAGNIFICENT MS. MARVEL #5! --ALANNA
I MIGHT BE ABLE TO HELP WITH THAT.
HOW?
I'LL GO HAVE A LITTLE TALK WITH THEM.
NO-NO-NO-NO--
WE'LL COME UP WITH SOME KIND OF COVER STORY.
I'LL COME BY AND CONVINCE YOUR FOLKS TO... FREE YOU UP!
MAYBE OVER BRUNCH!
OH, CAP--
--THAT'S A BA-A-A-D IDEA.

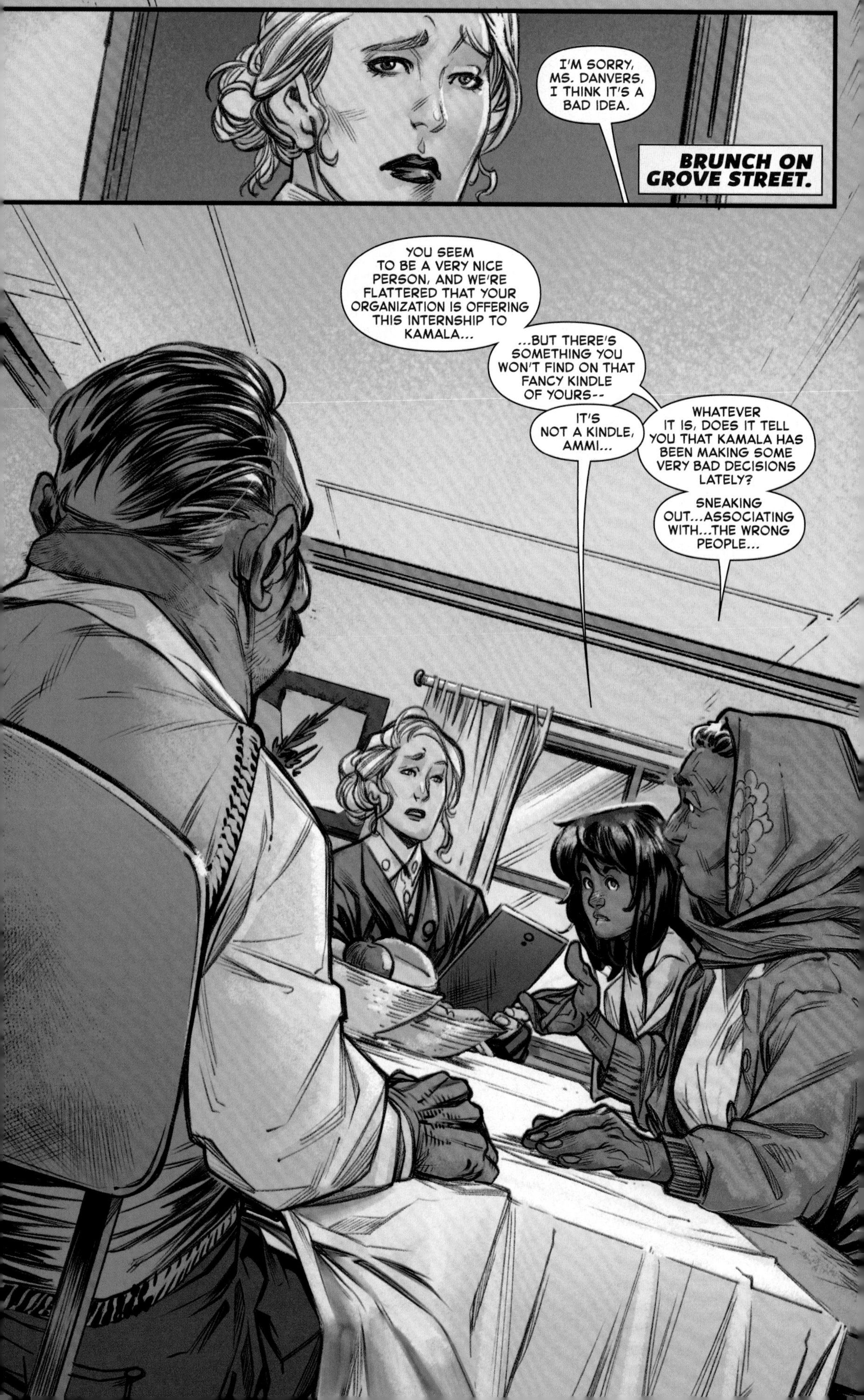
I'M SORRY, MS. DANVERS, I THINK IT'S A BAD IDEA.
BRUNCH ON GROVE STREET.
YOU SEEM TO BE A VERY NICE PERSON, AND WE'RE FLATTERED THAT YOUR ORGANIZATION IS OFFERING THIS INTERNSHIP TO KAMALA...
...BUT THERE'S SOMETHING YOU WON'T FIND ON THAT FANCY KINDLE OF YOURS--
IT'S NOT A KINDLE, AMMI...
WHATEVER IT IS, DOES IT TELL YOU THAT KAMALA HAS BEEN MAKING SOME VERY BAD DECISIONS LATELY?
SNEAKING OUT...ASSOCIATING WITH...THE WRONG PEOPLE...

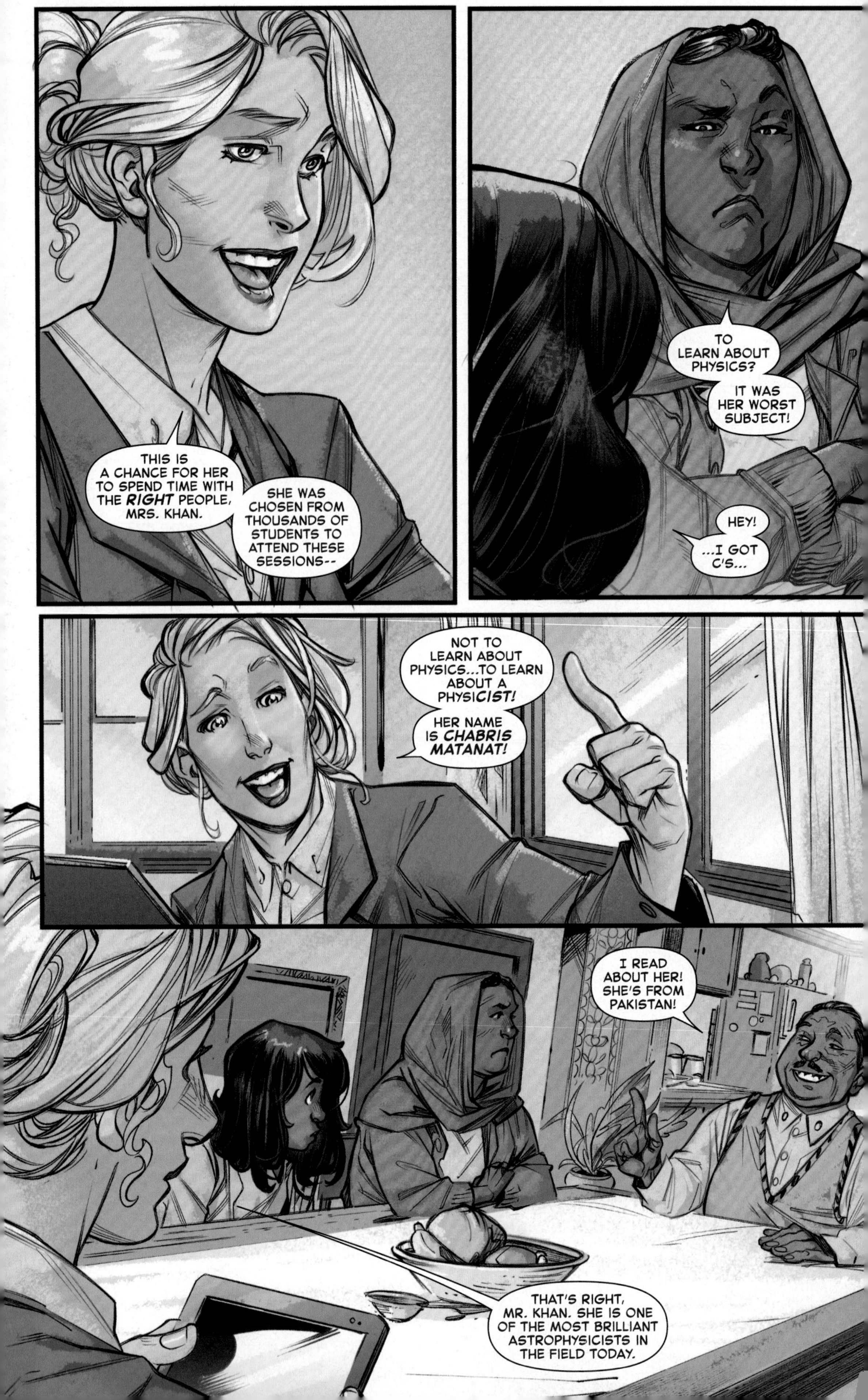
THIS IS A CHANCE FOR HER TO SPEND TIME WITH THE RIGHT PEOPLE, MRS. KHAN.
SHE WAS CHOSEN FROM THOUSANDS OF STUDENTS TO ATTEND THESE SESSIONS--
TO LEARN ABOUT PHYSICS?
IT WAS HER WORST SUBJECT!
HEY!
...I GOT C'S...
NOT TO LEARN ABOUT PHYSICS...TO LEARN ABOUT A PHYSICIST!
HER NAME IS CHABRIS MATANAT!
I READ ABOUT HER! SHE'S FROM PAKISTAN!
THAT'S RIGHT, MR. KHAN. SHE IS ONE OF THE MOST BRILLIANT ASTROPHYSICISTS IN THE FIELD TODAY.

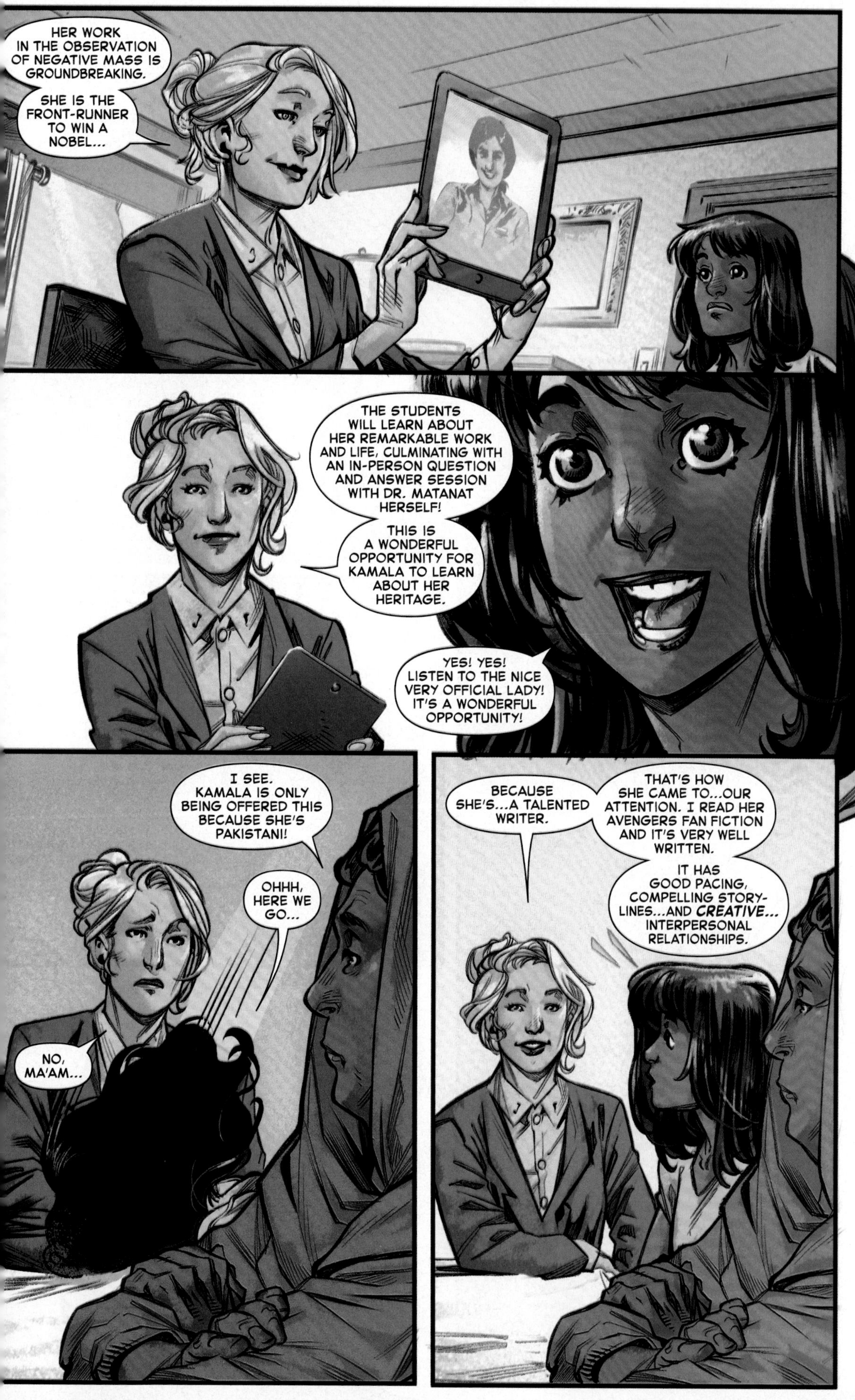
HER WORK IN THE OBSERVATION OF NEGATIVE MASS IS GROUNDBREAKING.
SHE IS THE FRONT-RUNNER TO WIN A NOBEL...
THE STUDENTS WILL LEARN ABOUT HER REMARKABLE WORK AND LIFE, CULMINATING WITH AN IN-PERSON QUESTION AND ANSWER SESSION WITH DR. MATANAT HERSELF!
THIS IS A WONDERFUL OPPORTUNITY FOR KAMALA TO LEARN ABOUT HER HERITAGE.
YES! YES! LISTEN TO THE NICE VERY OFFICIAL LADY! IT'S A WONDERFUL OPPORTUNITY!
I SEE. KAMALA IS ONLY BEING OFFERED THIS BECAUSE SHE'S PAKISTANI!
OHHH, HERE WE GO...
NO, MA'AM...
BECAUSE SHE'S...A TALENTED WRITER.
THAT'S HOW SHE CAME TO...OUR ATTENTION. I READ HER AVENGERS FAN FICTION AND IT'S VERY WELL WRITTEN.
IT HAS GOOD PACING, COMPELLING STORY-LINES...AND CREATIVE... INTERPERSONAL RELATIONSHIPS.

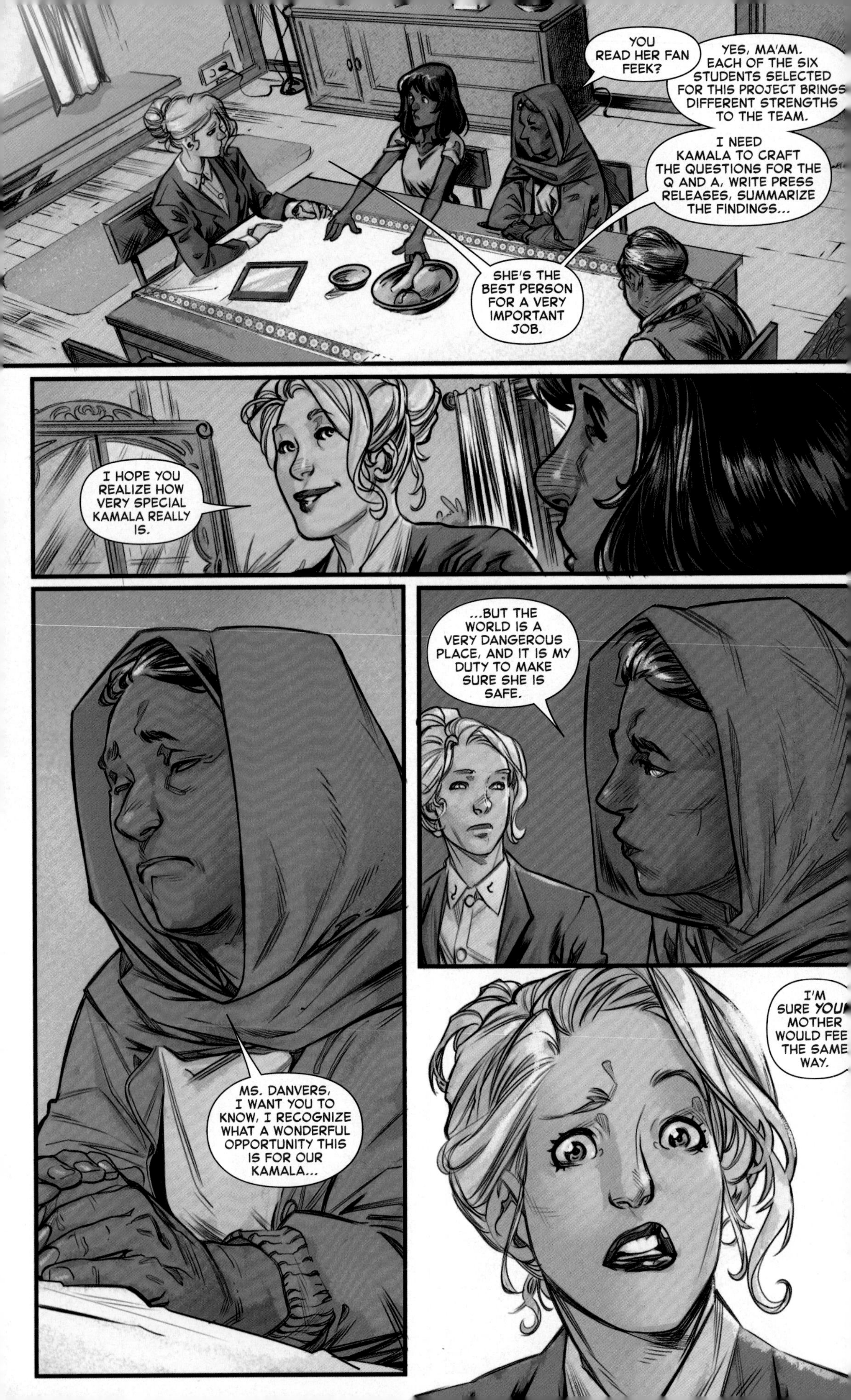
YOU READ HER FAN FEEK?
YES, MA'AM. EACH OF THE SIX STUDENTS SELECTED FOR THIS PROJECT BRINGS DIFFERENT STRENGTHS TO THE TEAM.
I NEED KAMALA TO CRAFT THE QUESTIONS FOR THE Q AND A, WRITE PRESS RELEASES, SUMMARIZE THE FINDINGS...
SHE'S THE BEST PERSON FOR A VERY IMPORTANT JOB.
I HOPE YOU REALIZE HOW VERY SPECIAL KAMALA REALLY IS.
MS. DANVERS, I WANT YOU TO KNOW, I RECOGNIZE WHAT A WONDERFUL OPPORTUNITY THIS IS FOR OUR KAMALA...
...BUT THE WORLD IS A VERY DANGEROUS PLACE, AND IT IS MY DUTY TO MAKE SURE SHE IS SAFE.
I'M SURE YOU MOTHER WOULD FEE THE SAME WAY.

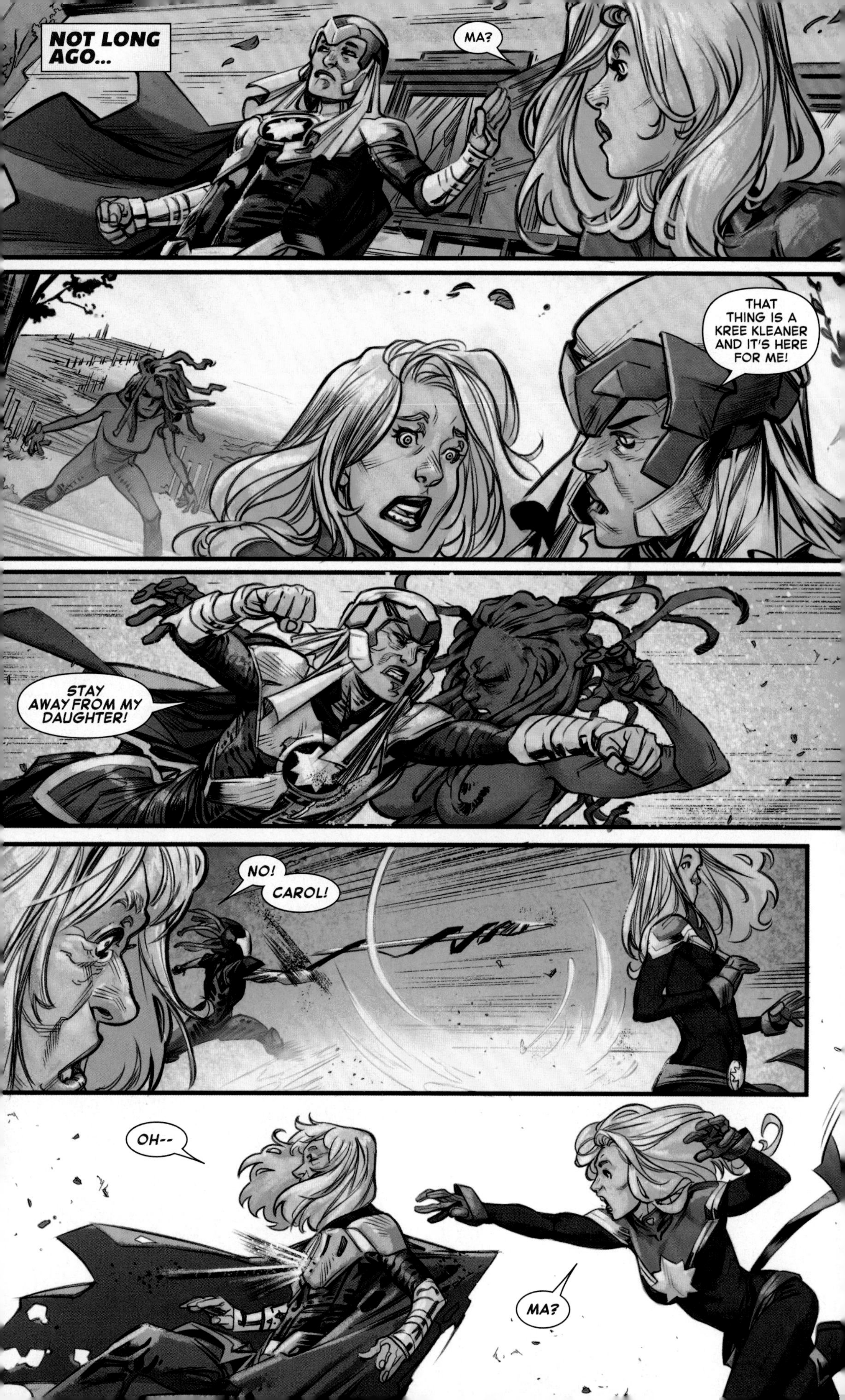
NOT LONG AGO...
MA?
THAT THING IS A KREE KLEANER AND IT'S HERE FOR ME!
STAY AWAY FROM MY DAUGHTER!
NO!
CAROL!
OH--
MA?

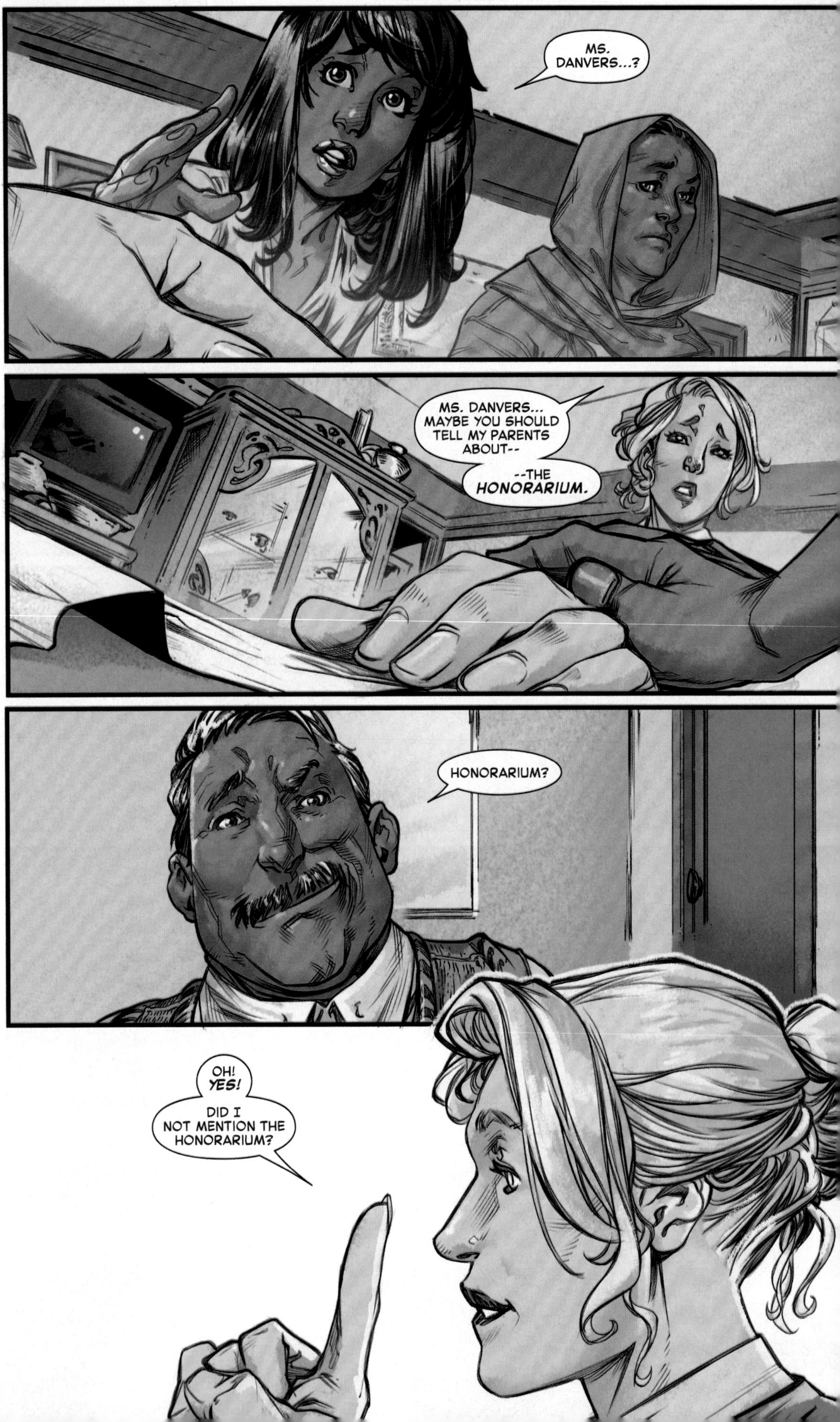
MS. DANVERS...?
MS. DANVERS... MAYBE YOU SHOULD TELL MY PARENTS ABOUT--
--THE *HONORARIUM.*
HONORARIUM?
OH! *YES!*
DID I NOT MENTION THE HONORARIUM?

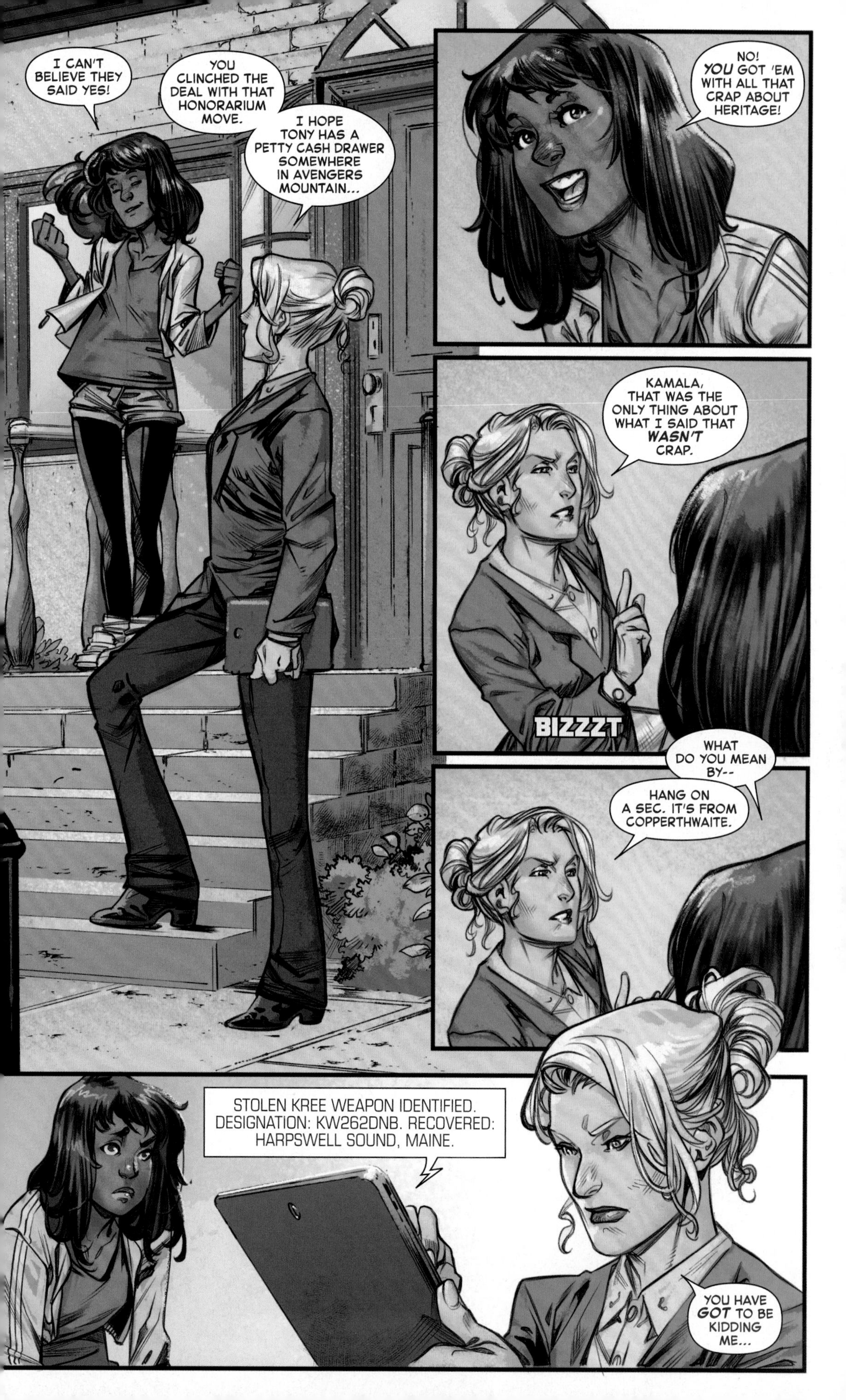

I CAN'T BELIEVE THEY SAID YES!
YOU CLINCHED THE DEAL WITH THAT HONORARIUM MOVE.
I HOPE TONY HAS A PETTY CASH DRAWER SOMEWHERE IN AVENGERS MOUNTAIN...
NO! YOU GOT 'EM WITH ALL THAT CRAP ABOUT HERITAGE!
KAMALA, THAT WAS THE ONLY THING ABOUT WHAT I SAID THAT WASN'T CRAP.
BIZZZT
WHAT DO YOU MEAN BY--
HANG ON A SEC. IT'S FROM COPPERTHWAITE.
STOLEN KREE WEAPON IDENTIFIED. DESIGNATION: KW262DNB. RECOVERED: HARPSWELL SOUND, MAINE.
YOU HAVE GOT TO BE KIDDING ME...

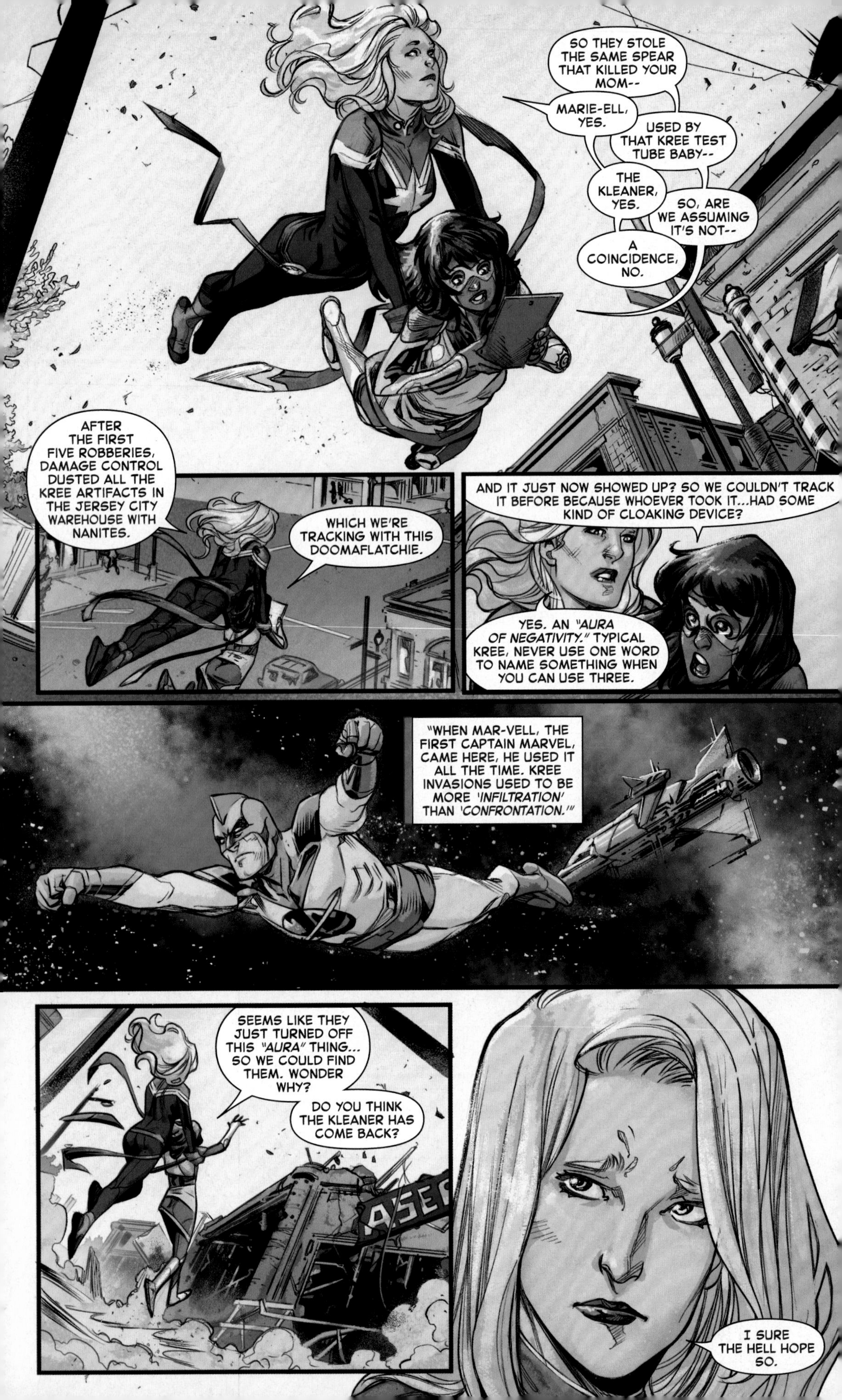
SO THEY STOLE THE SAME SPEAR THAT KILLED YOUR MOM--
MARIE-ELL, YES.
USED BY THAT KREE TEST TUBE BABY--
THE KLEANER, YES.
SO, ARE WE ASSUMING IT'S NOT--
A COINCIDENCE, NO.
AFTER THE FIRST FIVE ROBBERIES, DAMAGE CONTROL DUSTED ALL THE KREE ARTIFACTS IN THE JERSEY CITY WAREHOUSE WITH NANITES.
WHICH WE'RE TRACKING WITH THIS DOOMAFLATCHIE.
AND IT JUST NOW SHOWED UP? SO WE COULDN'T TRACK IT BEFORE BECAUSE WHOEVER TOOK IT...HAD SOME KIND OF CLOAKING DEVICE?
YES. AN *"AURA OF NEGATIVITY."* TYPICAL KREE, NEVER USE ONE WORD TO NAME SOMETHING WHEN YOU CAN USE THREE.
"WHEN MAR-VELL, THE FIRST CAPTAIN MARVEL, CAME HERE, HE USED IT ALL THE TIME. KREE INVASIONS USED TO BE MORE *'INFILTRATION'* THAN *'CONFRONTATION.'"*
SEEMS LIKE THEY JUST TURNED OFF THIS *"AURA"* THING... SO WE COULD FIND THEM. WONDER WHY?
DO YOU THINK THE KLEANER HAS COME BACK?
ASE
I SURE THE HELL HOPE SO.

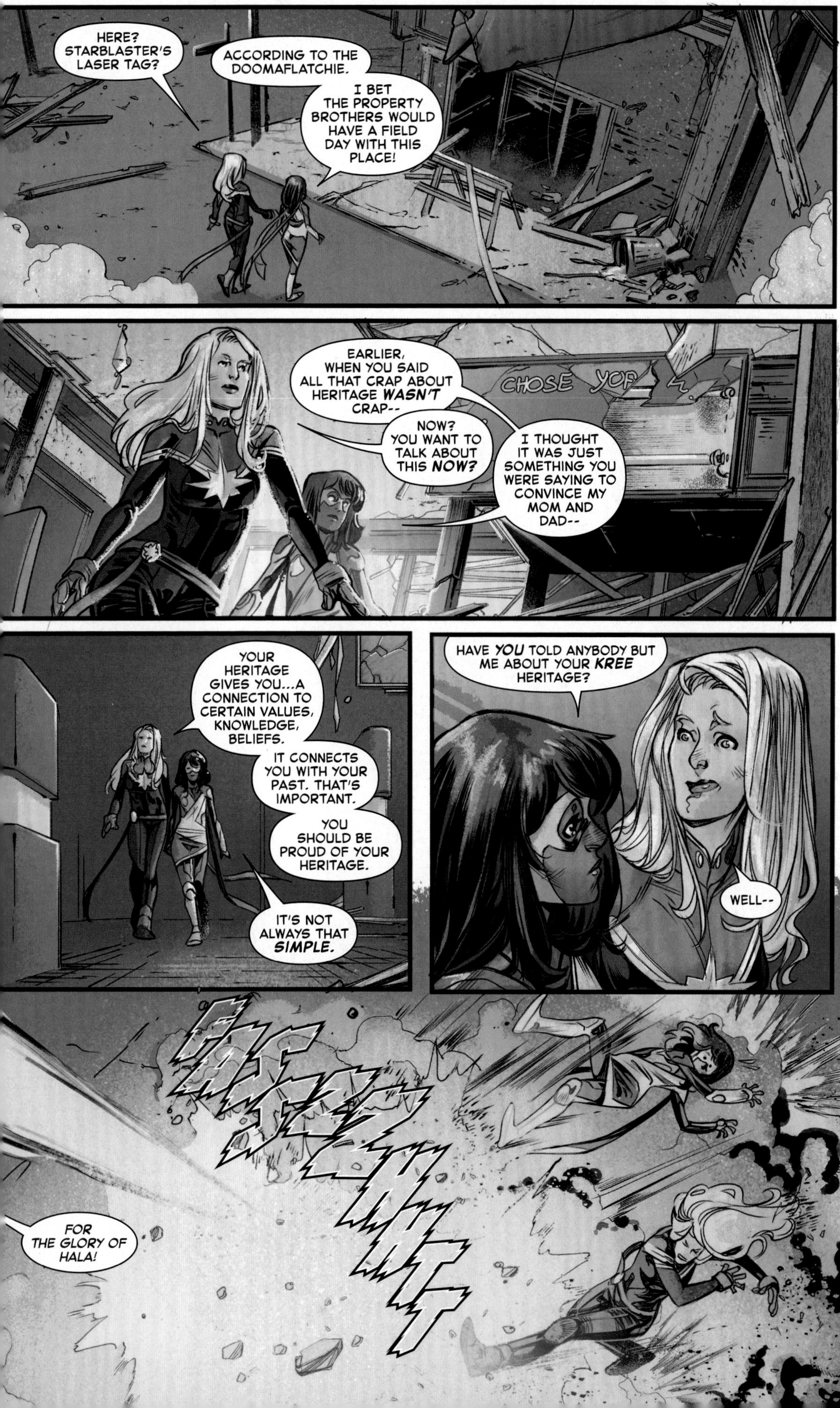
HERE? STARBLASTER'S LASER TAG?
ACCORDING TO THE DOOMAFLATCHIE.
I BET THE PROPERTY BROTHERS WOULD HAVE A FIELD DAY WITH THIS PLACE!
CHOSE YOF
EARLIER, WHEN YOU SAID ALL THAT CRAP ABOUT HERITAGE WASN'T CRAP--
NOW? YOU WANT TO TALK ABOUT THIS NOW?
I THOUGHT IT WAS JUST SOMETHING YOU WERE SAYING TO CONVINCE MY MOM AND DAD--
YOUR HERITAGE GIVES YOU...A CONNECTION TO CERTAIN VALUES, KNOWLEDGE, BELIEFS.
IT CONNECTS YOU WITH YOUR PAST. THAT'S IMPORTANT.
YOU SHOULD BE PROUD OF YOUR HERITAGE.
IT'S NOT ALWAYS THAT SIMPLE.
HAVE YOU TOLD ANYBODY BUT ME ABOUT YOUR KREE HERITAGE?
WELL--
FOR THE GLORY OF HALA!

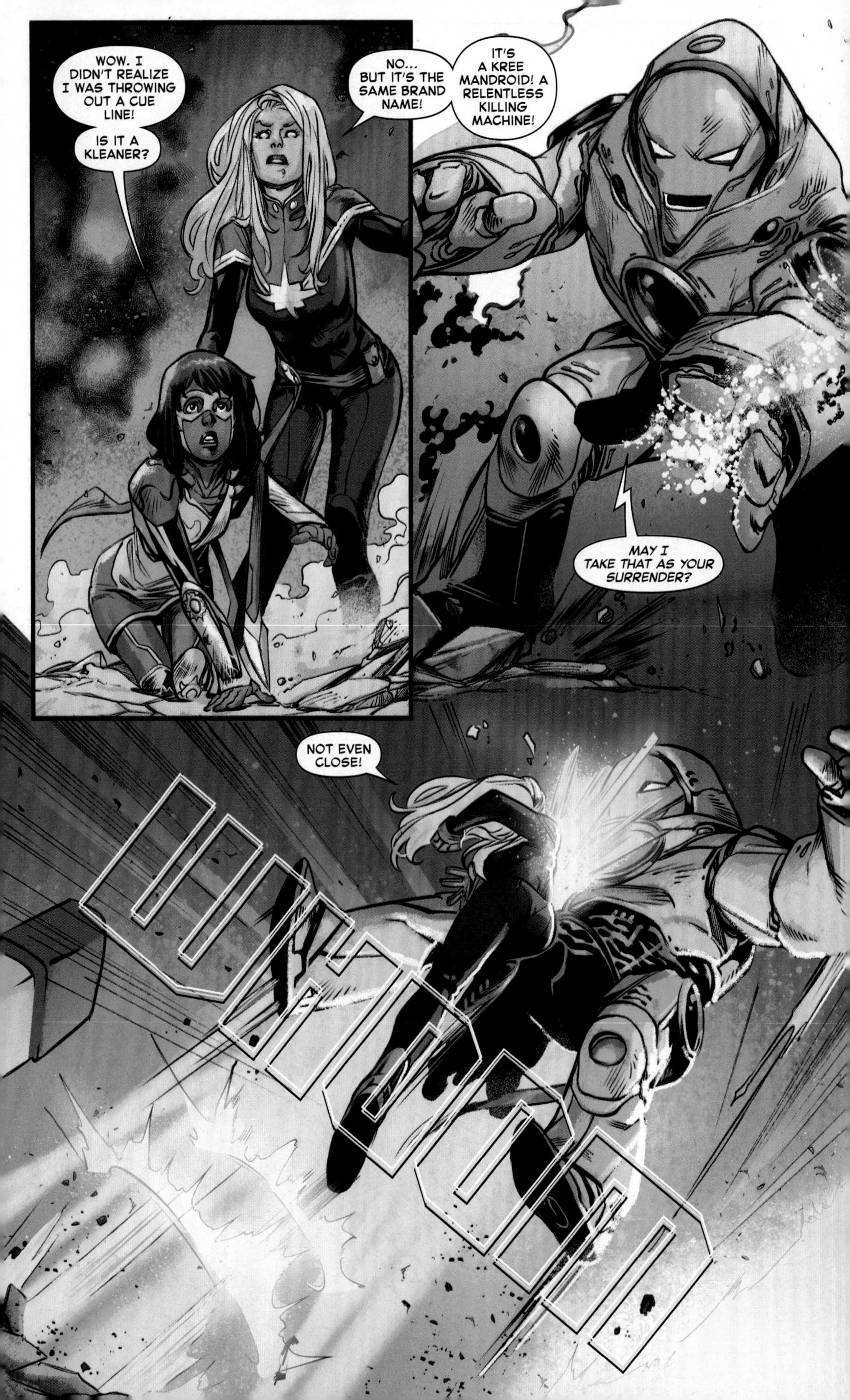
WOW. I DIDN'T REALIZE I WAS THROWING OUT A CUE LINE!
IS IT A KLEANER?
NO... BUT IT'S THE SAME BRAND NAME!
IT'S A KREE MANDROID! A RELENTLESS KILLING MACHINE!
MAY I TAKE THAT AS YOUR SURRENDER?
NOT EVEN CLOSE!

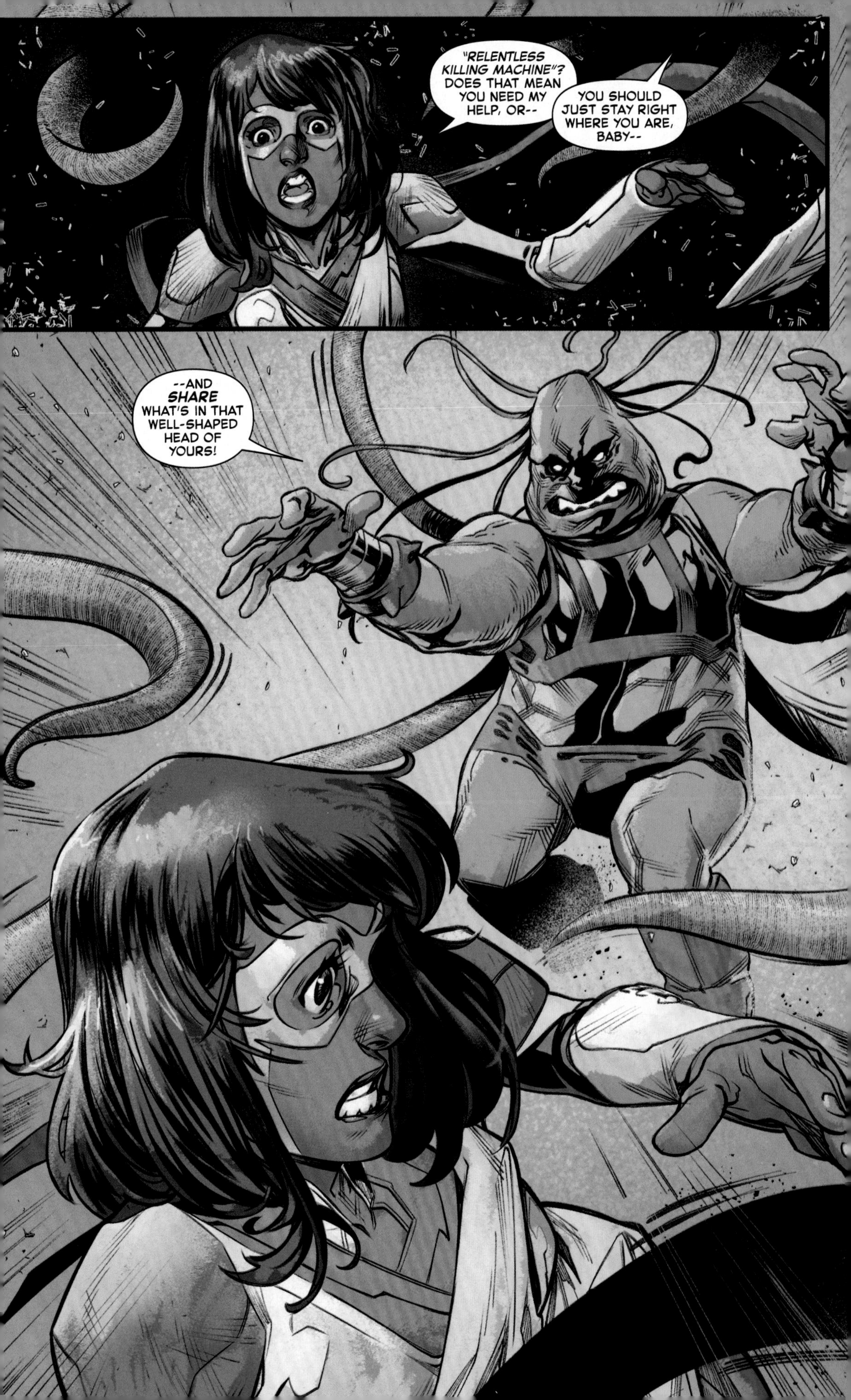
"RELENTLESS KILLING MACHINE"? DOES THAT MEAN YOU NEED MY HELP, OR--
YOU SHOULD JUST STAY RIGHT WHERE YOU ARE, BABY--
--AND SHARE WHAT'S IN THAT WELL-SHAPED HEAD OF YOURS!

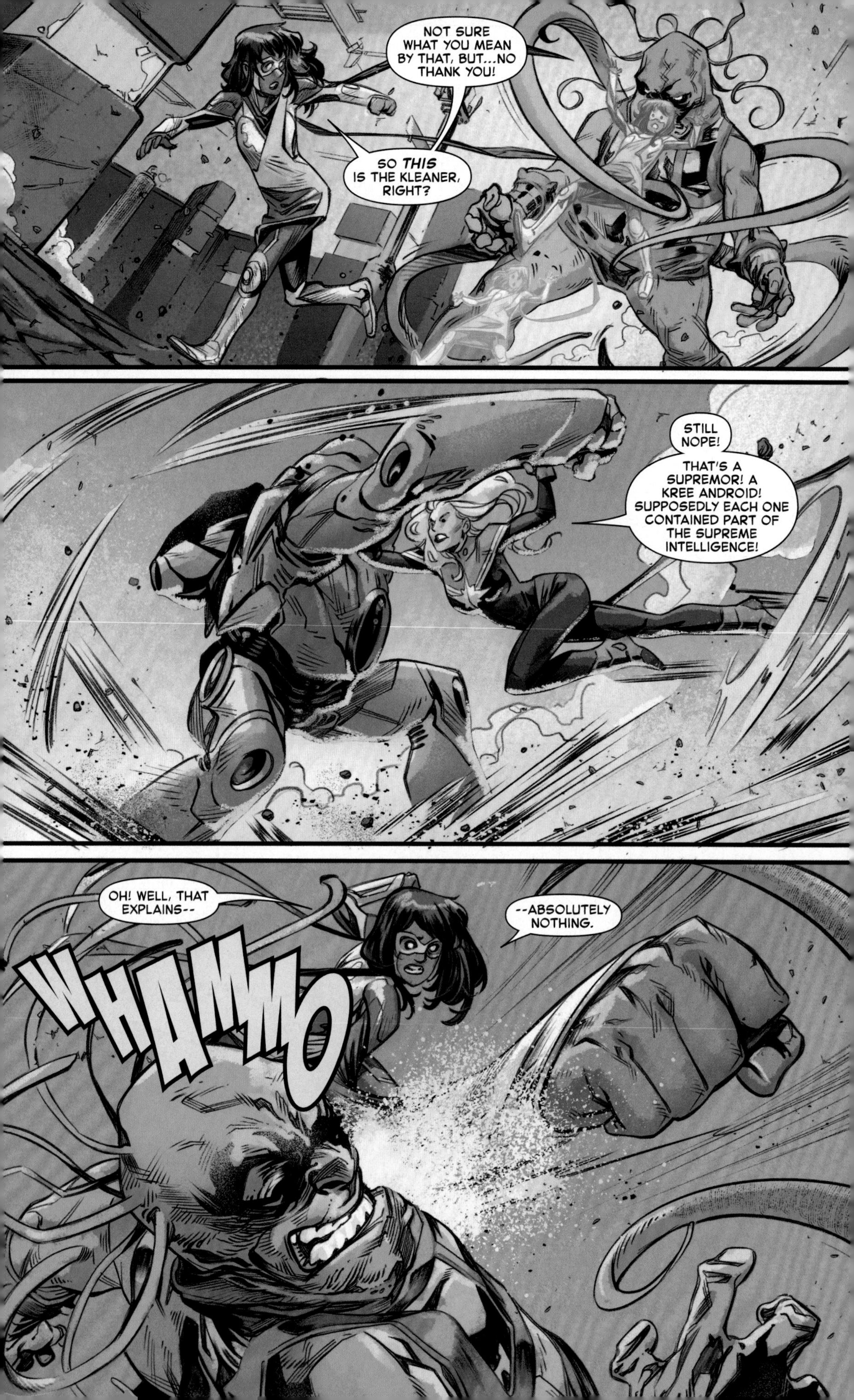
NOT SURE WHAT YOU MEAN BY THAT, BUT...NO THANK YOU!
SO THIS IS THE KLEANER, RIGHT?
STILL NOPE!
THAT'S A SUPREMOR! A KREE ANDROID! SUPPOSEDLY EACH ONE CONTAINED PART OF THE SUPREME INTELLIGENCE!
OH! WELL, THAT EXPLAINS--
--ABSOLUTELY NOTHING.
WHAMMO

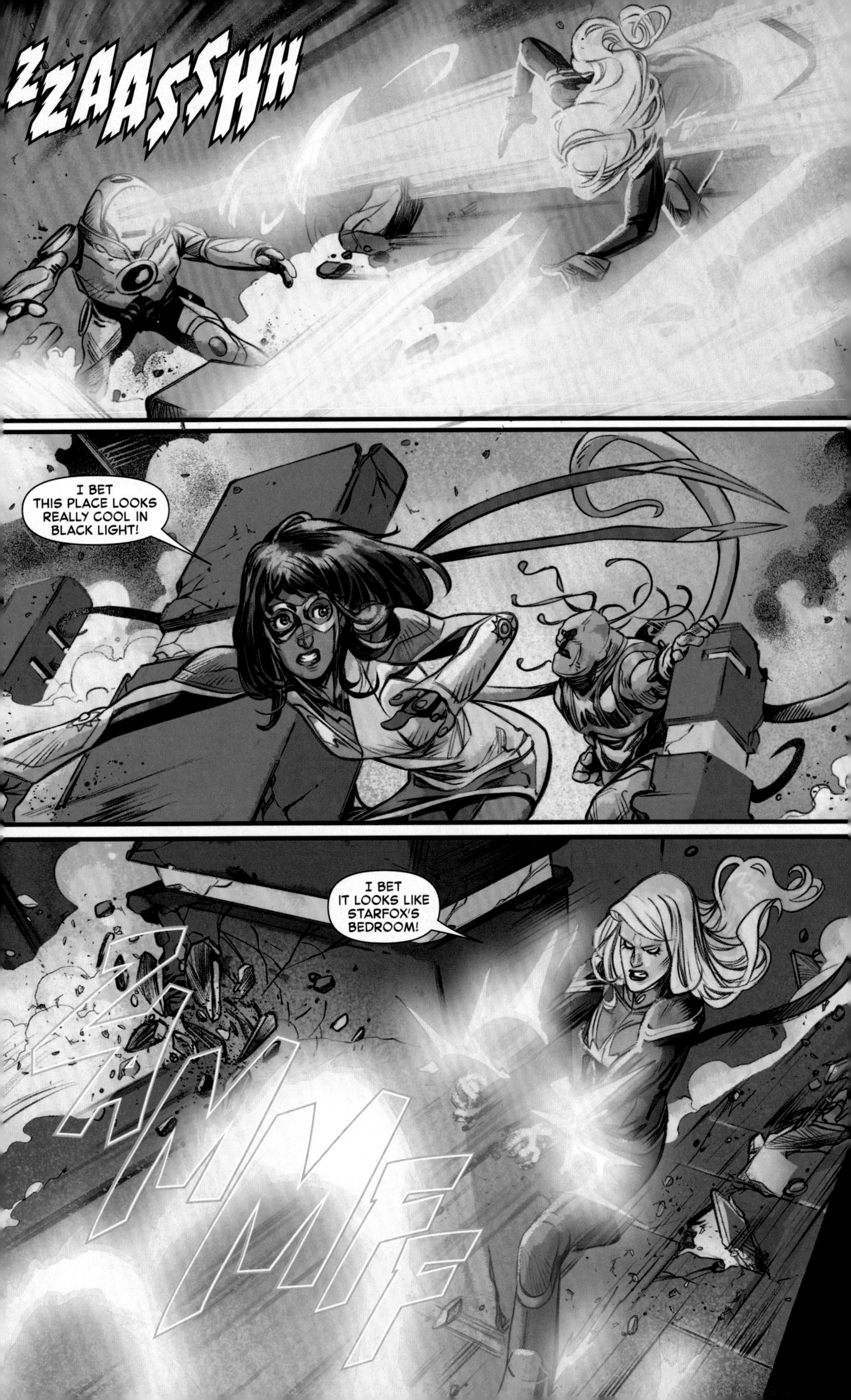
ZZAASSHH
I BET THIS PLACE LOOKS REALLY COOL IN BLACK LIGHT!
I BET IT LOOKS LIKE STARFOX'S BEDROOM!
ZHMMF

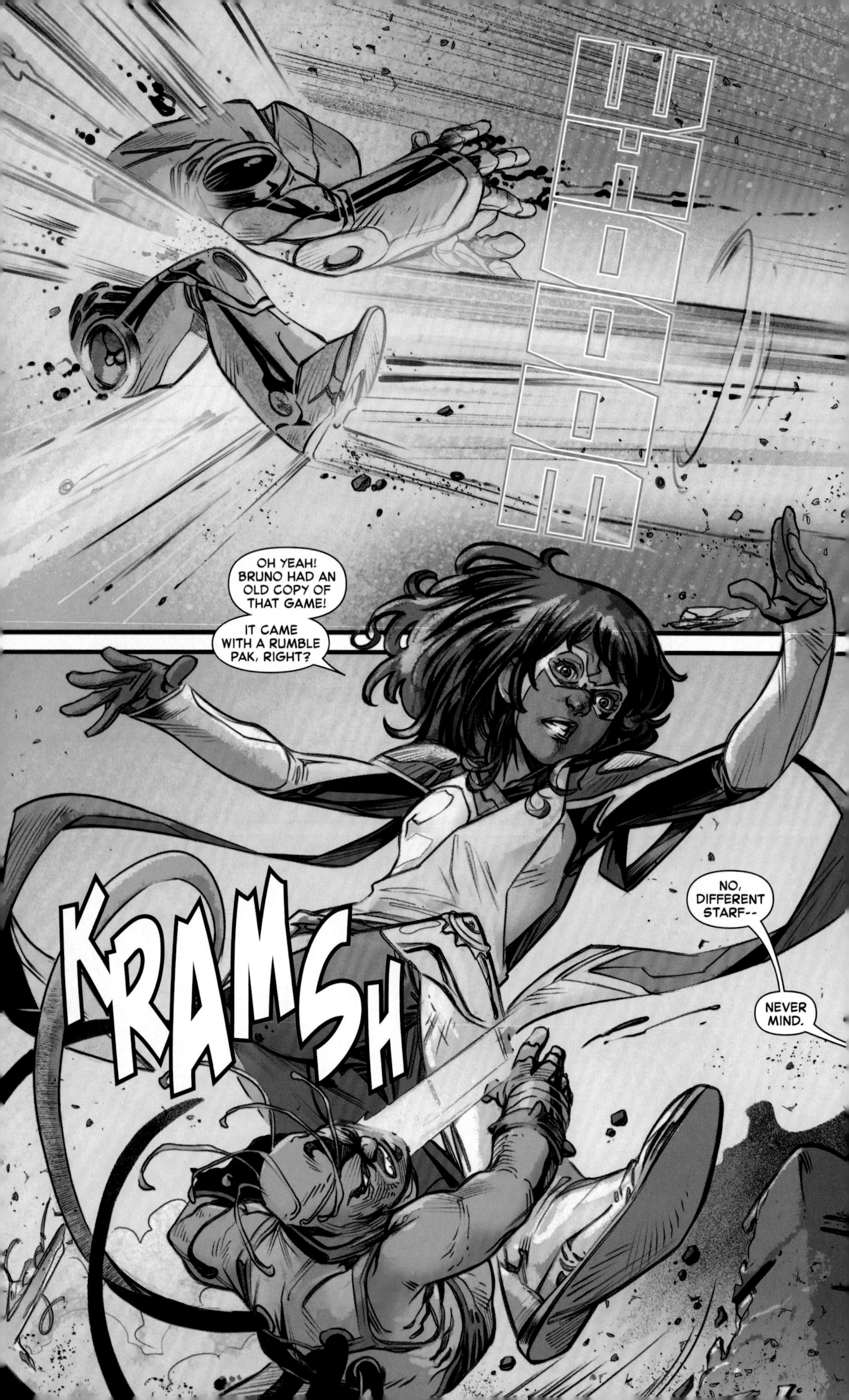
OH YEAH! BRUNO HAD AN OLD COPY OF THAT GAME!
IT CAME WITH A RUMBLE PAK, RIGHT?
NO, DIFFERENT STARF--
NEVER MIND.
KRAMSH

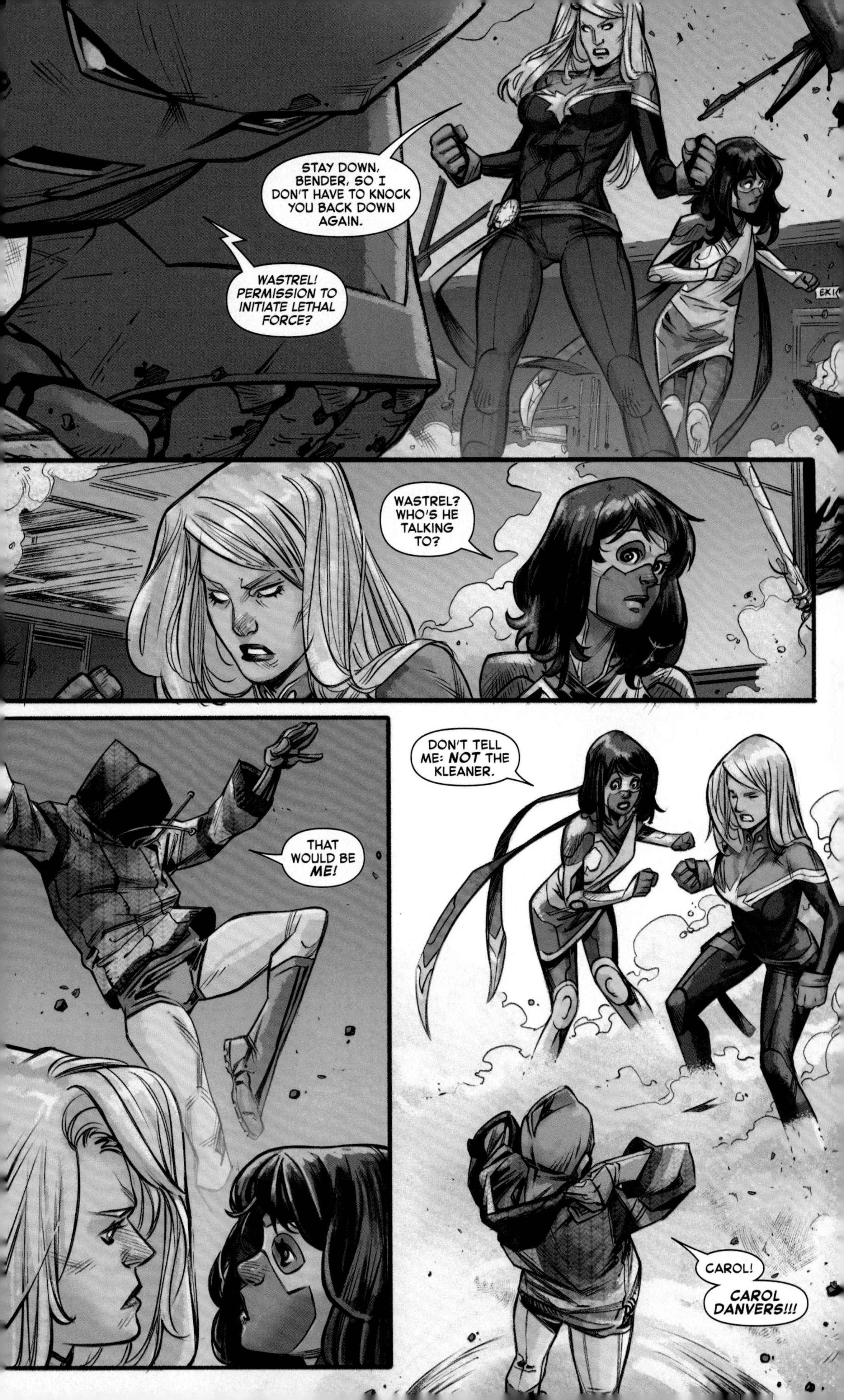
STAY DOWN, BENDER, SO I DON'T HAVE TO KNOCK YOU BACK DOWN AGAIN.
WASTREL! PERMISSION TO INITIATE LETHAL FORCE?
EXI
WASTREL? WHO'S HE TALKING TO?
DON'T TELL ME: *NOT* THE KLEANER.
THAT WOULD BE *ME!*
CAROL!
CAROL DANVERS!!!

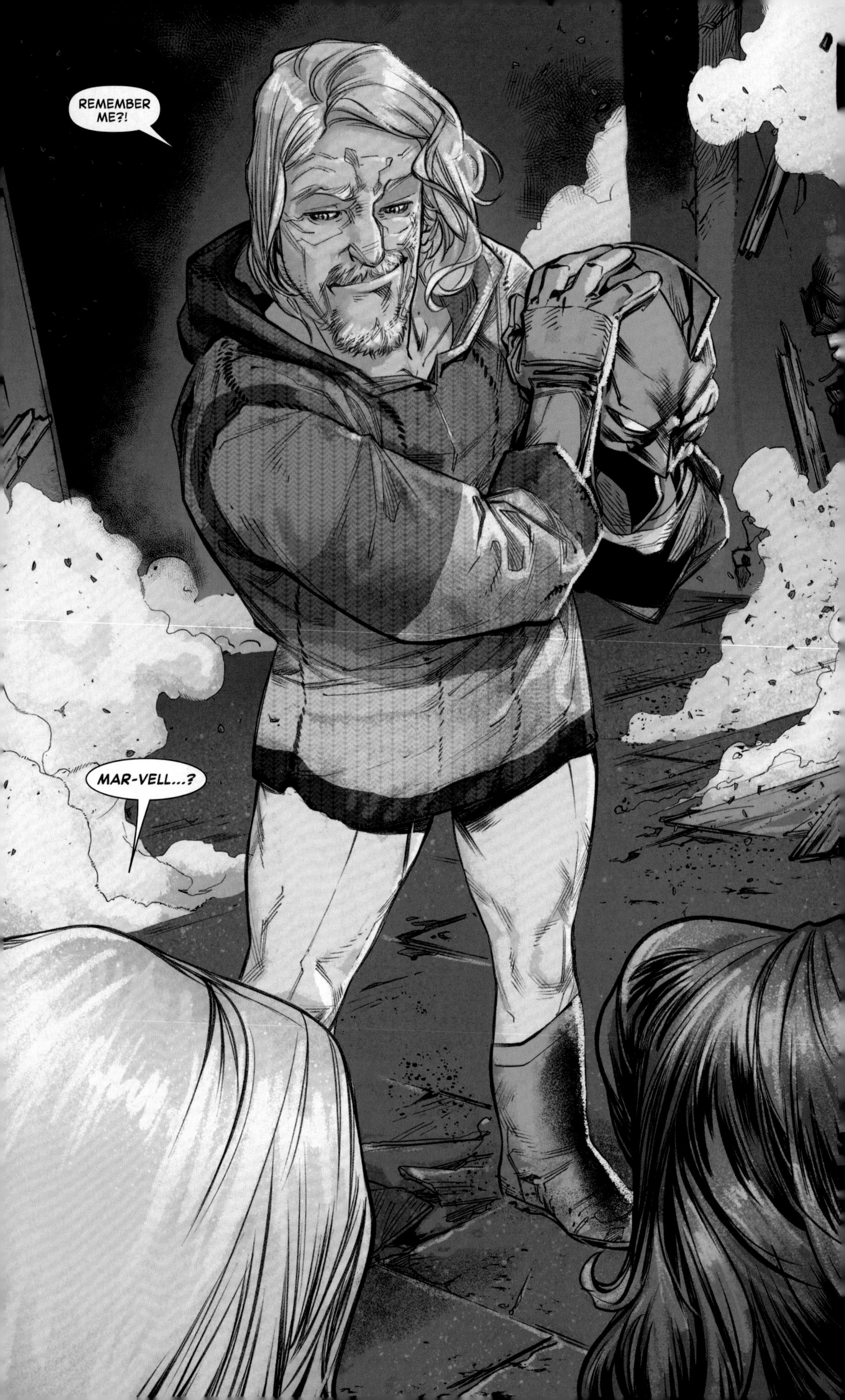
REMEMBER ME?!
MAR-VELL...?

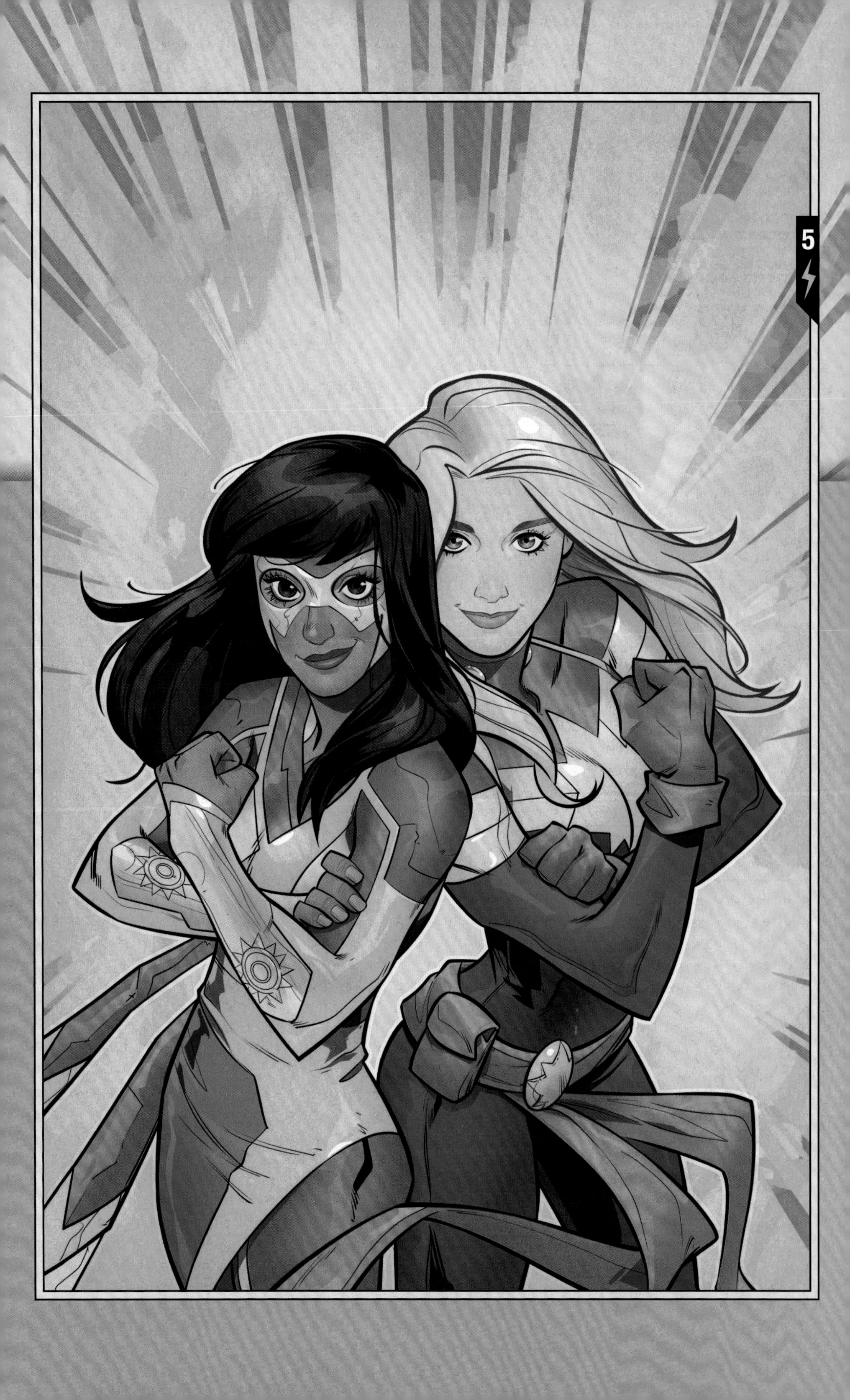

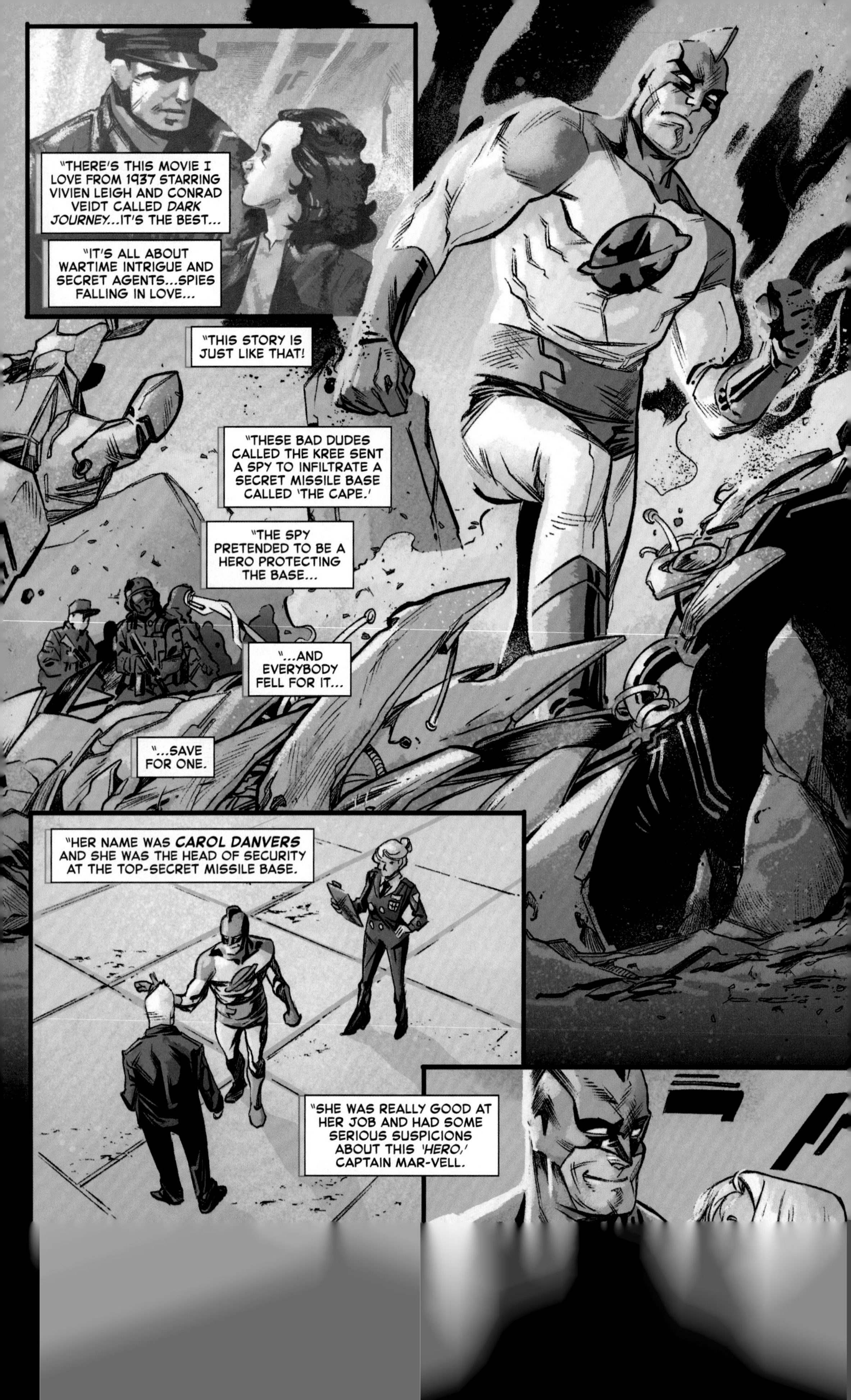
"THERE'S THIS MOVIE I LOVE FROM 1937 STARRING VIVIEN LEIGH AND CONRAD VEIDT CALLED *DARK JOURNEY*...IT'S THE BEST...
"IT'S ALL ABOUT WARTIME INTRIGUE AND SECRET AGENTS...SPIES FALLING IN LOVE...
"THIS STORY IS JUST LIKE THAT!
"THESE BAD DUDES CALLED THE KREE SENT A SPY TO INFILTRATE A SECRET MISSILE BASE CALLED 'THE CAPE.'
"THE SPY PRETENDED TO BE A HERO PROTECTING THE BASE...
"...AND EVERYBODY FELL FOR IT...
"...SAVE FOR ONE.
"HER NAME WAS ***CAROL DANVERS*** AND SHE WAS THE HEAD OF SECURITY AT THE TOP-SECRET MISSILE BASE.
"SHE WAS REALLY GOOD AT HER JOB AND HAD SOME SERIOUS SUSPICIONS ABOUT THIS *'HERO,'* CAPTAIN MAR-VELL.

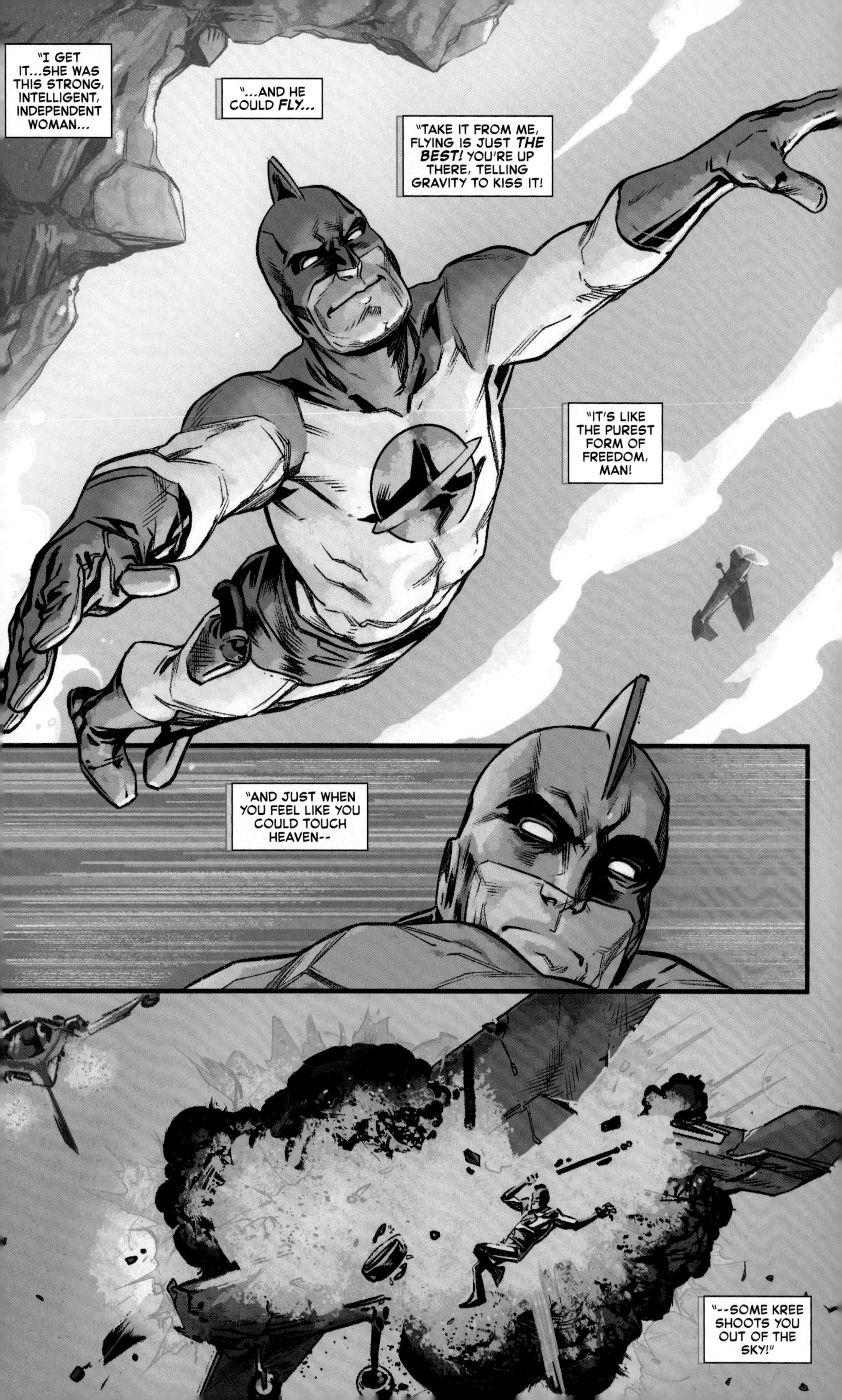
"I GET IT...SHE WAS THIS STRONG, INTELLIGENT, INDEPENDENT WOMAN...
"...AND HE COULD *FLY*...
"TAKE IT FROM ME, FLYING IS JUST ***THE BEST!*** YOU'RE UP THERE, TELLING GRAVITY TO KISS IT!
"IT'S LIKE THE PUREST FORM OF FREEDOM, MAN!
"AND JUST WHEN YOU FEEL LIKE YOU COULD TOUCH HEAVEN--
"--SOME KREE SHOOTS YOU OUT OF THE SKY!"

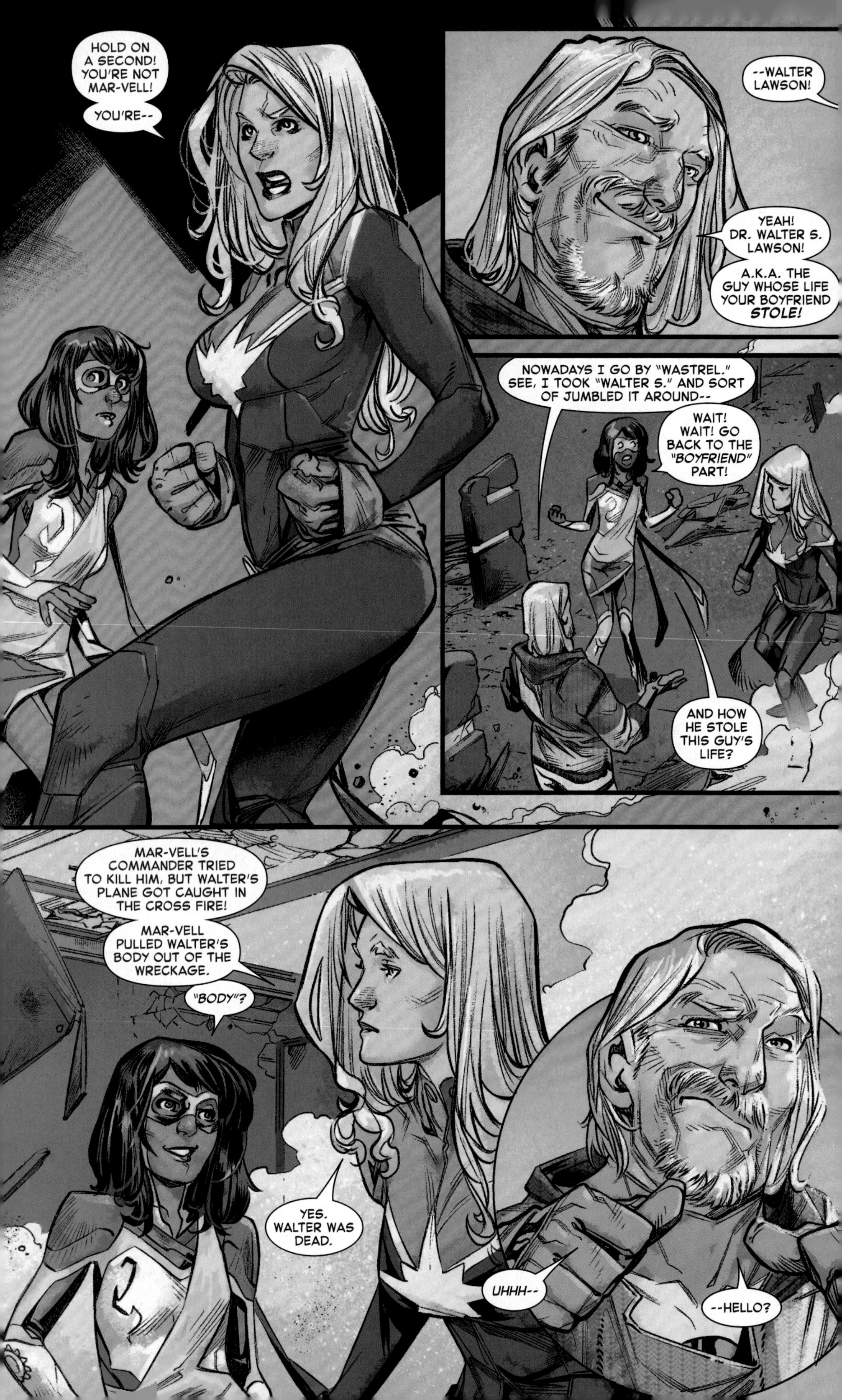
HOLD ON A SECOND! YOU'RE NOT MAR-VELL!
YOU'RE--
--WALTER LAWSON!
YEAH! DR. WALTER S. LAWSON!
A.K.A. THE GUY WHOSE LIFE YOUR BOYFRIEND STOLE!
NOWADAYS I GO BY "WASTREL." SEE, I TOOK "WALTER S." AND SORT OF JUMBLED IT AROUND--
WAIT! WAIT! GO BACK TO THE "BOYFRIEND" PART!
AND HOW HE STOLE THIS GUY'S LIFE?
MAR-VELL'S COMMANDER TRIED TO KILL HIM, BUT WALTER'S PLANE GOT CAUGHT IN THE CROSS FIRE!
MAR-VELL PULLED WALTER'S BODY OUT OF THE WRECKAGE.
"BODY"?
YES. WALTER WAS DEAD.
UHHH--
--HELLO?

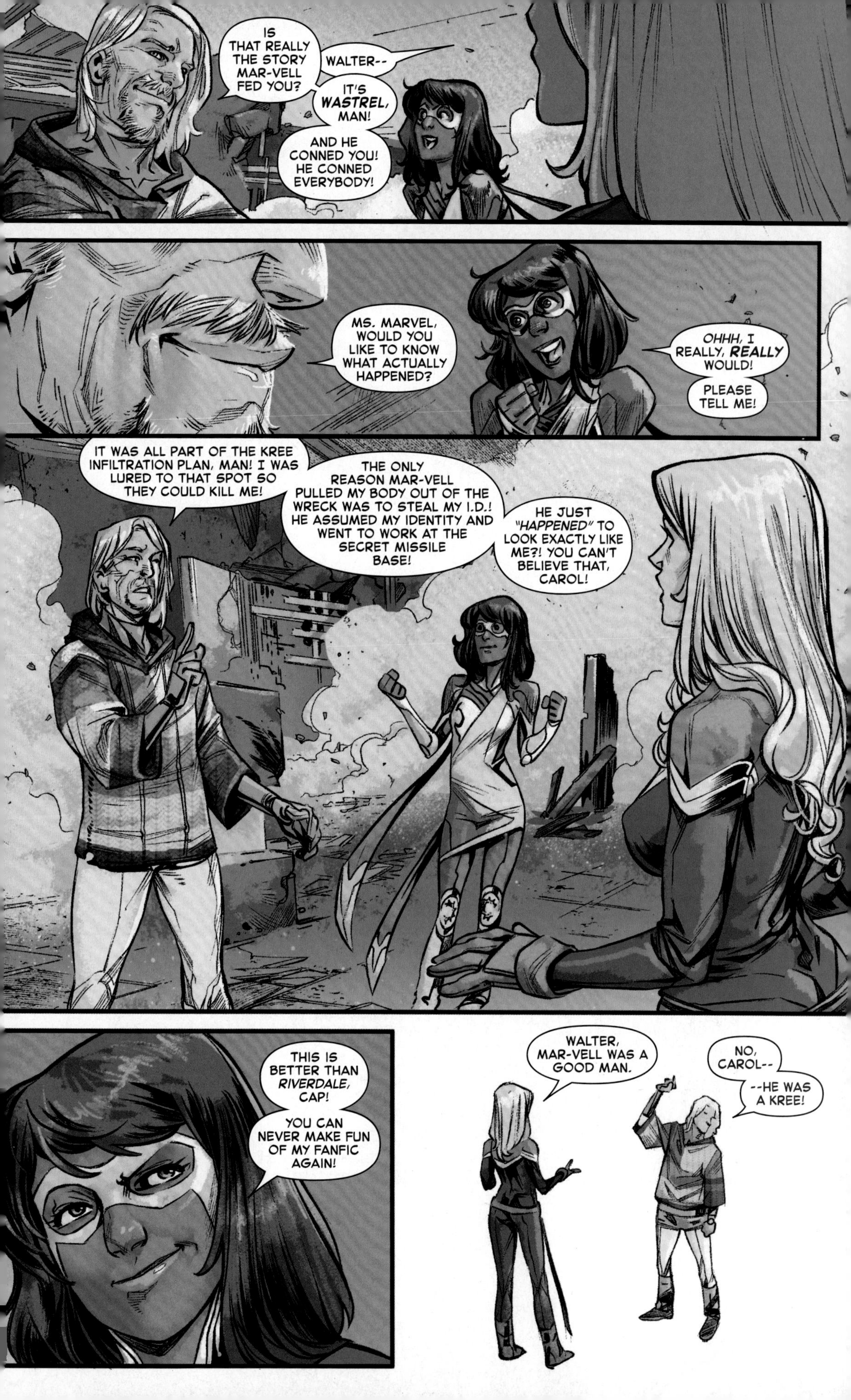
IS THAT REALLY THE STORY MAR-VELL FED YOU?
WALTER--
IT'S *WASTREL*, MAN!
AND HE CONNED YOU! HE CONNED EVERYBODY!
MS. MARVEL, WOULD YOU LIKE TO KNOW WHAT ACTUALLY HAPPENED?
OHHH, I REALLY, ***REALLY*** WOULD!
PLEASE TELL ME!
IT WAS ALL PART OF THE KREE INFILTRATION PLAN, MAN! I WAS LURED TO THAT SPOT SO THEY COULD KILL ME!
THE ONLY REASON MAR-VELL PULLED MY BODY OUT OF THE WRECK WAS TO STEAL MY I.D.! HE ASSUMED MY IDENTITY AND WENT TO WORK AT THE SECRET MISSILE BASE!
HE JUST *"HAPPENED"* TO LOOK EXACTLY LIKE ME?! YOU CAN'T BELIEVE THAT, CAROL!
THIS IS BETTER THAN *RIVERDALE*, CAP!
YOU CAN NEVER MAKE FUN OF MY FANFIC AGAIN!
WALTER, MAR-VELL WAS A GOOD MAN.
NO, CAROL--
--HE WAS A KREE!

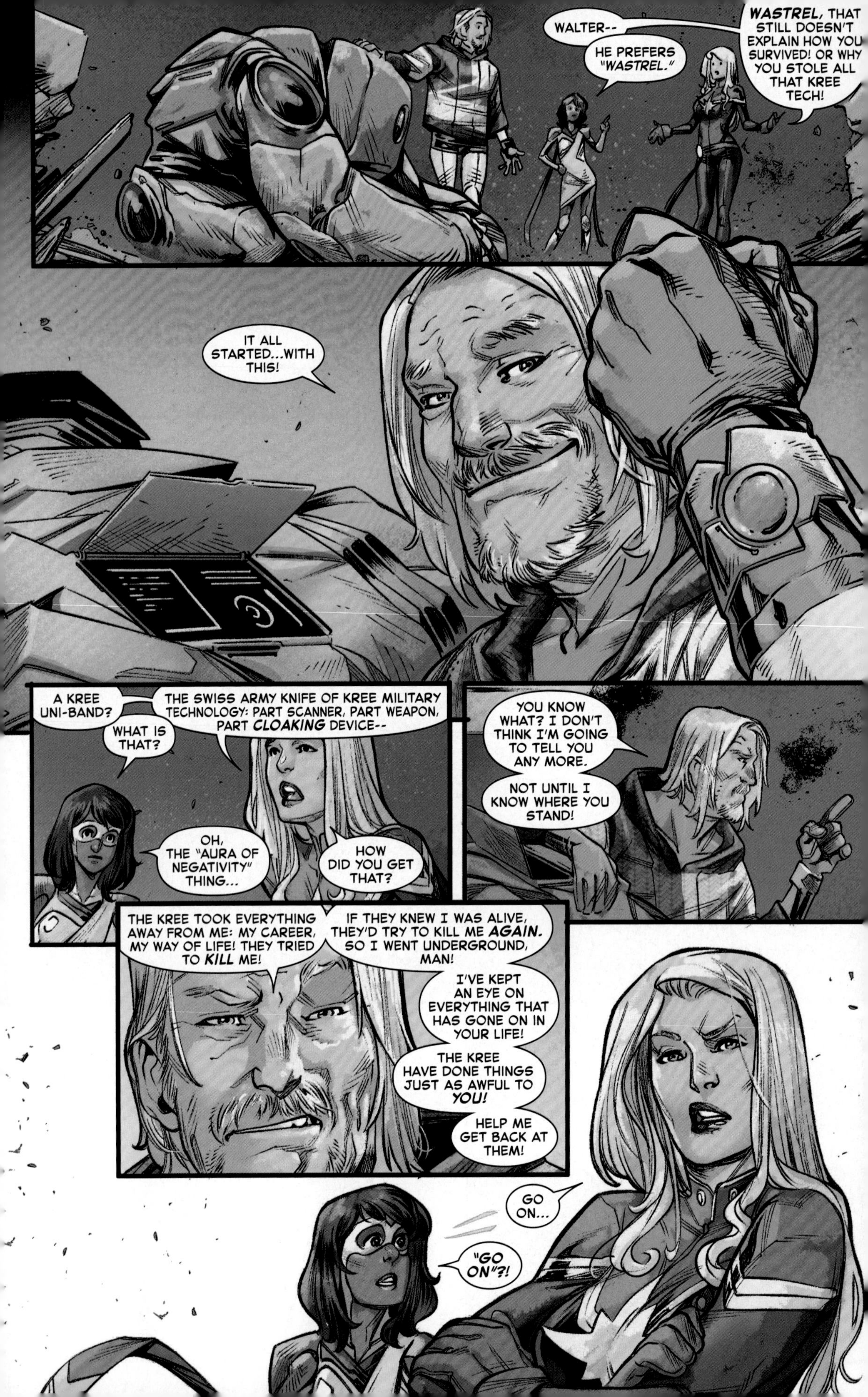
WALTER--
WASTREL, THAT STILL DOESN'T EXPLAIN HOW YOU SURVIVED! OR WHY YOU STOLE ALL THAT KREE TECH!
HE PREFERS "WASTREL."
IT ALL STARTED...WITH THIS!
A KREE UNI-BAND?
WHAT IS THAT?
THE SWISS ARMY KNIFE OF KREE MILITARY TECHNOLOGY: PART SCANNER, PART WEAPON, PART CLOAKING DEVICE--
OH, THE "AURA OF NEGATIVITY" THING...
HOW DID YOU GET THAT?
YOU KNOW WHAT? I DON'T THINK I'M GOING TO TELL YOU ANY MORE.
NOT UNTIL I KNOW WHERE YOU STAND!
THE KREE TOOK EVERYTHING AWAY FROM ME: MY CAREER, MY WAY OF LIFE! THEY TRIED TO KILL ME!
IF THEY KNEW I WAS ALIVE, THEY'D TRY TO KILL ME AGAIN. SO I WENT UNDERGROUND, MAN!
I'VE KEPT AN EYE ON EVERYTHING THAT HAS GONE ON IN YOUR LIFE!
THE KREE HAVE DONE THINGS JUST AS AWFUL TO YOU!
HELP ME GET BACK AT THEM!
GO ON...
"GO ON"?!

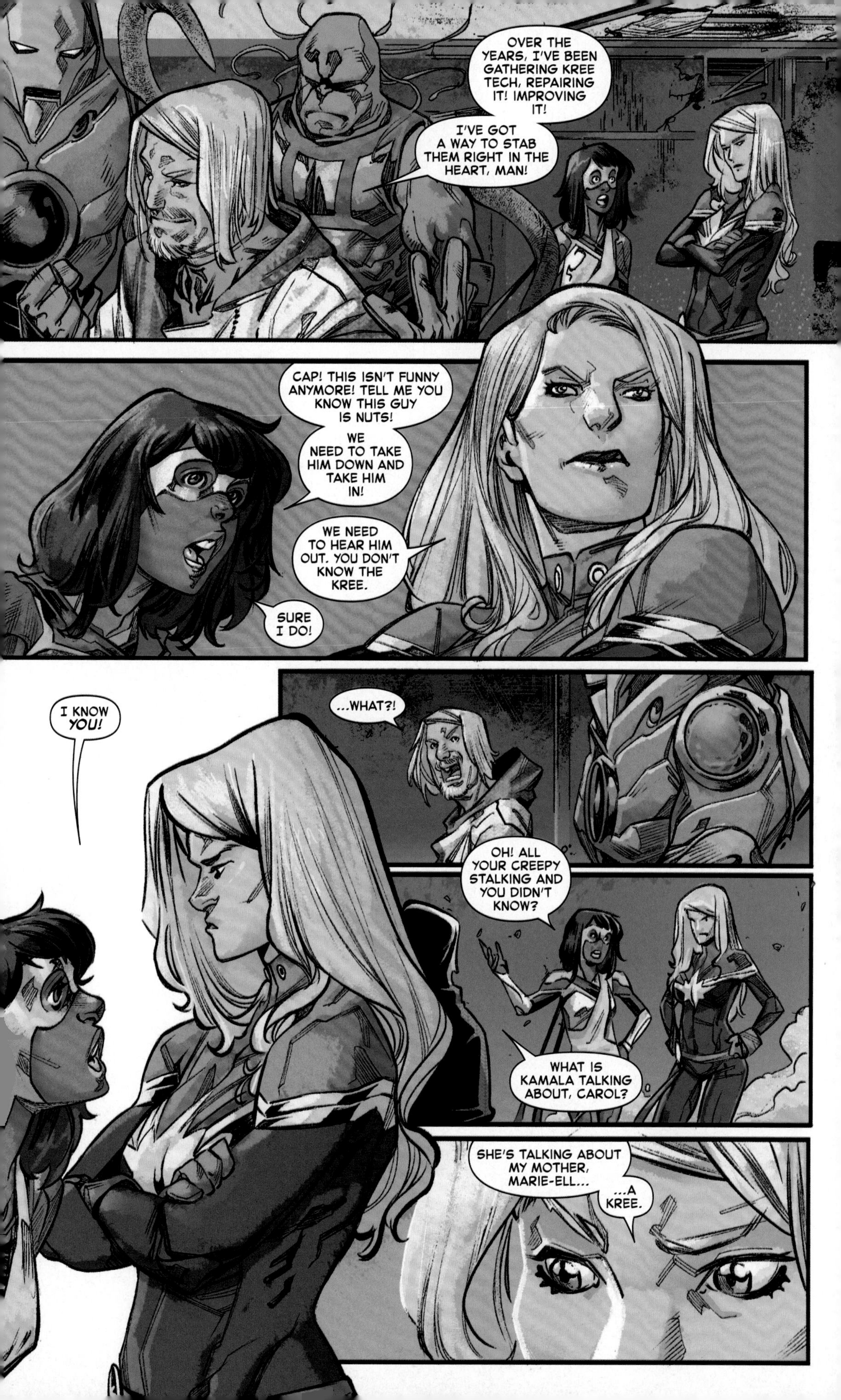

OVER THE YEARS, I'VE BEEN GATHERING KREE TECH, REPAIRING IT! IMPROVING IT!
I'VE GOT A WAY TO STAB THEM RIGHT IN THE HEART, MAN!
CAP! THIS ISN'T FUNNY ANYMORE! TELL ME YOU KNOW THIS GUY IS NUTS!
WE NEED TO TAKE HIM DOWN AND TAKE HIM IN!
WE NEED TO HEAR HIM OUT. YOU DON'T KNOW THE KREE.
SURE I DO!
I KNOW *YOU!*
...WHAT?!
OH! ALL YOUR CREEPY STALKING AND YOU DIDN'T KNOW?
WHAT IS KAMALA TALKING ABOUT, CAROL?
SHE'S TALKING ABOUT MY MOTHER, MARIE-ELL...
...A KREE.

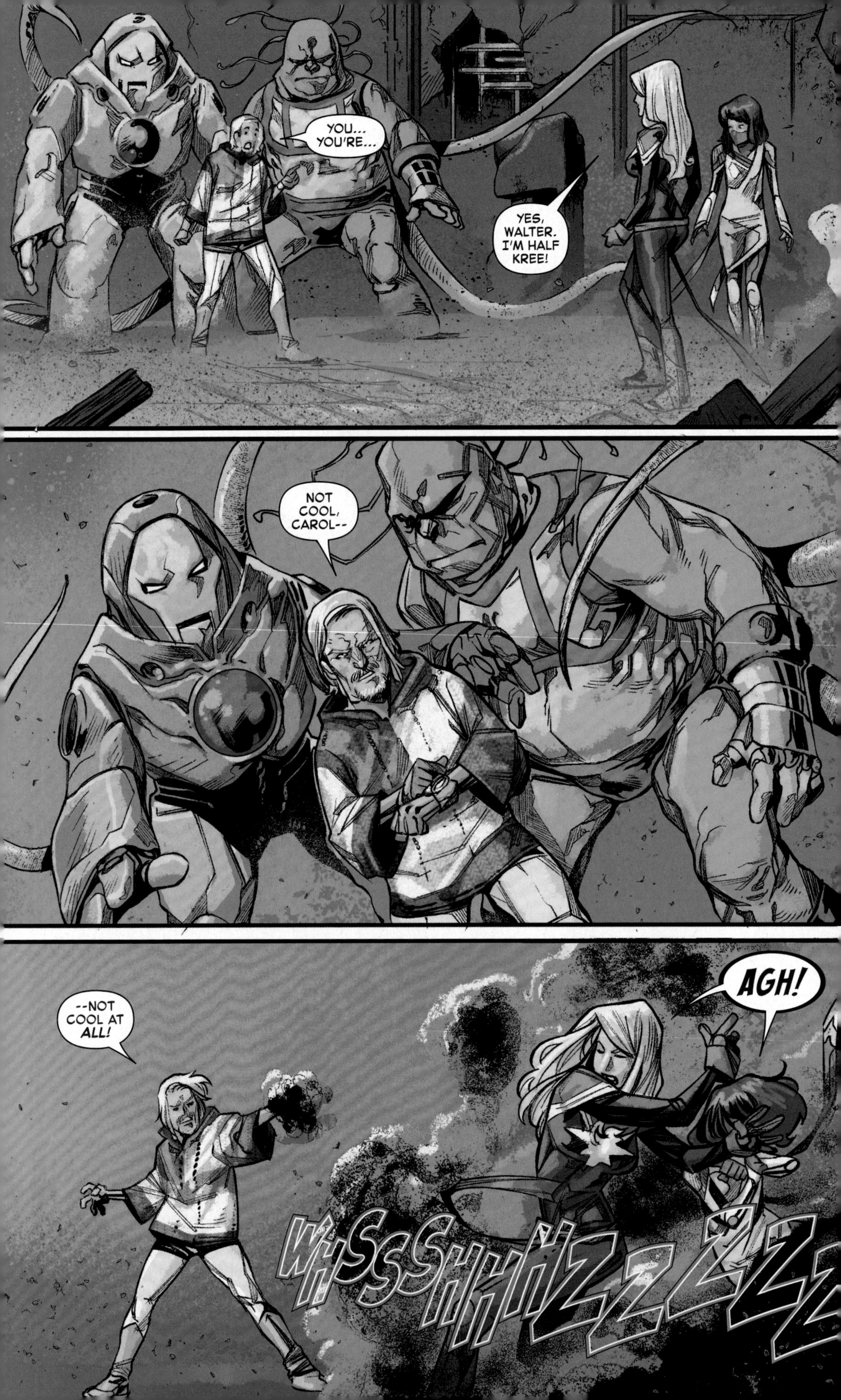
YOU... YOU'RE...
YES, WALTER. I'M HALF KREE!
NOT COOL, CAROL--
--NOT COOL AT ALL!
AGH!
WHSSSHHHZZZZZ

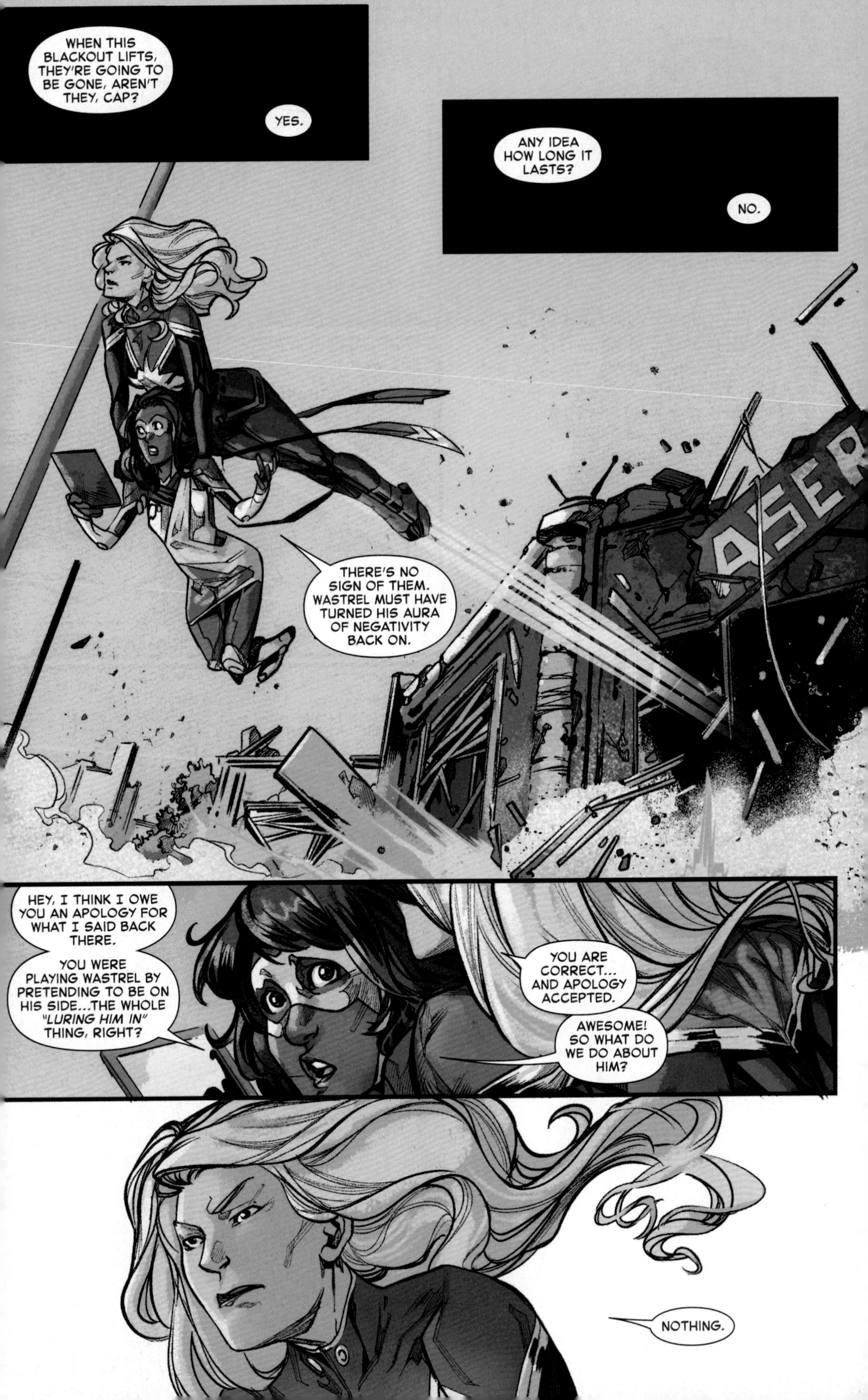
WHEN THIS BLACKOUT LIFTS, THEY'RE GOING TO BE GONE, AREN'T THEY, CAP?
YES.
ANY IDEA HOW LONG IT LASTS?
NO.
THERE'S NO SIGN OF THEM. WASTREL MUST HAVE TURNED HIS AURA OF NEGATIVITY BACK ON.
HEY, I THINK I OWE YOU AN APOLOGY FOR WHAT I SAID BACK THERE.
YOU WERE PLAYING WASTREL BY PRETENDING TO BE ON HIS SIDE...THE WHOLE *"LURING HIM IN"* THING, RIGHT?
YOU ARE CORRECT... AND APOLOGY ACCEPTED.
AWESOME! SO WHAT DO WE DO ABOUT HIM?
NOTHING.

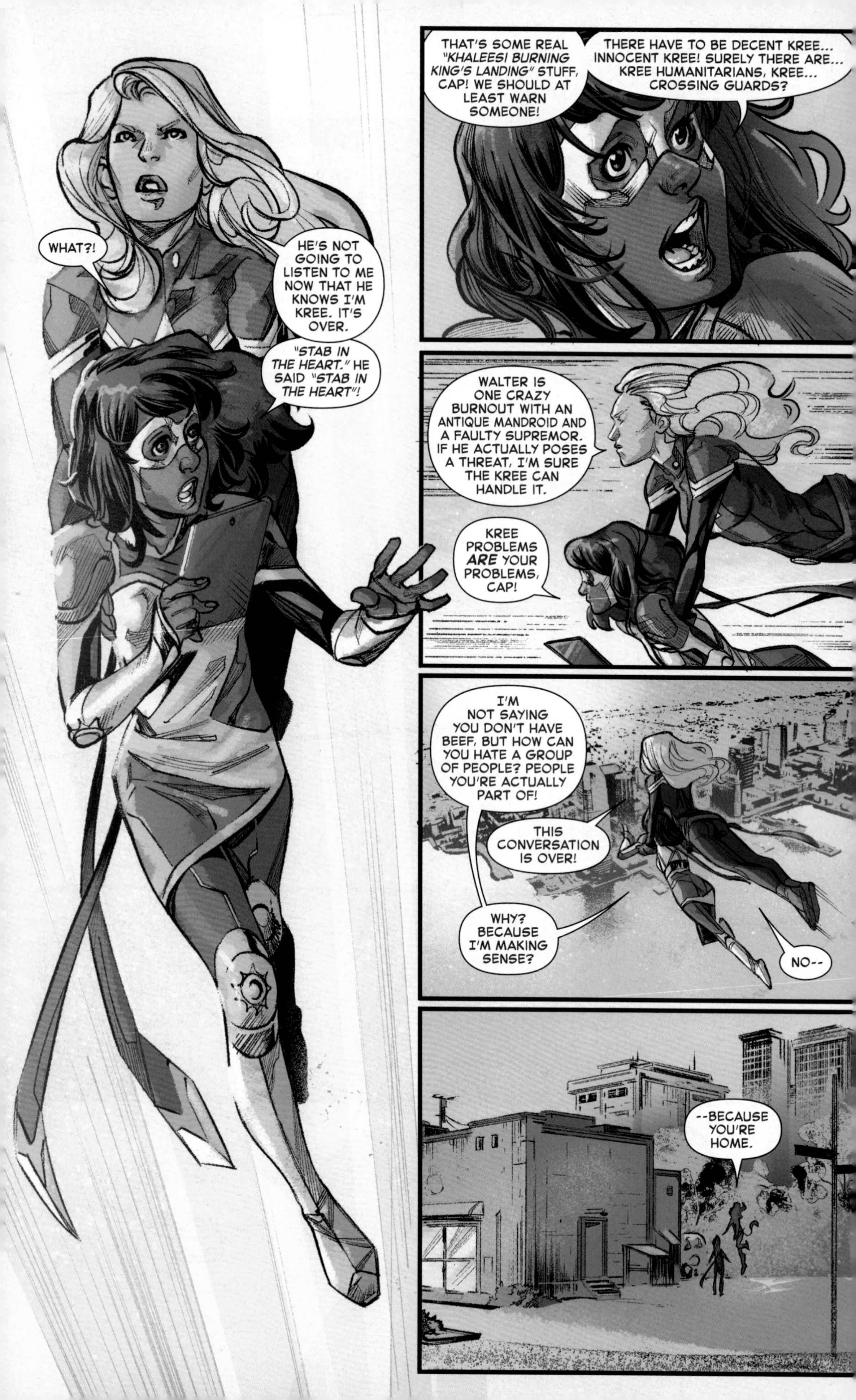

WHAT?!
HE'S NOT GOING TO LISTEN TO ME NOW THAT HE KNOWS I'M KREE. IT'S OVER.
"STAB IN THE HEART." HE SAID "STAB IN THE HEART"!
THAT'S SOME REAL "KHALEESI BURNING KING'S LANDING" STUFF, CAP! WE SHOULD AT LEAST WARN SOMEONE!
THERE HAVE TO BE DECENT KREE... INNOCENT KREE! SURELY THERE ARE... KREE HUMANITARIANS, KREE... CROSSING GUARDS?
WALTER IS ONE CRAZY BURNOUT WITH AN ANTIQUE MANDROID AND A FAULTY SUPREMOR. IF HE ACTUALLY POSES A THREAT, I'M SURE THE KREE CAN HANDLE IT.
KREE PROBLEMS ARE YOUR PROBLEMS, CAP!
I'M NOT SAYING YOU DON'T HAVE BEEF, BUT HOW CAN YOU HATE A GROUP OF PEOPLE? PEOPLE YOU'RE ACTUALLY PART OF!
THIS CONVERSATION IS OVER!
WHY? BECAUSE I'M MAKING SENSE?
NO--
--BECAUSE YOU'RE HOME.

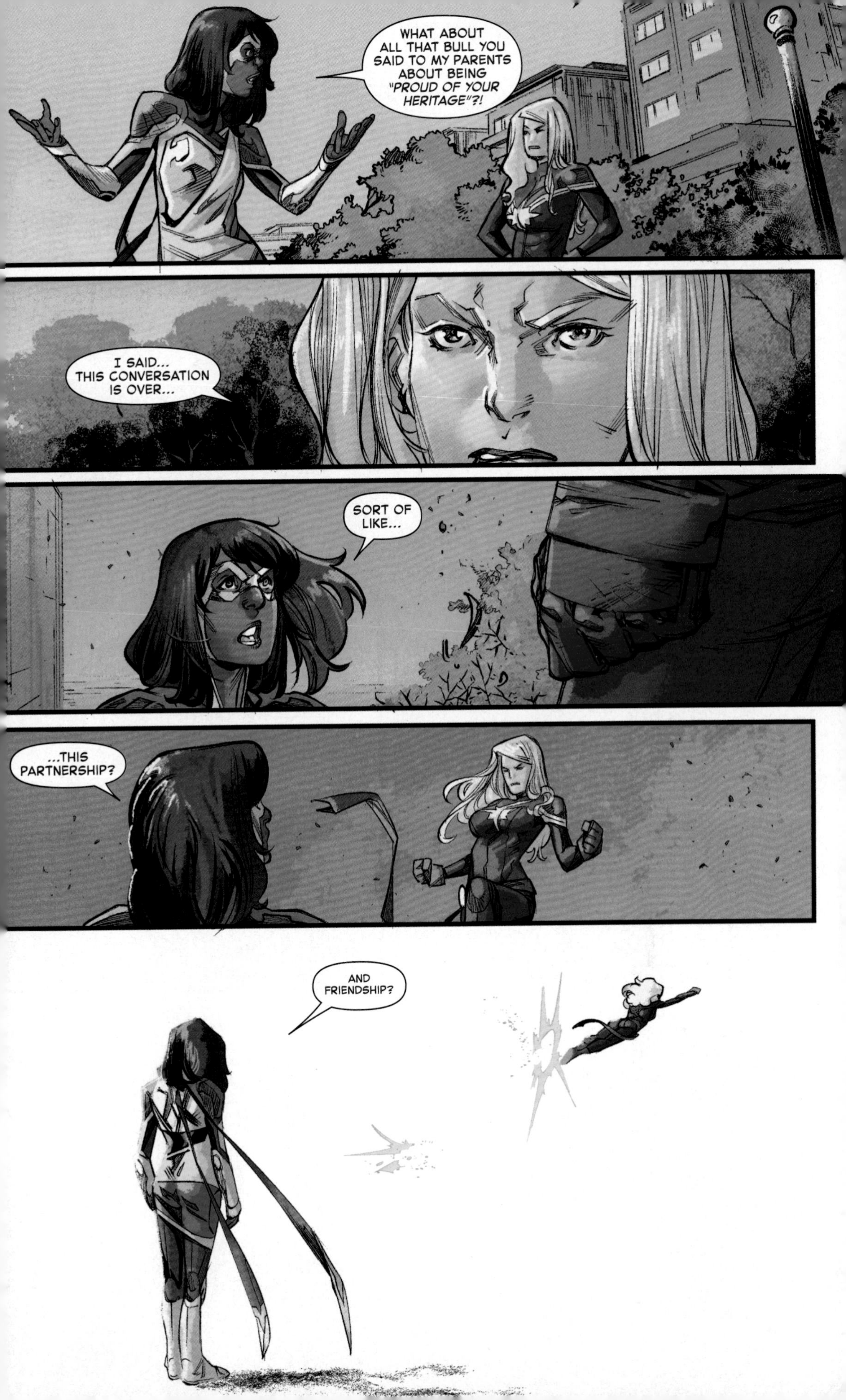
WHAT ABOUT ALL THAT BULL YOU SAID TO MY PARENTS ABOUT BEING "PROUD OF YOUR HERITAGE"?!
I SAID... THIS CONVERSATION IS OVER...
SORT OF LIKE...
...THIS PARTNERSHIP?
AND FRIENDSHIP?

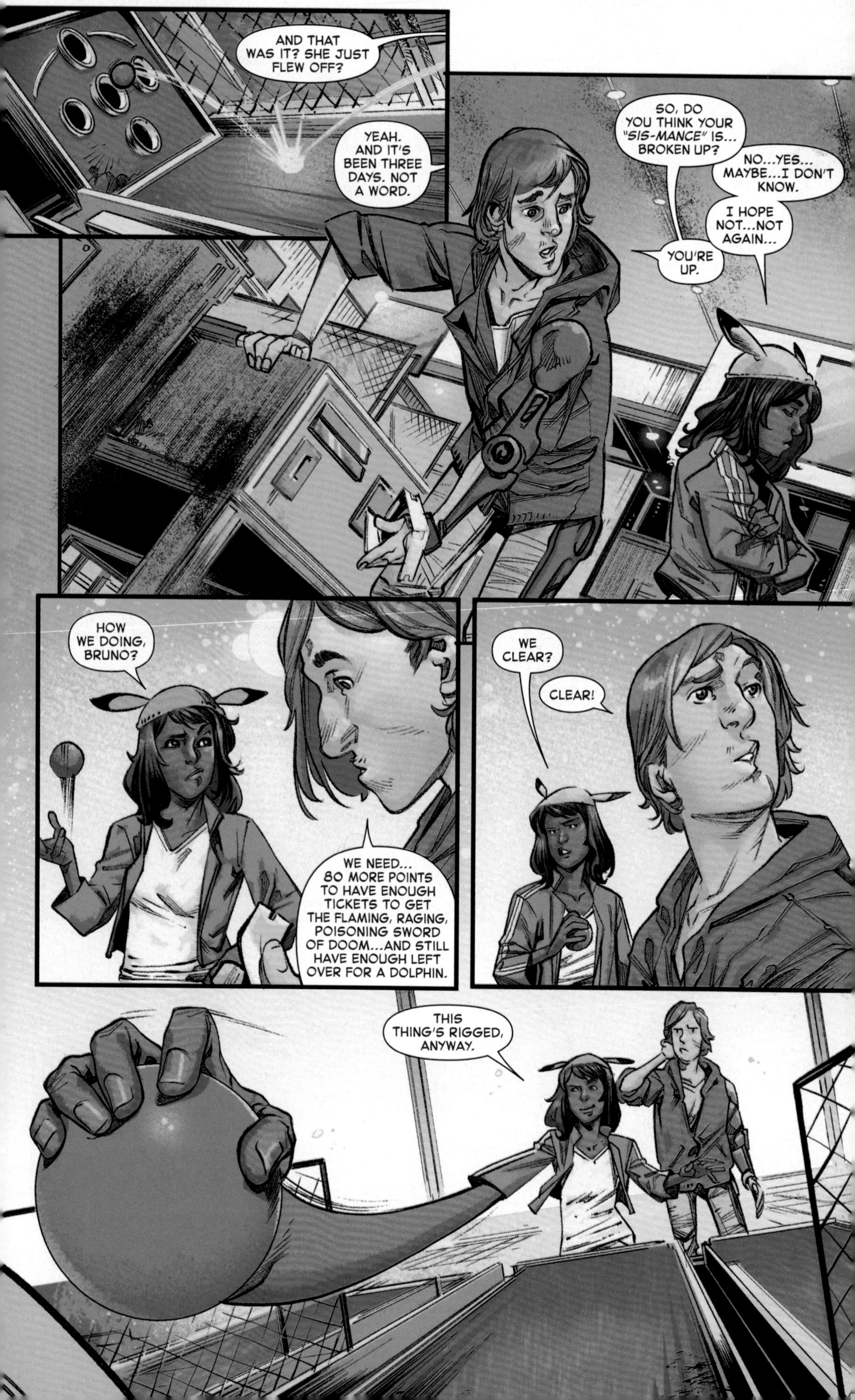
AND THAT WAS IT? SHE JUST FLEW OFF?
YEAH. AND IT'S BEEN THREE DAYS. NOT A WORD.
SO, DO YOU THINK YOUR "SIS-MANCE" IS... BROKEN UP?
NO...YES... MAYBE...I DON'T KNOW.
I HOPE NOT...NOT AGAIN...
YOU'RE UP.
HOW WE DOING, BRUNO?
WE NEED... 80 MORE POINTS TO HAVE ENOUGH TICKETS TO GET THE FLAMING, RAGING, POISONING SWORD OF DOOM...AND STILL HAVE ENOUGH LEFT OVER FOR A DOLPHIN.
WE CLEAR?
CLEAR!
THIS THING'S RIGGED, ANYWAY.

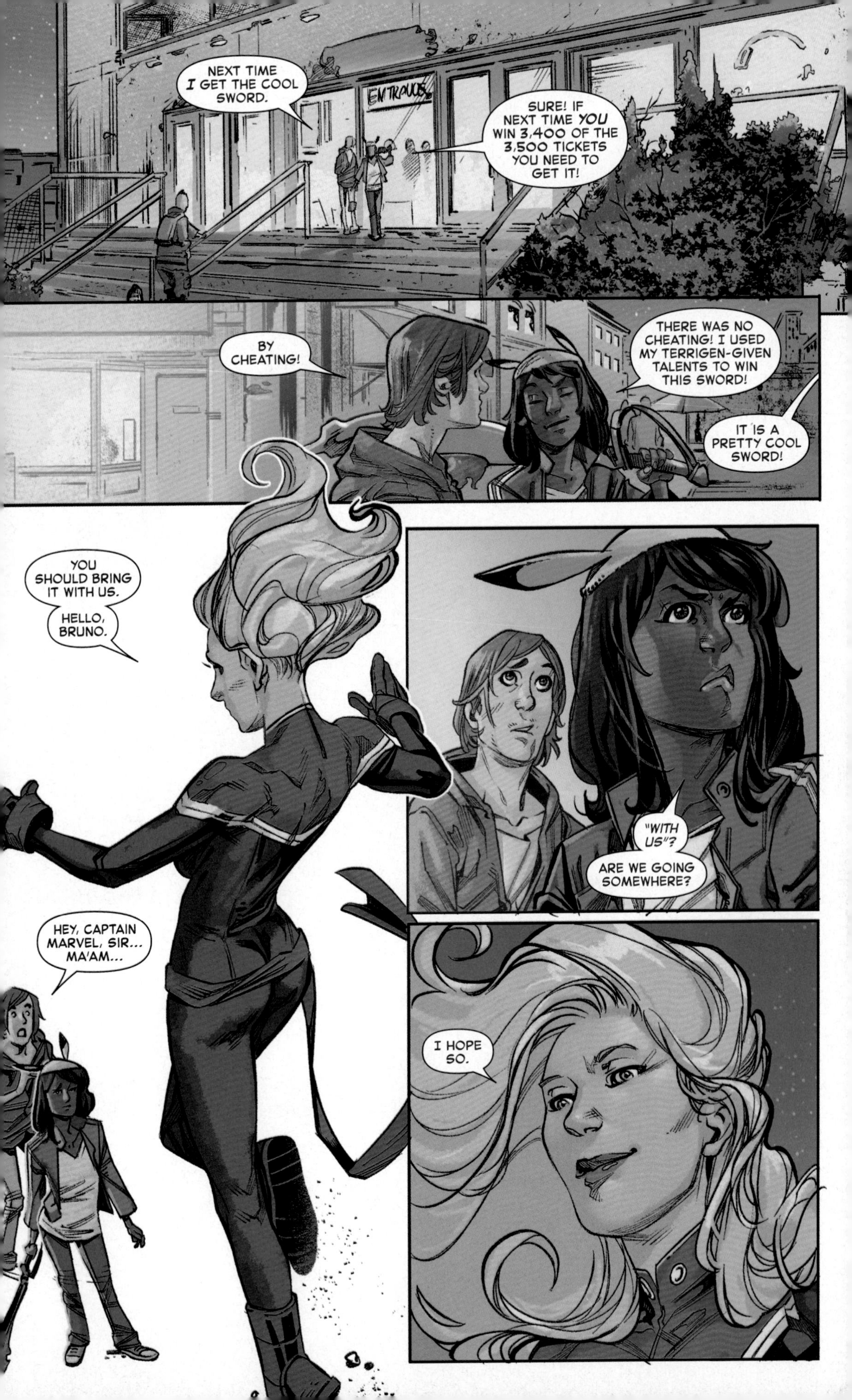
NEXT TIME I GET THE COOL SWORD.
SURE! IF NEXT TIME YOU WIN 3,400 OF THE 3,500 TICKETS YOU NEED TO GET IT!
BY CHEATING!
THERE WAS NO CHEATING! I USED MY TERRIGEN-GIVEN TALENTS TO WIN THIS SWORD!
IT IS A PRETTY COOL SWORD!
YOU SHOULD BRING IT WITH US.
HELLO, BRUNO.
"WITH US"?
ARE WE GOING SOMEWHERE?
HEY, CAPTAIN MARVEL, SIR... MA'AM...
I HOPE SO.

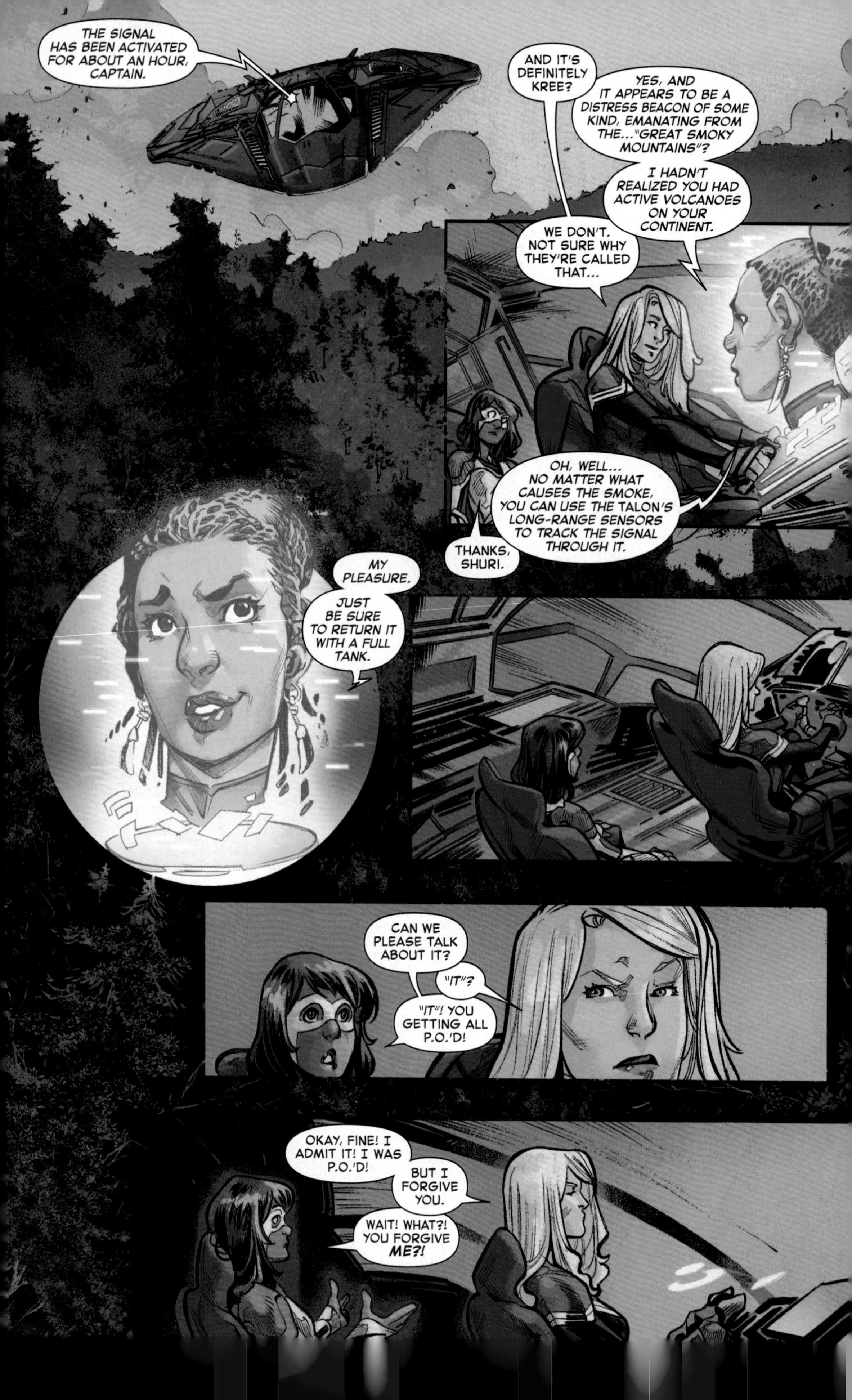
THE SIGNAL HAS BEEN ACTIVATED FOR ABOUT AN HOUR, CAPTAIN.
AND IT'S DEFINITELY KREE?
YES, AND IT APPEARS TO BE A DISTRESS BEACON OF SOME KIND, EMANATING FROM THE..."GREAT SMOKY MOUNTAINS"?
I HADN'T REALIZED YOU HAD ACTIVE VOLCANOES ON YOUR CONTINENT.
WE DON'T. NOT SURE WHY THEY'RE CALLED THAT...
OH, WELL... NO MATTER WHAT CAUSES THE SMOKE, YOU CAN USE THE TALON'S LONG-RANGE SENSORS TO TRACK THE SIGNAL THROUGH IT.
THANKS, SHURI.
MY PLEASURE.
JUST BE SURE TO RETURN IT WITH A FULL TANK.
CAN WE PLEASE TALK ABOUT IT?
"IT"?
"IT"! YOU GETTING ALL P.O.'D!
OKAY, FINE! I ADMIT IT! I WAS P.O.'D!
BUT I FORGIVE YOU.
WAIT! WHAT?! YOU FORGIVE ME?!

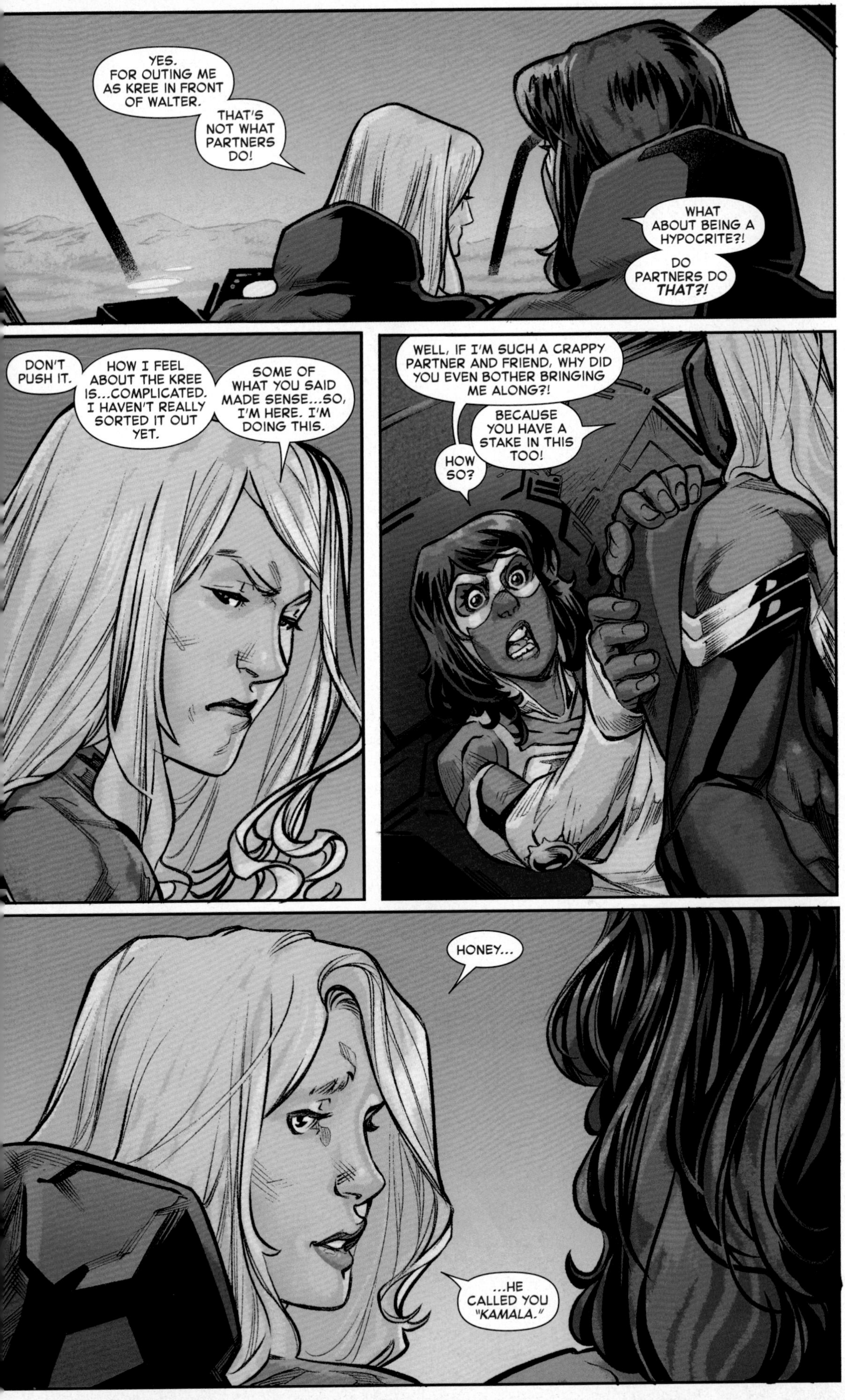
YES. FOR OUTING ME AS KREE IN FRONT OF WALTER.
THAT'S NOT WHAT PARTNERS DO!
WHAT ABOUT BEING A HYPOCRITE?!
DO PARTNERS DO *THAT?!*
DON'T PUSH IT.
HOW I FEEL ABOUT THE KREE IS...COMPLICATED. I HAVEN'T REALLY SORTED IT OUT YET.
SOME OF WHAT YOU SAID MADE SENSE...SO, I'M HERE. I'M DOING THIS.
WELL, IF I'M SUCH A CRAPPY PARTNER AND FRIEND, WHY DID YOU EVEN BOTHER BRINGING ME ALONG?!
BECAUSE YOU HAVE A STAKE IN THIS TOO!
HOW SO?
HONEY...
...HE CALLED YOU "*KAMALA.*"

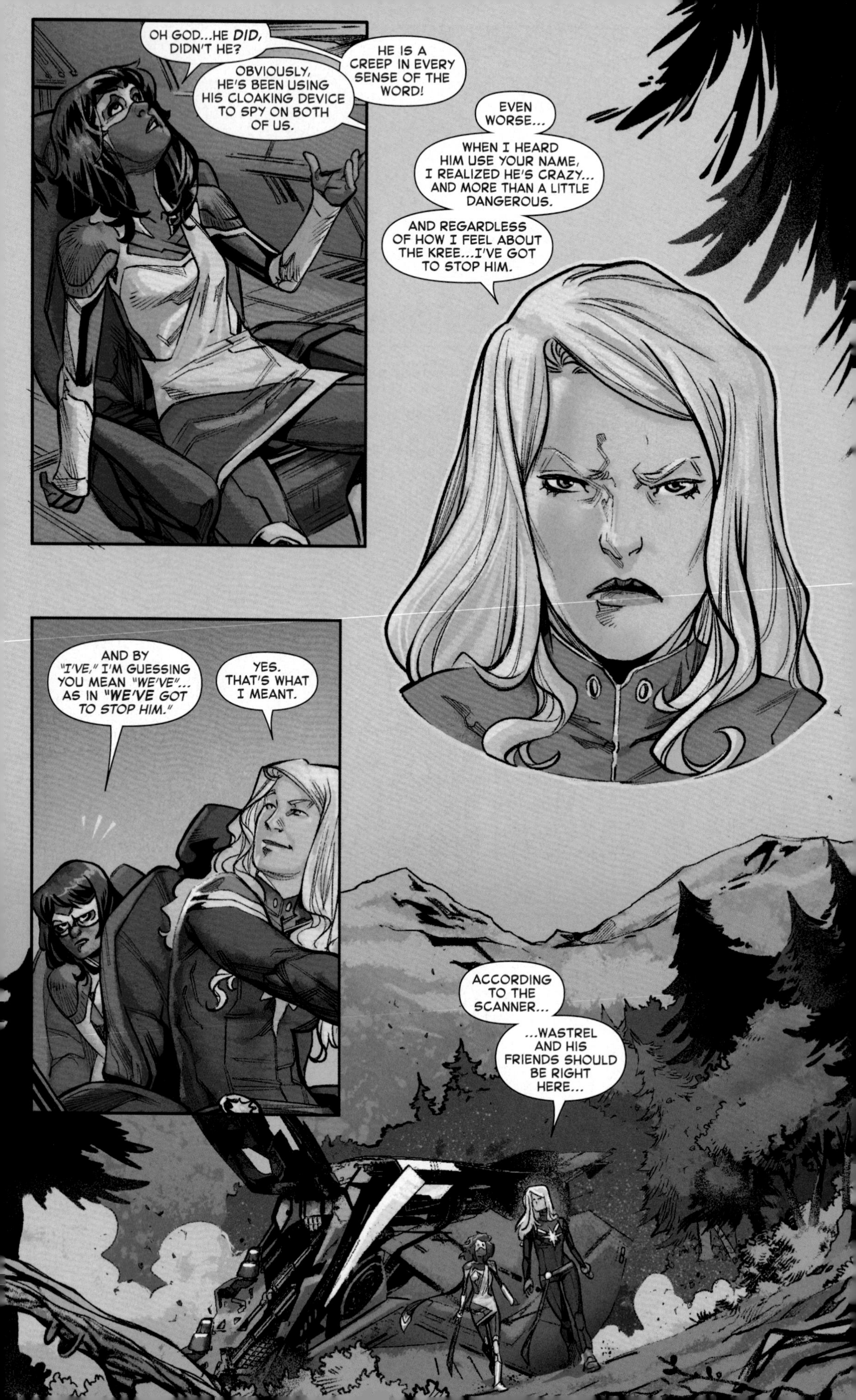

OH GOD...HE *DID*, DIDN'T HE?
OBVIOUSLY, HE'S BEEN USING HIS CLOAKING DEVICE TO SPY ON BOTH OF US.
HE IS A CREEP IN EVERY SENSE OF THE WORD!
EVEN WORSE...
WHEN I HEARD HIM USE YOUR NAME, I REALIZED HE'S CRAZY... AND MORE THAN A LITTLE DANGEROUS.
AND REGARDLESS OF HOW I FEEL ABOUT THE KREE...I'VE GOT TO STOP HIM.
AND BY *"I'VE,"* I'M GUESSING YOU MEAN *"WE'VE"*... AS IN *"WE'VE GOT TO STOP HIM."*
YES. THAT'S WHAT I MEANT.
ACCORDING TO THE SCANNER...
...WASTREL AND HIS FRIENDS SHOULD BE RIGHT HERE...

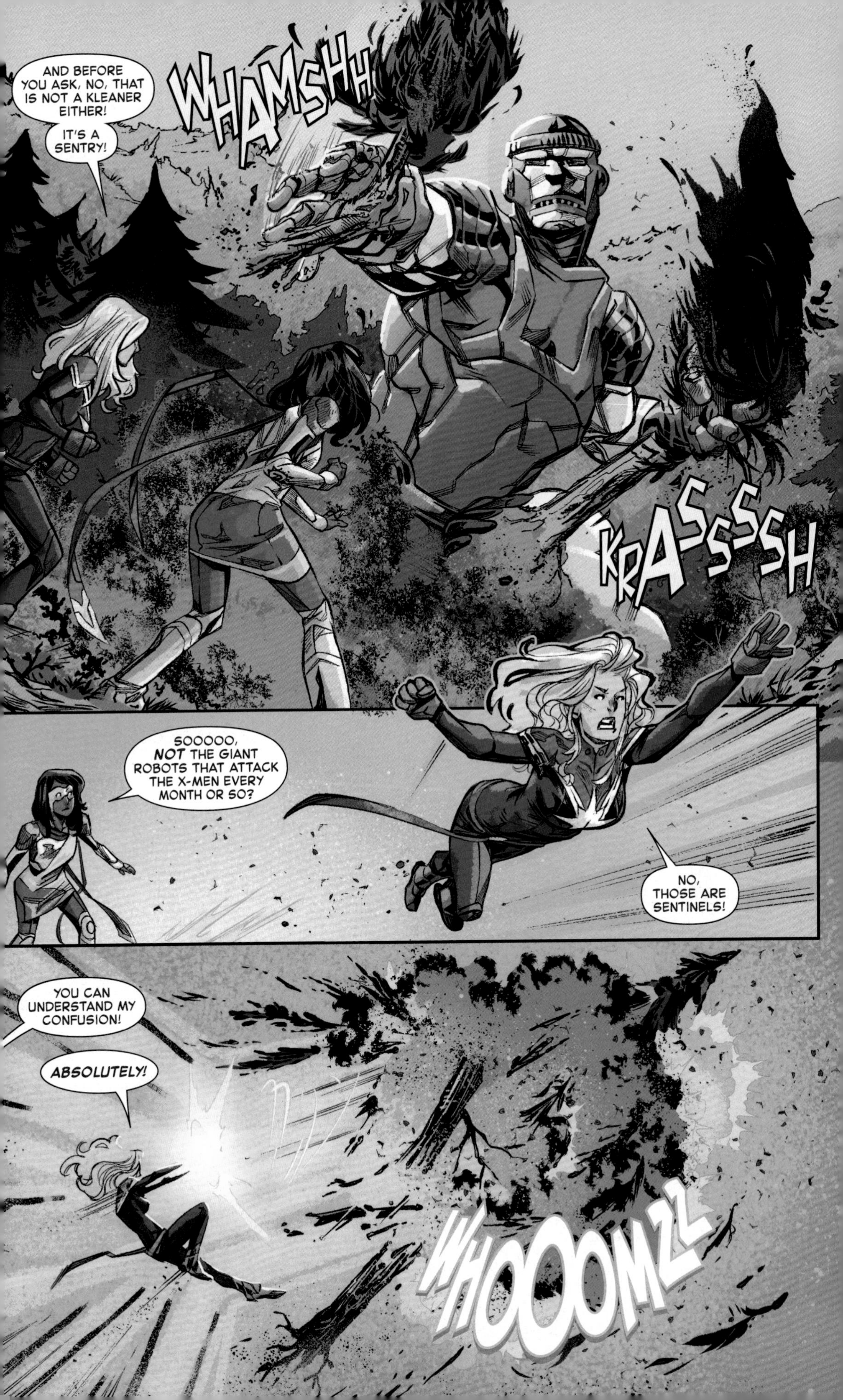
AND BEFORE YOU ASK, NO, THAT IS NOT A KLEANER EITHER!
IT'S A SENTRY!
WHAMSHH
KRASSSSH
SOOOOO, NOT THE GIANT ROBOTS THAT ATTACK THE X-MEN EVERY MONTH OR SO?
NO, THOSE ARE SENTINELS!
YOU CAN UNDERSTAND MY CONFUSION!
ABSOLUTELY!
WHOOOMZZ

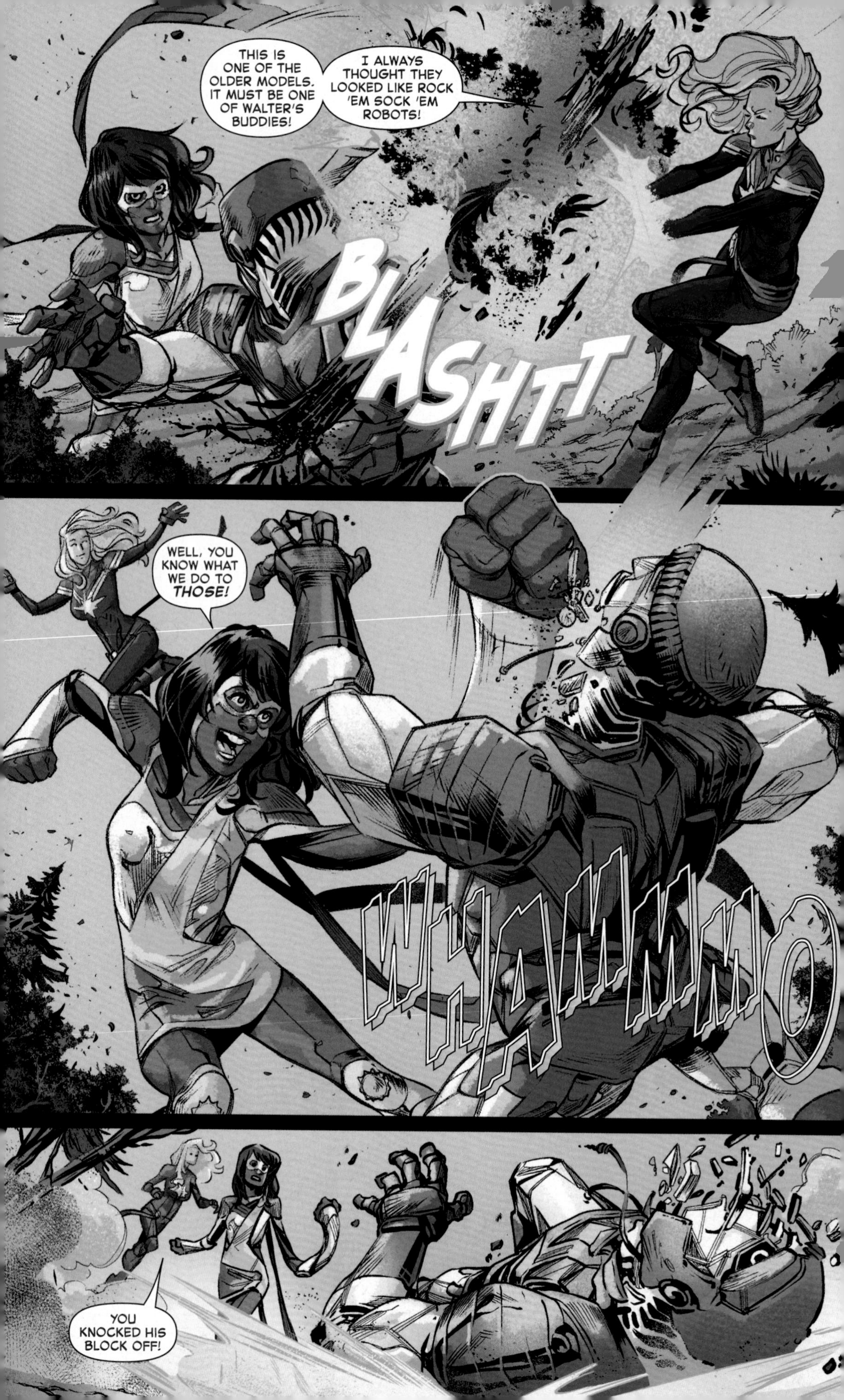
THIS IS ONE OF THE OLDER MODELS. IT MUST BE ONE OF WALTER'S BUDDIES!
I ALWAYS THOUGHT THEY LOOKED LIKE ROCK 'EM SOCK 'EM ROBOTS!
BLASHTT
WELL, YOU KNOW WHAT WE DO TO *THOSE!*
WHAMMMO
YOU KNOCKED HIS BLOCK OFF!

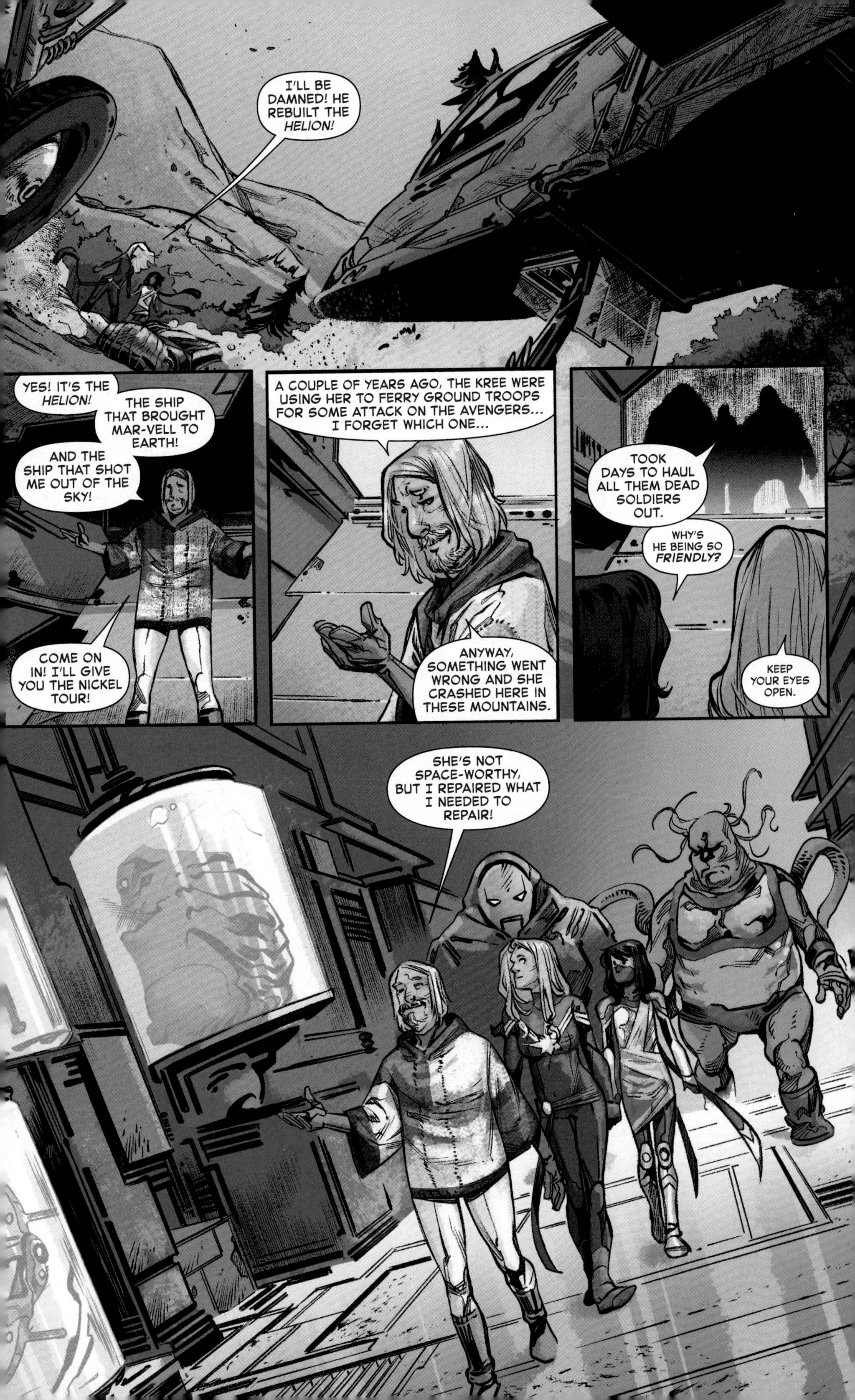

I'LL BE DAMNED! HE REBUILT THE *HELION!*
YES! IT'S THE *HELION!*
THE SHIP THAT BROUGHT MAR-VELL TO EARTH!
AND THE SHIP THAT SHOT ME OUT OF THE SKY!
COME ON IN! I'LL GIVE YOU THE NICKEL TOUR!
A COUPLE OF YEARS AGO, THE KREE WERE USING HER TO FERRY GROUND TROOPS FOR SOME ATTACK ON THE AVENGERS... I FORGET WHICH ONE...
ANYWAY, SOMETHING WENT WRONG AND SHE CRASHED HERE IN THESE MOUNTAINS.
TOOK DAYS TO HAUL ALL THEM DEAD SOLDIERS OUT.
WHY'S HE BEING SO *FRIENDLY?*
KEEP YOUR EYES OPEN.
SHE'S NOT SPACE-WORTHY, BUT I REPAIRED WHAT I NEEDED TO REPAIR!

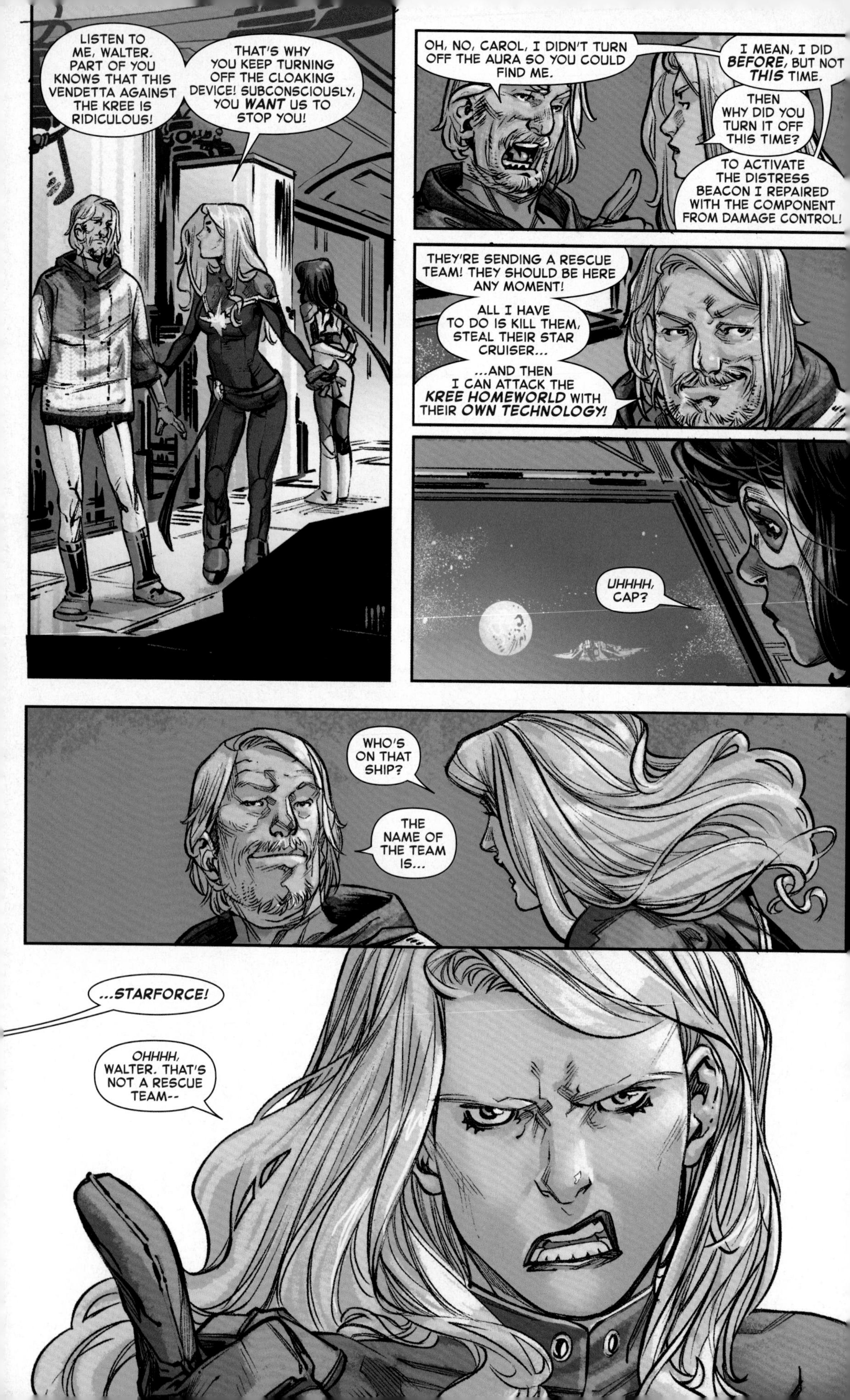
LISTEN TO ME, WALTER. PART OF YOU KNOWS THAT THIS VENDETTA AGAINST THE KREE IS RIDICULOUS!
THAT'S WHY YOU KEEP TURNING OFF THE CLOAKING DEVICE! SUBCONSCIOUSLY, YOU WANT US TO STOP YOU!
OH, NO, CAROL, I DIDN'T TURN OFF THE AURA SO YOU COULD FIND ME.
I MEAN, I DID BEFORE, BUT NOT THIS TIME.
THEN WHY DID YOU TURN IT OFF THIS TIME?
TO ACTIVATE THE DISTRESS BEACON I REPAIRED WITH THE COMPONENT FROM DAMAGE CONTROL!
THEY'RE SENDING A RESCUE TEAM! THEY SHOULD BE HERE ANY MOMENT!
ALL I HAVE TO DO IS KILL THEM, STEAL THEIR STAR CRUISER...
...AND THEN I CAN ATTACK THE KREE HOMEWORLD WITH THEIR OWN TECHNOLOGY!
UHHHH, CAP?
WHO'S ON THAT SHIP?
THE NAME OF THE TEAM IS...
...STARFORCE!
OHHHH, WALTER. THAT'S NOT A RESCUE TEAM--

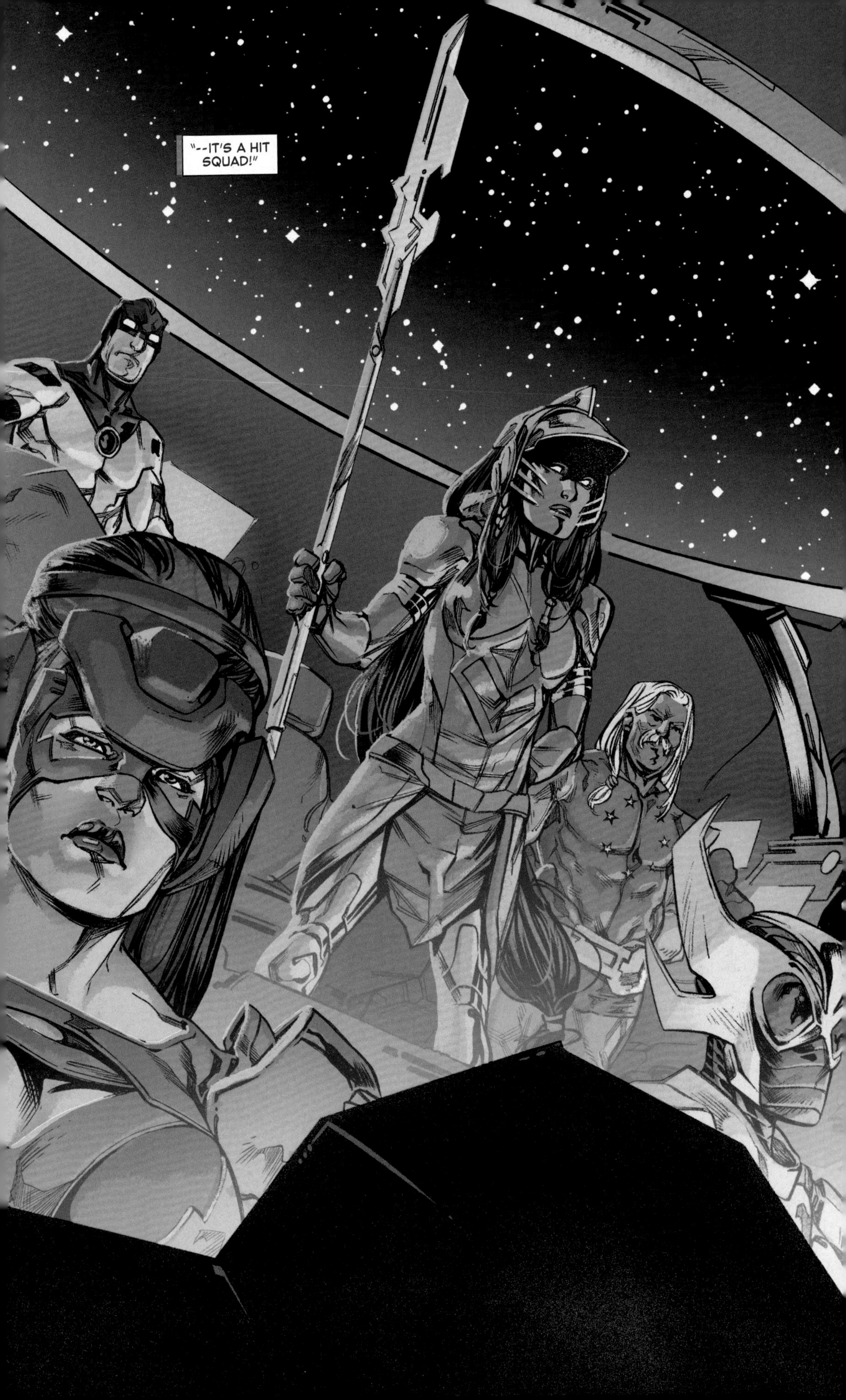
"--IT'S A HIT SQUAD!"

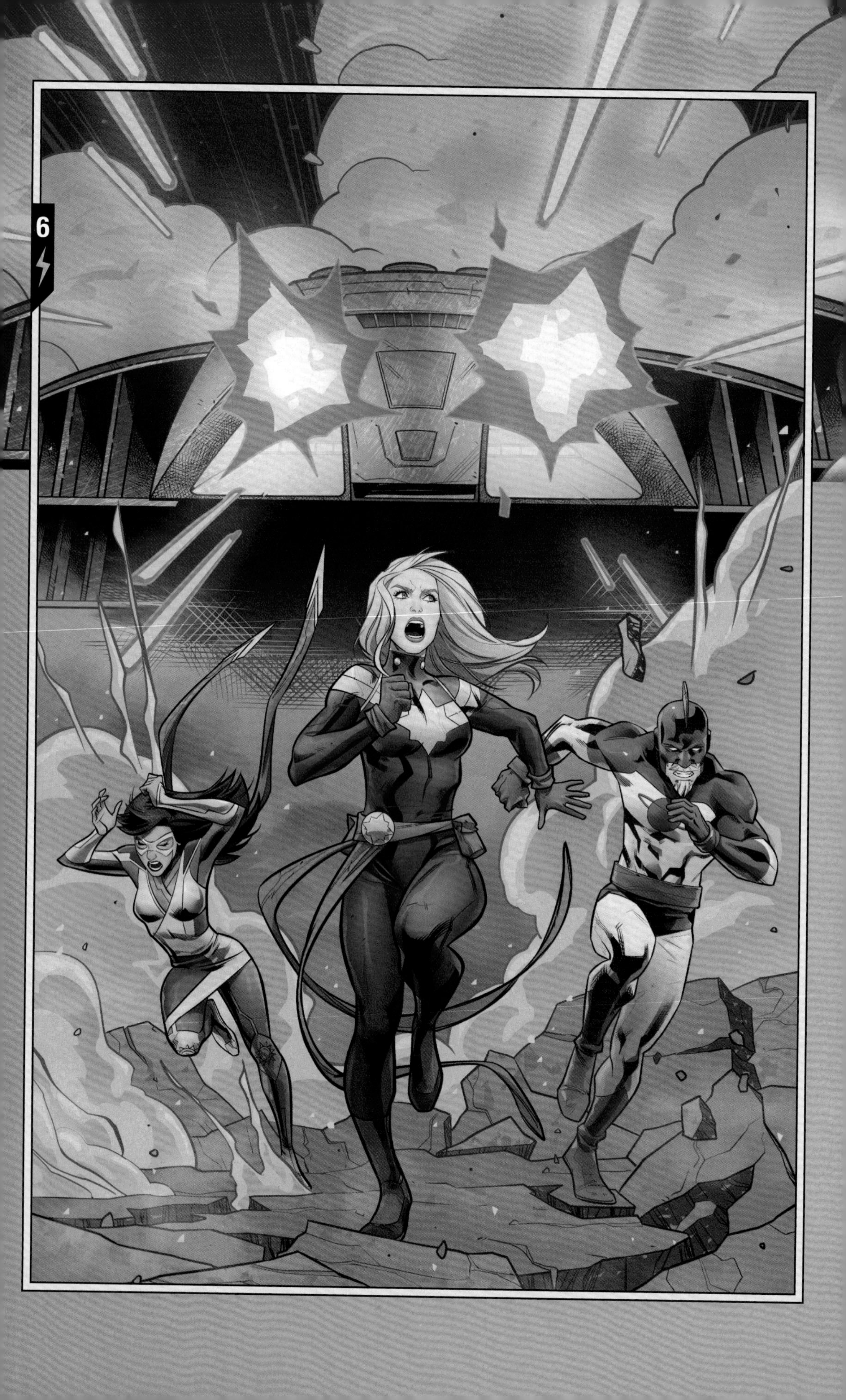

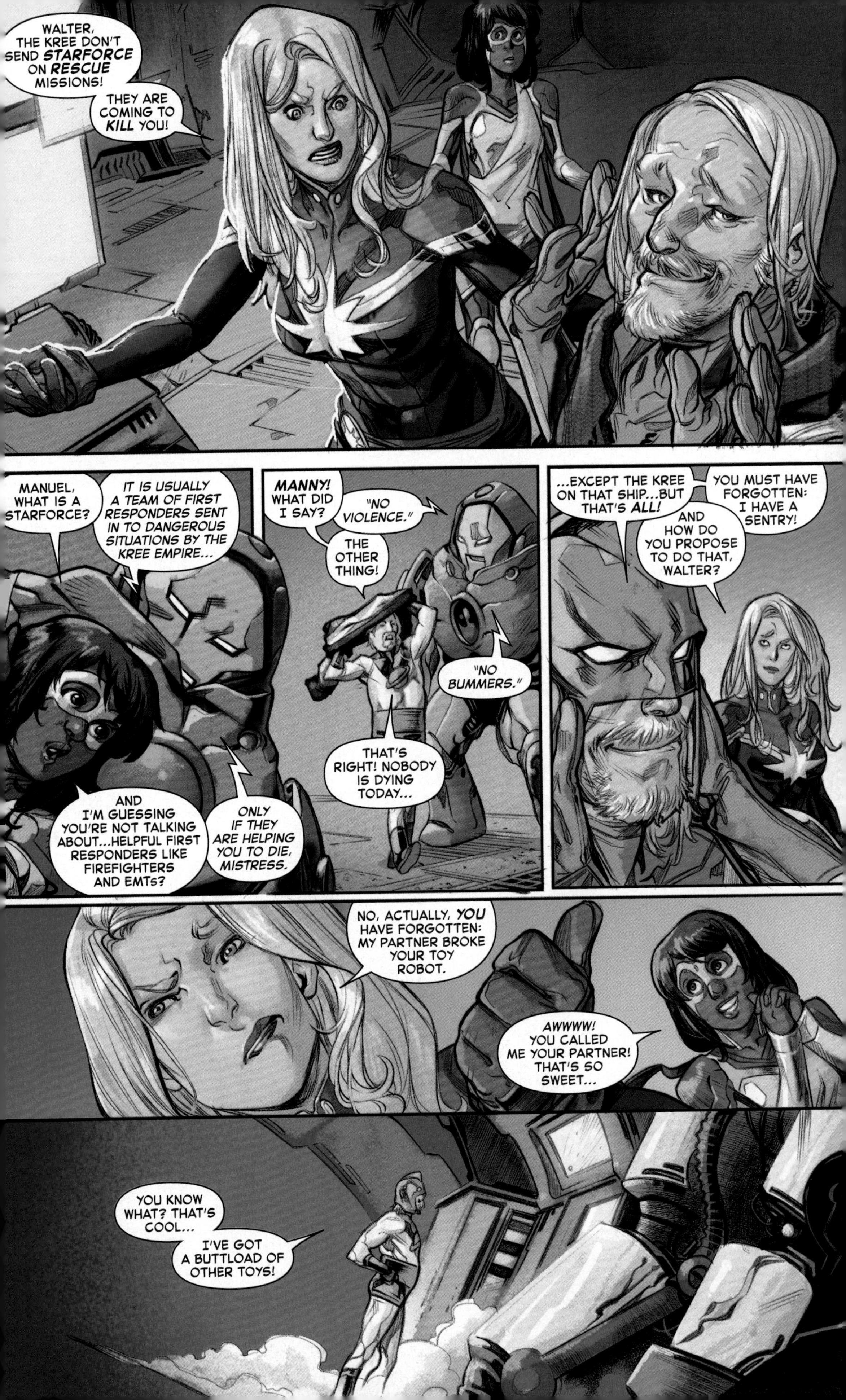
WALTER, THE KREE DON'T SEND STARFORCE ON RESCUE MISSIONS!
THEY ARE COMING TO KILL YOU!
MANUEL, WHAT IS A STARFORCE?
IT IS USUALLY A TEAM OF FIRST RESPONDERS SENT IN TO DANGEROUS SITUATIONS BY THE KREE EMPIRE...
AND I'M GUESSING YOU'RE NOT TALKING ABOUT...HELPFUL FIRST RESPONDERS LIKE FIREFIGHTERS AND EMTs?
ONLY IF THEY ARE HELPING YOU TO DIE, MISTRESS.
MANNY! WHAT DID I SAY?
"NO VIOLENCE."
THE OTHER THING!
"NO BUMMERS."
THAT'S RIGHT! NOBODY IS DYING TODAY...
...EXCEPT THE KREE ON THAT SHIP...BUT THAT'S ALL!
AND HOW DO YOU PROPOSE TO DO THAT, WALTER?
YOU MUST HAVE FORGOTTEN: I HAVE A SENTRY!
NO, ACTUALLY, YOU HAVE FORGOTTEN: MY PARTNER BROKE YOUR TOY ROBOT.
AWWWW! YOU CALLED ME YOUR PARTNER! THAT'S SO SWEET...
YOU KNOW WHAT? THAT'S COOL...
I'VE GOT A BUTTLOAD OF OTHER TOYS!

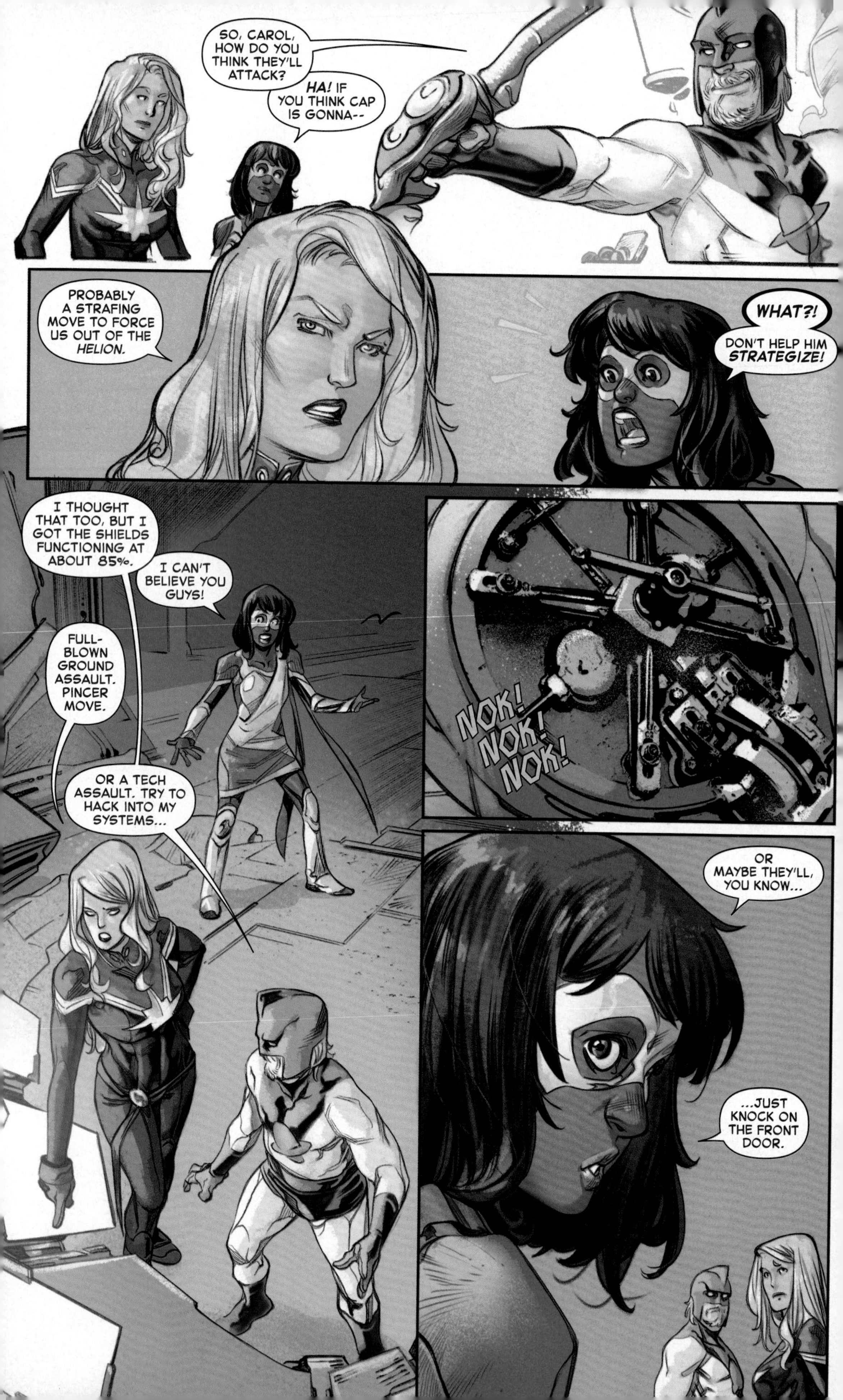
SO, CAROL, HOW DO YOU THINK THEY'LL ATTACK?
HA! IF YOU THINK CAP IS GONNA--
PROBABLY A STRAFING MOVE TO FORCE US OUT OF THE HELION.
WHAT?!
DON'T HELP HIM STRATEGIZE!
I THOUGHT THAT TOO, BUT I GOT THE SHIELDS FUNCTIONING AT ABOUT 85%.
I CAN'T BELIEVE YOU GUYS!
FULL-BLOWN GROUND ASSAULT. PINCER MOVE.
OR A TECH ASSAULT. TRY TO HACK INTO MY SYSTEMS...
NOK! NOK! NOK!
OR MAYBE THEY'LL, YOU KNOW...
...JUST KNOCK ON THE FRONT DOOR.

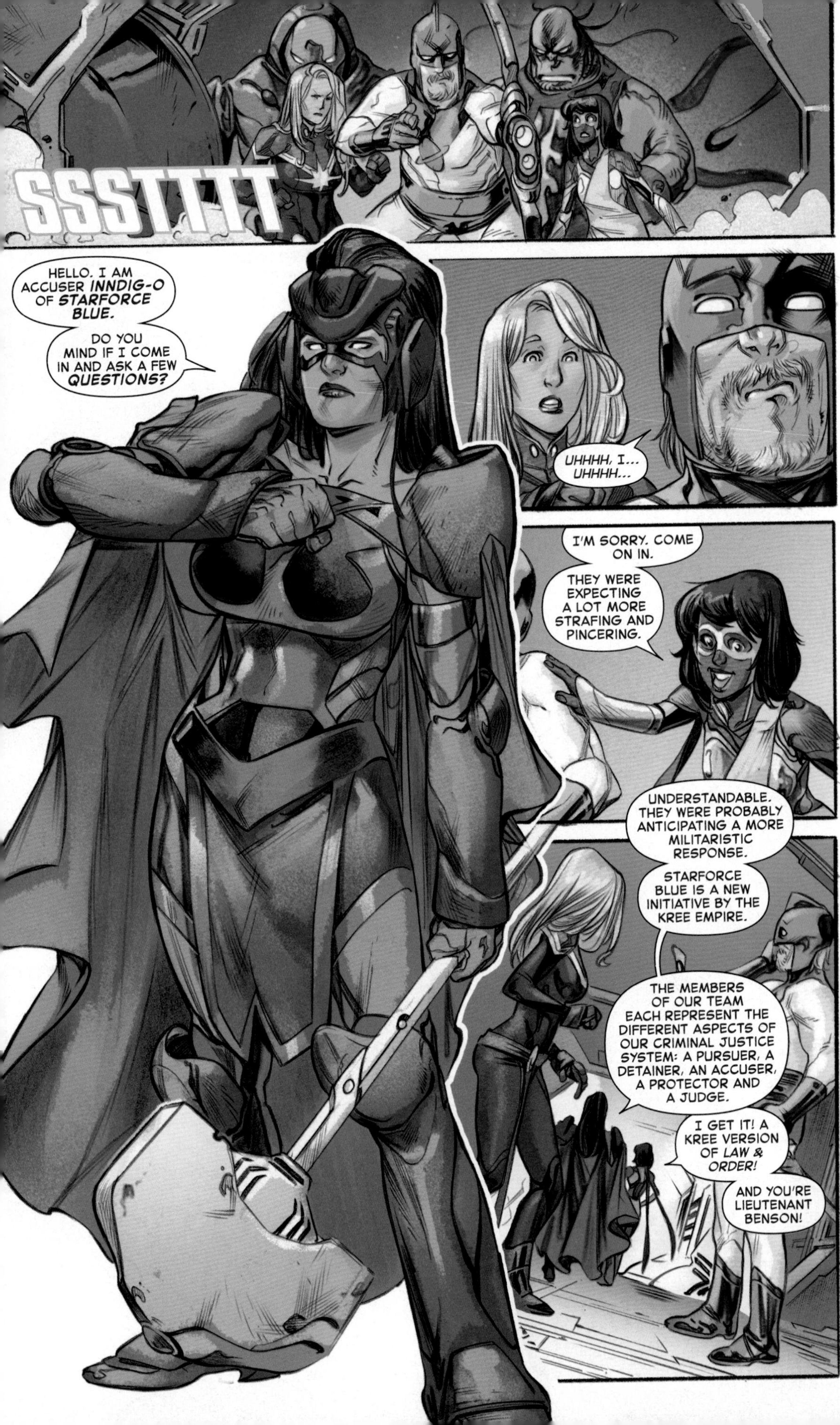
SSSTTTTT
HELLO. I AM ACCUSER INNDIG-O OF STARFORCE BLUE.
DO YOU MIND IF I COME IN AND ASK A FEW QUESTIONS?
UHHHH, I... UHHHH...
I'M SORRY. COME ON IN.
THEY WERE EXPECTING A LOT MORE STRAFING AND PINCERING.
UNDERSTANDABLE. THEY WERE PROBABLY ANTICIPATING A MORE MILITARISTIC RESPONSE.
STARFORCE BLUE IS A NEW INITIATIVE BY THE KREE EMPIRE.
THE MEMBERS OF OUR TEAM EACH REPRESENT THE DIFFERENT ASPECTS OF OUR CRIMINAL JUSTICE SYSTEM: A PURSUER, A DETAINER, AN ACCUSER, A PROTECTOR AND A JUDGE.
I GET IT! A KREE VERSION OF LAW & ORDER!
AND YOU'RE LIEUTENANT BENSON!

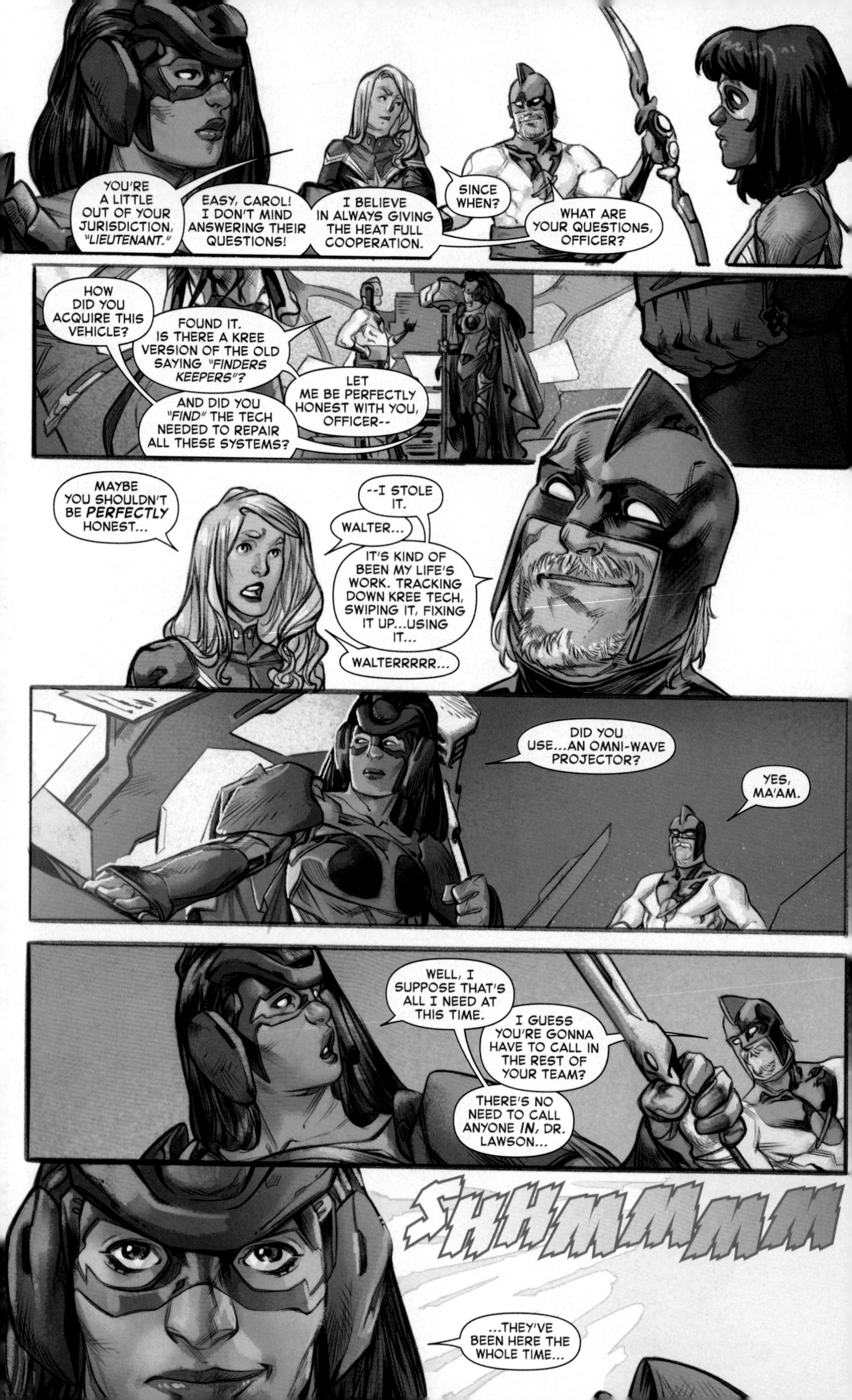
YOU'RE A LITTLE OUT OF YOUR JURISDICTION, "LIEUTENANT."
EASY, CAROL! I DON'T MIND ANSWERING THEIR QUESTIONS!
I BELIEVE IN ALWAYS GIVING THE HEAT FULL COOPERATION.
SINCE WHEN?
WHAT ARE YOUR QUESTIONS, OFFICER?
HOW DID YOU ACQUIRE THIS VEHICLE?
FOUND IT. IS THERE A KREE VERSION OF THE OLD SAYING "FINDERS KEEPERS"?
AND DID YOU "FIND" THE TECH NEEDED TO REPAIR ALL THESE SYSTEMS?
LET ME BE PERFECTLY HONEST WITH YOU, OFFICER--
MAYBE YOU SHOULDN'T BE PERFECTLY HONEST...
--I STOLE IT.
WALTER...
IT'S KIND OF BEEN MY LIFE'S WORK. TRACKING DOWN KREE TECH, SWIPING IT, FIXING IT UP...USING IT...
WALTERRRRR...
DID YOU USE...AN OMNI-WAVE PROJECTOR?
YES, MA'AM.
WELL, I SUPPOSE THAT'S ALL I NEED AT THIS TIME.
I GUESS YOU'RE GONNA HAVE TO CALL IN THE REST OF YOUR TEAM?
THERE'S NO NEED TO CALL ANYONE IN, DR. LAWSON...
SHHMMMMM
...THEY'VE BEEN HERE THE WHOLE TIME...

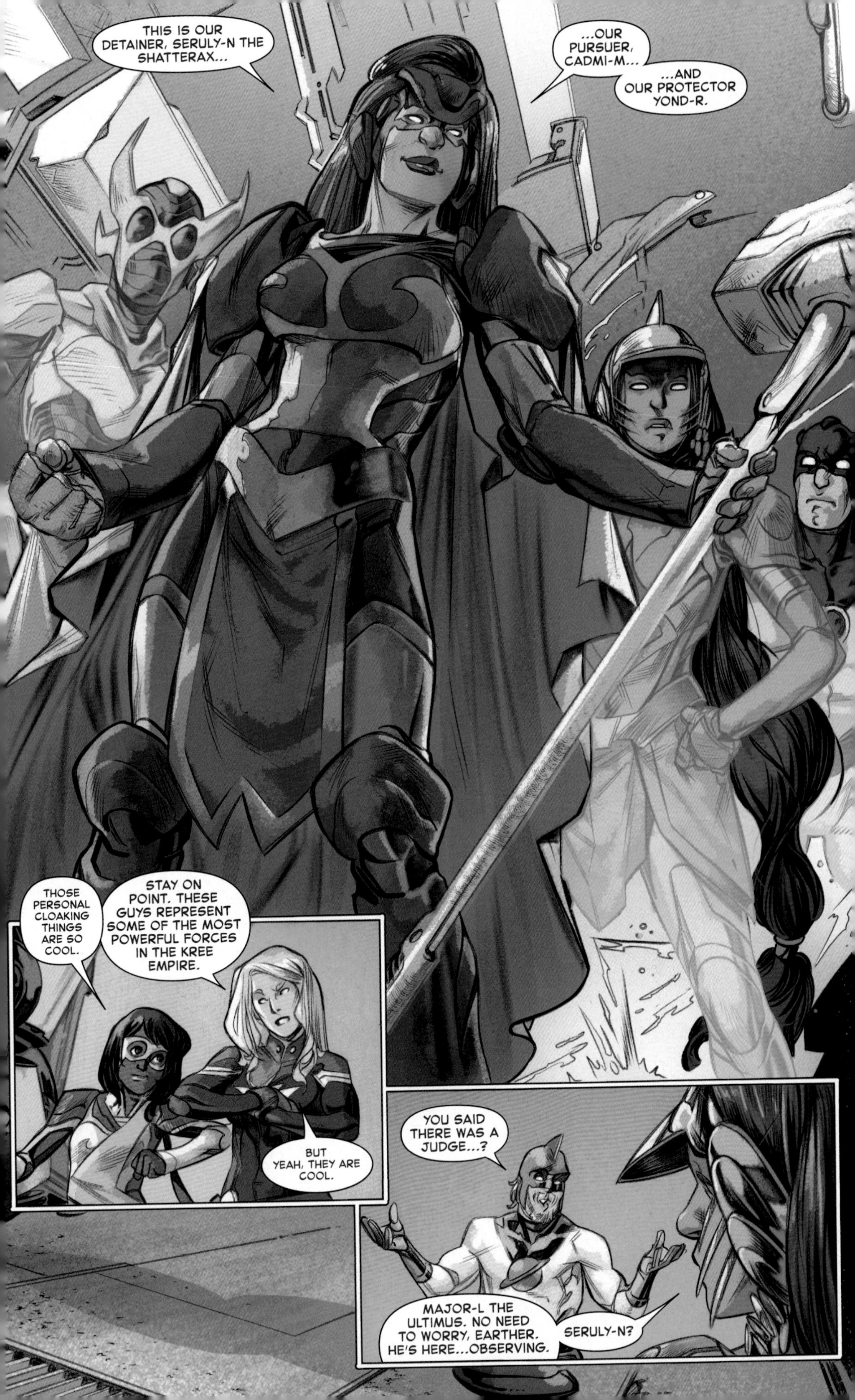
THIS IS OUR DETAINER, SERULY-N THE SHATTERAX...
...OUR PURSUER, CADMI-M...
...AND OUR PROTECTOR YOND-R.
THOSE PERSONAL CLOAKING THINGS ARE SO COOL.
STAY ON POINT. THESE GUYS REPRESENT SOME OF THE MOST POWERFUL FORCES IN THE KREE EMPIRE.
BUT YEAH, THEY ARE COOL.
YOU SAID THERE WAS A JUDGE...?
MAJOR-L THE ULTIMUS. NO NEED TO WORRY, EARTHER. HE'S HERE...OBSERVING.
SERULY-N?

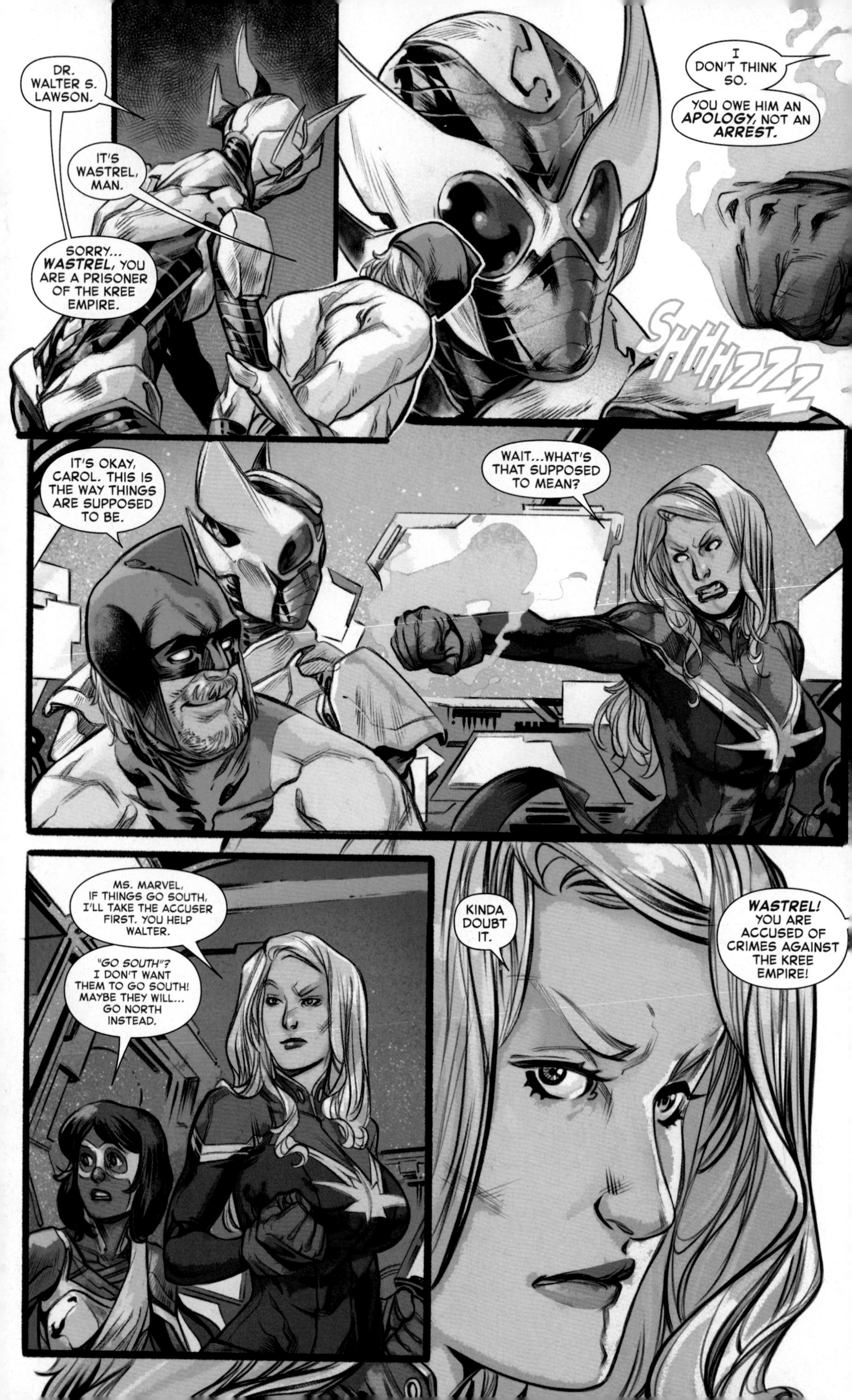
DR. WALTER S. LAWSON.
IT'S WASTREL, MAN.
SORRY... WASTREL, YOU ARE A PRISONER OF THE KREE EMPIRE.
I DON'T THINK SO.
YOU OWE HIM AN APOLOGY, NOT AN ARREST.
SHHHZZZz
IT'S OKAY, CAROL. THIS IS THE WAY THINGS ARE SUPPOSED TO BE.
WAIT...WHAT'S THAT SUPPOSED TO MEAN?
MS. MARVEL, IF THINGS GO SOUTH, I'LL TAKE THE ACCUSER FIRST. YOU HELP WALTER.
"GO SOUTH"? I DON'T WANT THEM TO GO SOUTH! MAYBE THEY WILL... GO NORTH INSTEAD.
KINDA DOUBT IT.
WASTREL! YOU ARE ACCUSED OF CRIMES AGAINST THE KREE EMPIRE!

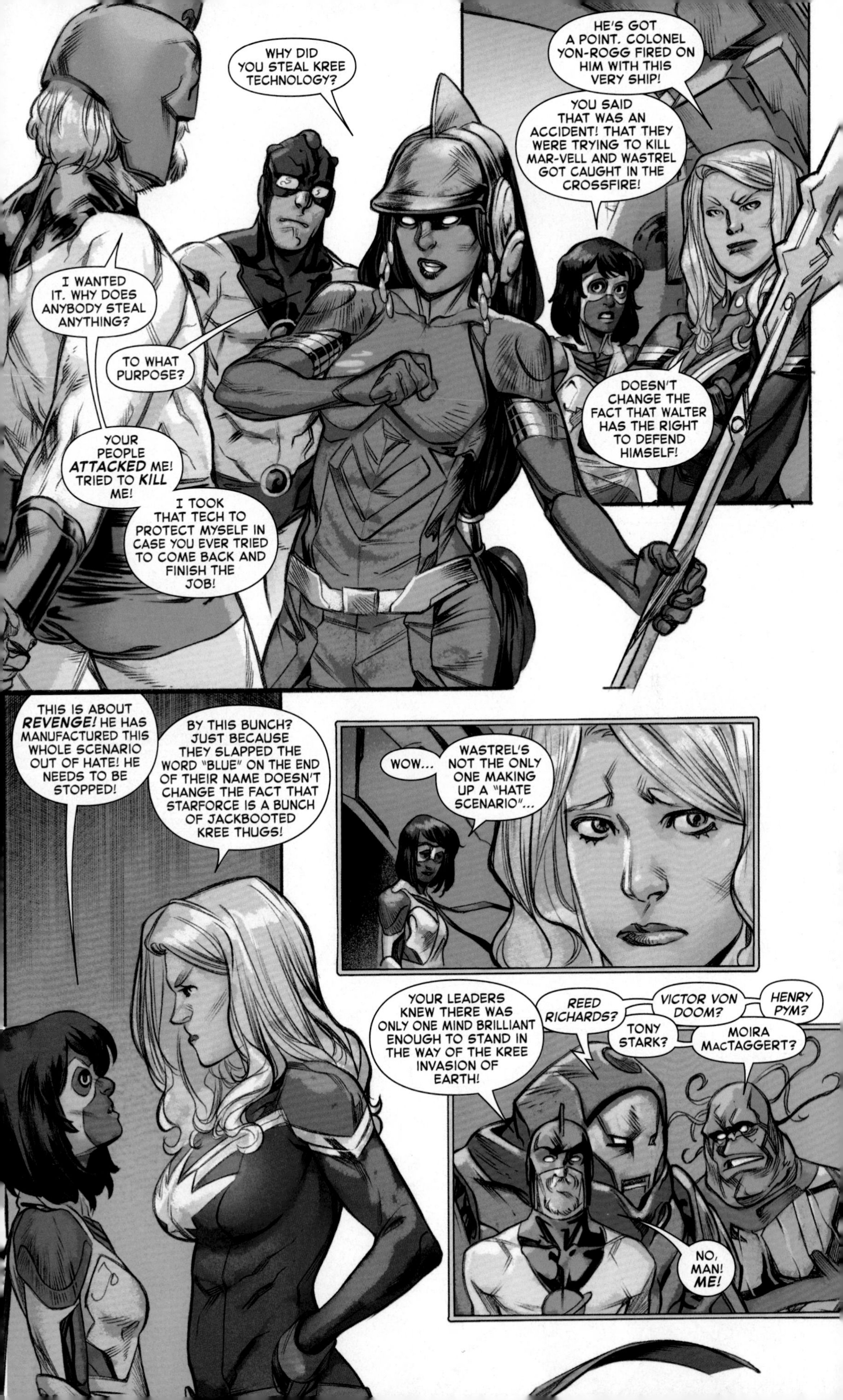

WHY DID YOU STEAL KREE TECHNOLOGY?
HE'S GOT A POINT. COLONEL YON-ROGG FIRED ON HIM WITH THIS VERY SHIP!
YOU SAID THAT WAS AN ACCIDENT! THAT THEY WERE TRYING TO KILL MAR-VELL AND WASTREL GOT CAUGHT IN THE CROSSFIRE!
I WANTED IT. WHY DOES ANYBODY STEAL ANYTHING?
TO WHAT PURPOSE?
DOESN'T CHANGE THE FACT THAT WALTER HAS THE RIGHT TO DEFEND HIMSELF!
YOUR PEOPLE ATTACKED ME! TRIED TO KILL ME!
I TOOK THAT TECH TO PROTECT MYSELF IN CASE YOU EVER TRIED TO COME BACK AND FINISH THE JOB!
THIS IS ABOUT REVENGE! HE HAS MANUFACTURED THIS WHOLE SCENARIO OUT OF HATE! HE NEEDS TO BE STOPPED!
BY THIS BUNCH? JUST BECAUSE THEY SLAPPED THE WORD "BLUE" ON THE END OF THEIR NAME DOESN'T CHANGE THE FACT THAT STARFORCE IS A BUNCH OF JACKBOOTED KREE THUGS!
WOW...
WASTREL'S NOT THE ONLY ONE MAKING UP A "HATE SCENARIO"...
YOUR LEADERS KNEW THERE WAS ONLY ONE MIND BRILLIANT ENOUGH TO STAND IN THE WAY OF THE KREE INVASION OF EARTH!
REED RICHARDS?
VICTOR VON DOOM?
HENRY PYM?
TONY STARK?
MOIRA MacTAGGERT?
NO, MAN! ME!

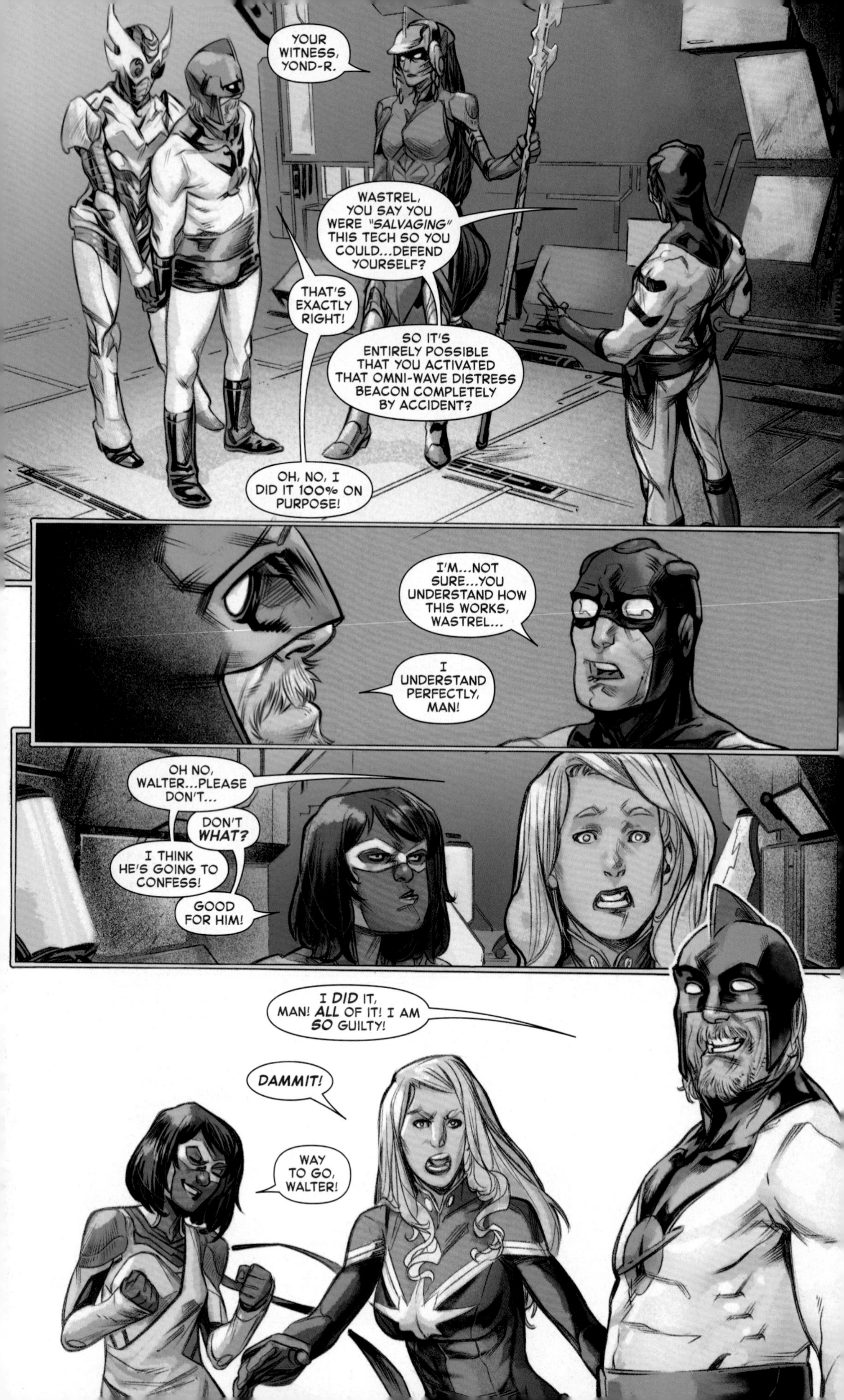
YOUR WITNESS, YOND-R.
WASTREL, YOU SAY YOU WERE "SALVAGING" THIS TECH SO YOU COULD...DEFEND YOURSELF?
THAT'S EXACTLY RIGHT!
SO IT'S ENTIRELY POSSIBLE THAT YOU ACTIVATED THAT OMNI-WAVE DISTRESS BEACON COMPLETELY BY ACCIDENT?
OH, NO, I DID IT 100% ON PURPOSE!
I'M...NOT SURE...YOU UNDERSTAND HOW THIS WORKS, WASTREL...
I UNDERSTAND PERFECTLY, MAN!
OH NO, WALTER...PLEASE DON'T...
DON'T *WHAT?*
I THINK HE'S GOING TO CONFESS!
GOOD FOR HIM!
I *DID* IT, MAN! *ALL* OF IT! I AM *SO* GUILTY!
DAMMIT!
WAY TO GO, WALTER!

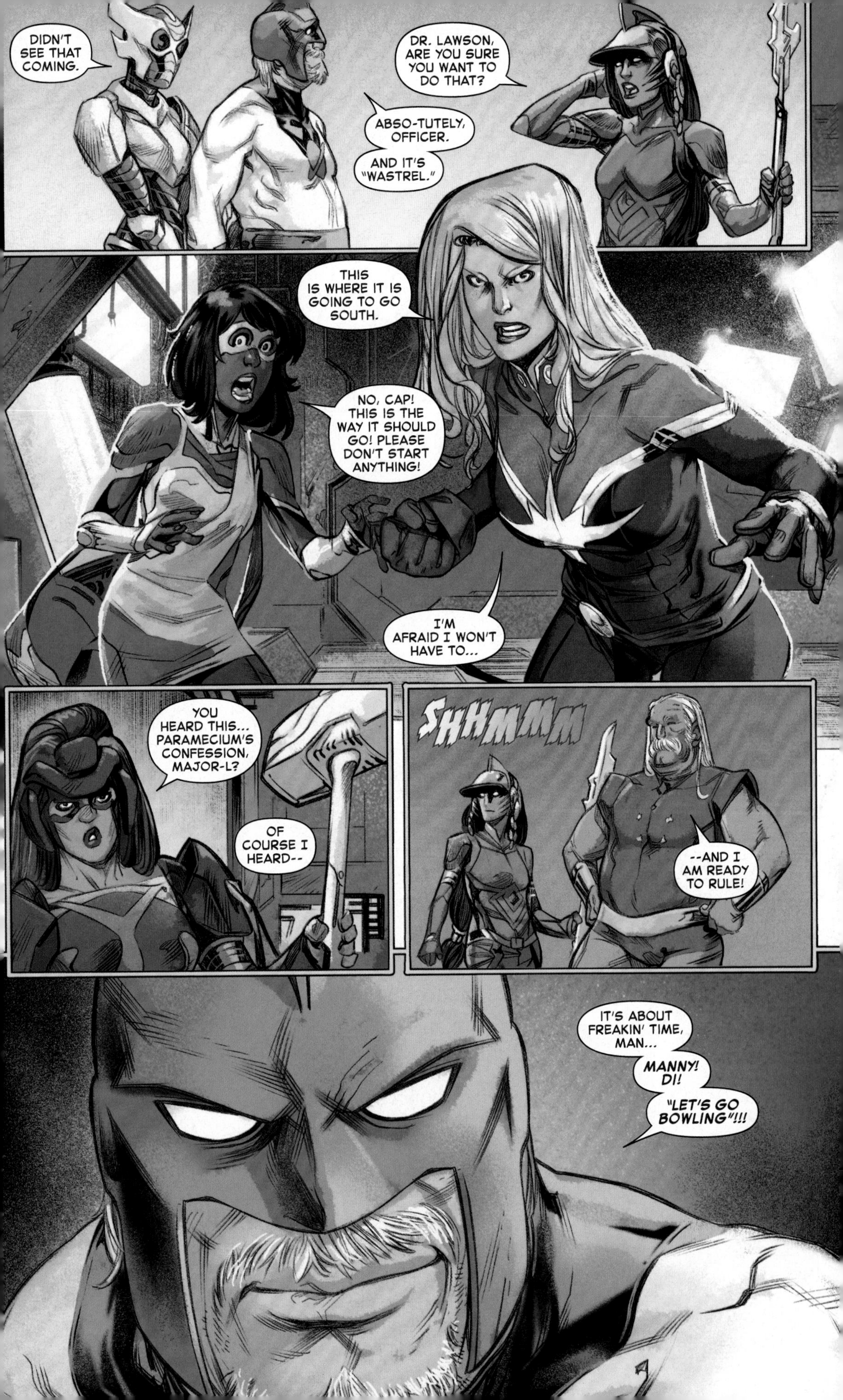
DIDN'T SEE THAT COMING.
DR. LAWSON, ARE YOU SURE YOU WANT TO DO THAT?
ABSO-TUTELY, OFFICER.
AND IT'S "WASTREL."
THIS IS WHERE IT IS GOING TO GO SOUTH.
NO, CAP! THIS IS THE WAY IT SHOULD GO! PLEASE DON'T START ANYTHING!
I'M AFRAID I WON'T HAVE TO...
YOU HEARD THIS... PARAMECIUM'S CONFESSION, MAJOR-L?
OF COURSE I HEARD--
SHHMMM
--AND I AM READY TO RULE!
IT'S ABOUT FREAKIN' TIME, MAN...
MANNY! DI!
"LET'S GO BOWLING"!!!

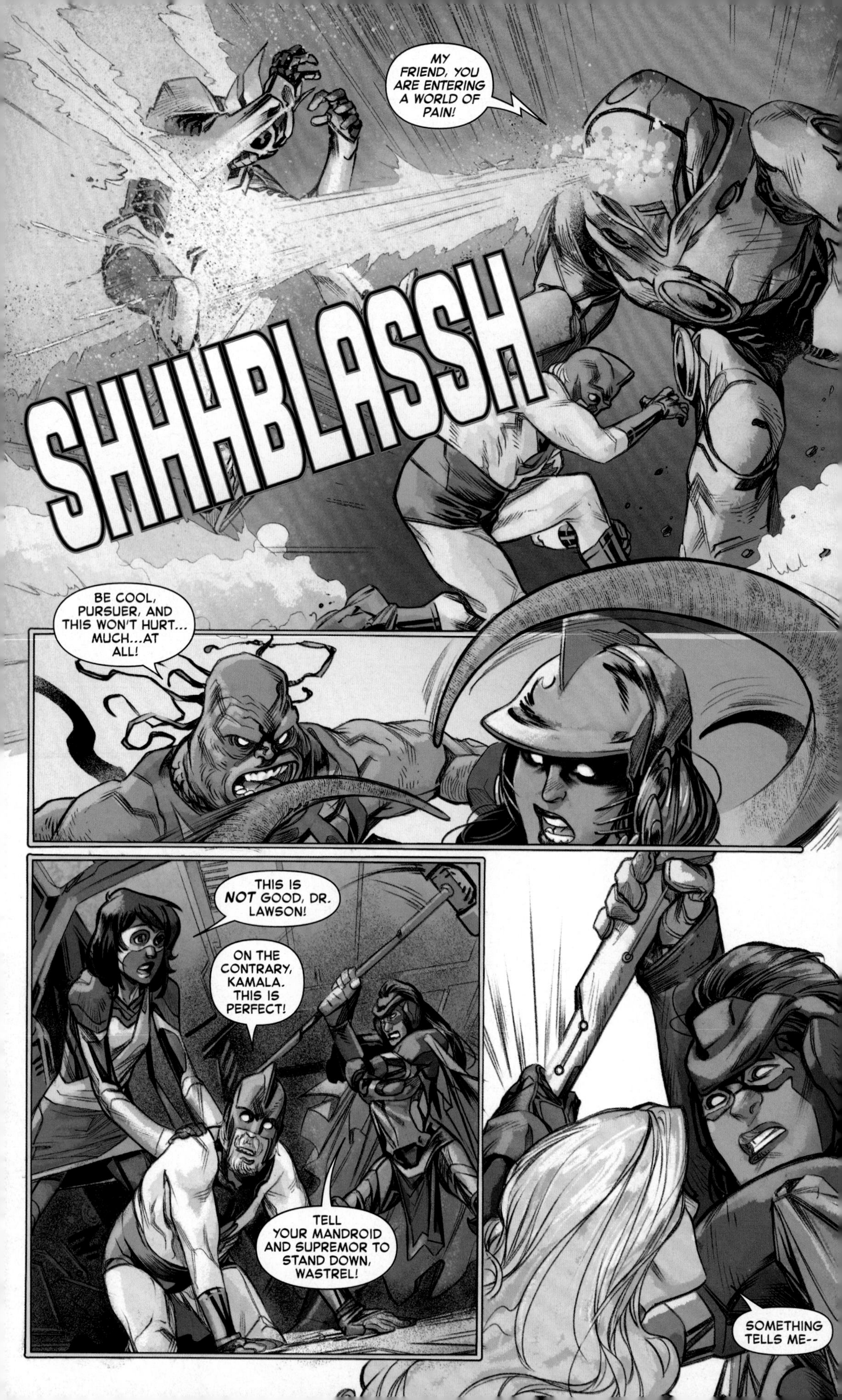
MY FRIEND, YOU ARE ENTERING A WORLD OF PAIN!
SHHHBLASSH
BE COOL, PURSUER, AND THIS WON'T HURT... MUCH...AT ALL!
THIS IS NOT GOOD, DR. LAWSON!
ON THE CONTRARY, KAMALA. THIS IS PERFECT!
TELL YOUR MANDROID AND SUPREMOR TO STAND DOWN, WASTREL!
SOMETHING TELLS ME--

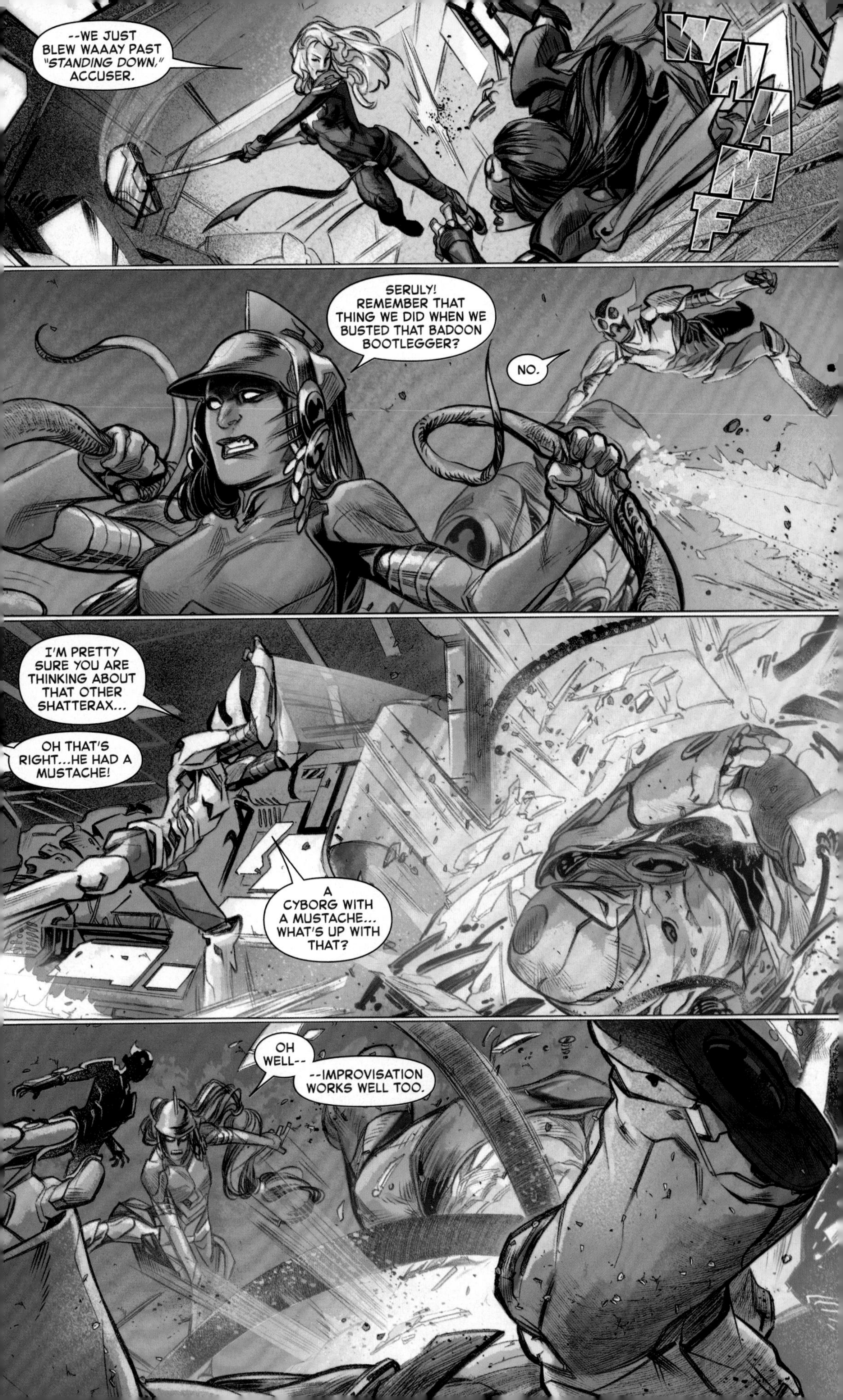
--WE JUST BLEW WAAAY PAST "STANDING DOWN," ACCUSER.
WHAMF
SERULY! REMEMBER THAT THING WE DID WHEN WE BUSTED THAT BADOON BOOTLEGGER?
NO.
I'M PRETTY SURE YOU ARE THINKING ABOUT THAT OTHER SHATTERAX...
OH THAT'S RIGHT...HE HAD A MUSTACHE!
A CYBORG WITH A MUSTACHE... WHAT'S UP WITH THAT?
OH WELL--
--IMPROVISATION WORKS WELL TOO.

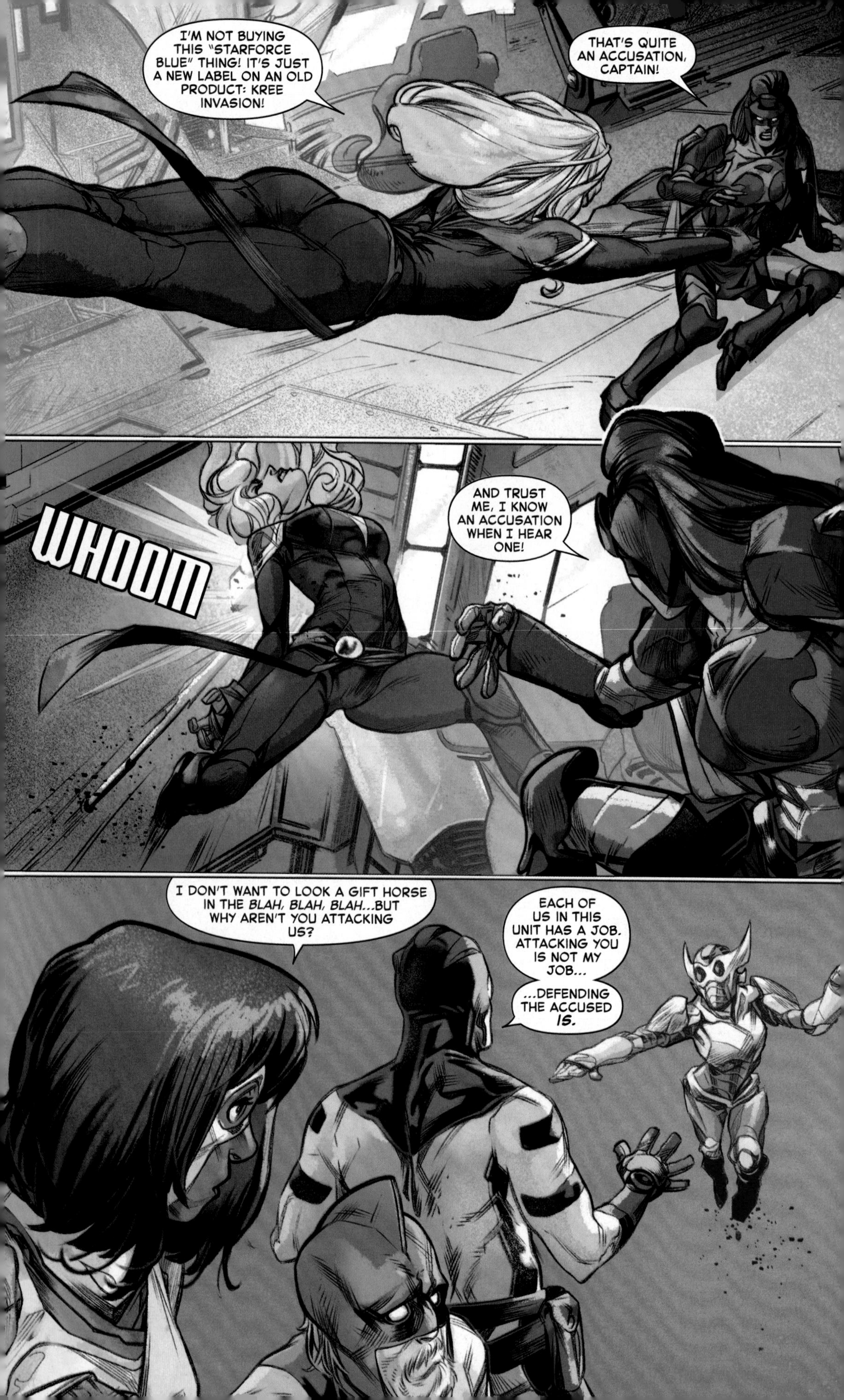
I'M NOT BUYING THIS "STARFORCE BLUE" THING! IT'S JUST A NEW LABEL ON AN OLD PRODUCT: KREE INVASION!
THAT'S QUITE AN ACCUSATION, CAPTAIN!
WHOOM
AND TRUST ME, I KNOW AN ACCUSATION WHEN I HEAR ONE!
I DON'T WANT TO LOOK A GIFT HORSE IN THE *BLAH, BLAH, BLAH*...BUT WHY AREN'T YOU ATTACKING US?
EACH OF US IN THIS UNIT HAS A JOB. ATTACKING YOU IS NOT MY JOB...
...DEFENDING THE ACCUSED *IS.*

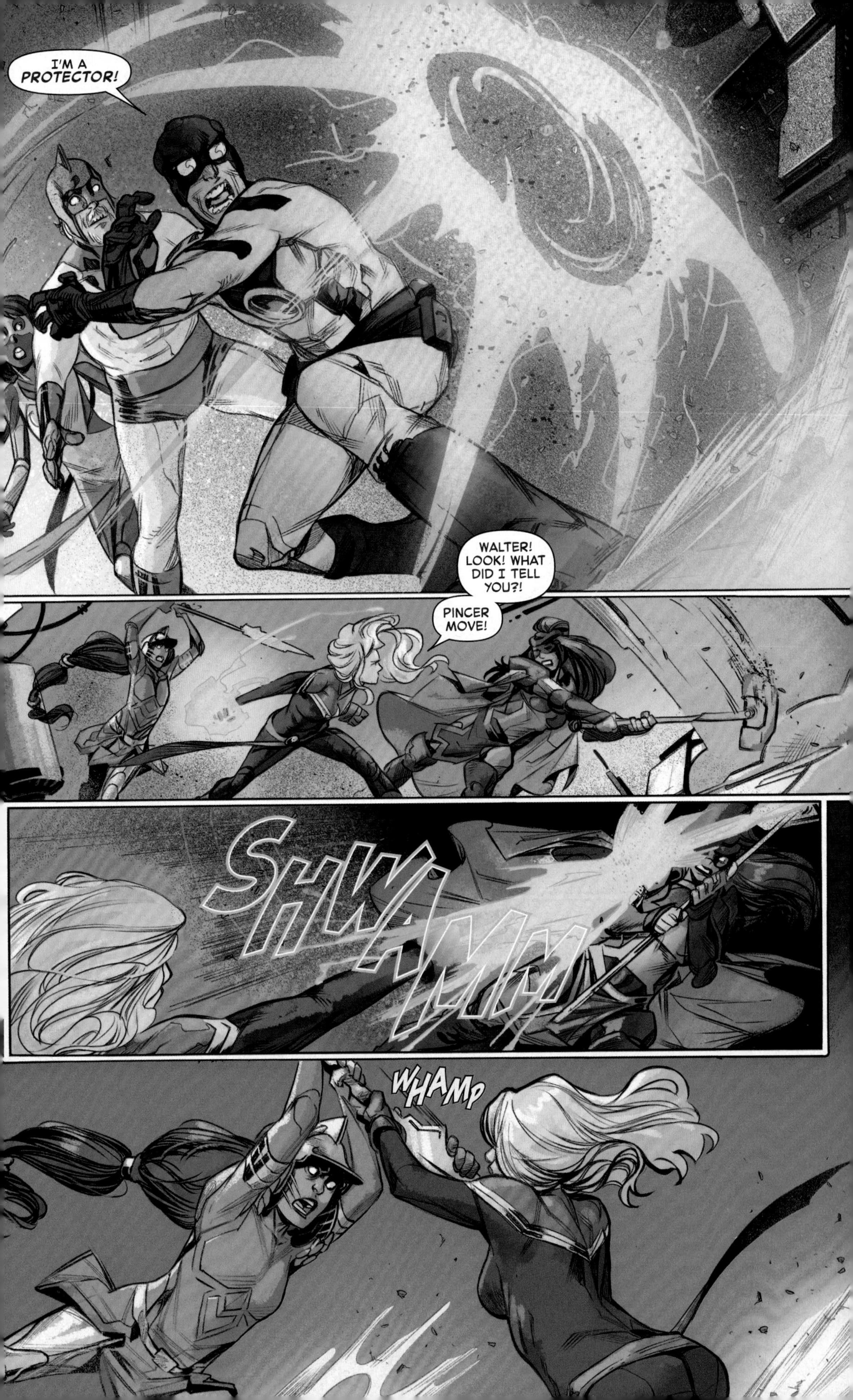
I'M A PROTECTOR!
WALTER! LOOK! WHAT DID I TELL YOU?!
PINCER MOVE!
SHWAMM
WHAMP

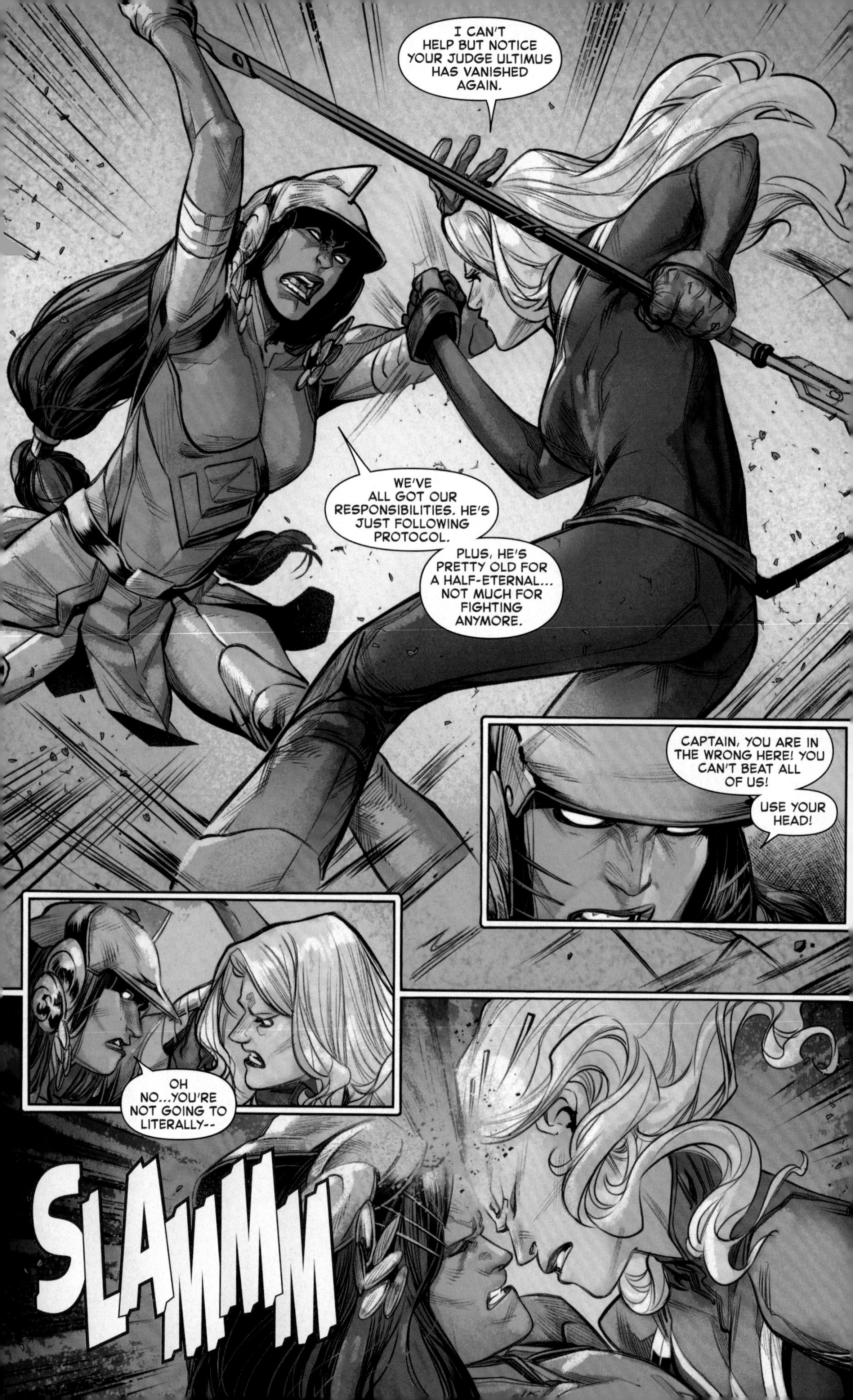
I CAN'T HELP BUT NOTICE YOUR JUDGE ULTIMUS HAS VANISHED AGAIN.
WE'VE ALL GOT OUR RESPONSIBILITIES. HE'S JUST FOLLOWING PROTOCOL.
PLUS, HE'S PRETTY OLD FOR A HALF-ETERNAL... NOT MUCH FOR FIGHTING ANYMORE.
CAPTAIN, YOU ARE IN THE WRONG HERE! YOU CAN'T BEAT ALL OF US!
USE YOUR HEAD!
OH NO...YOU'RE NOT GOING TO LITERALLY--
SLAMMM

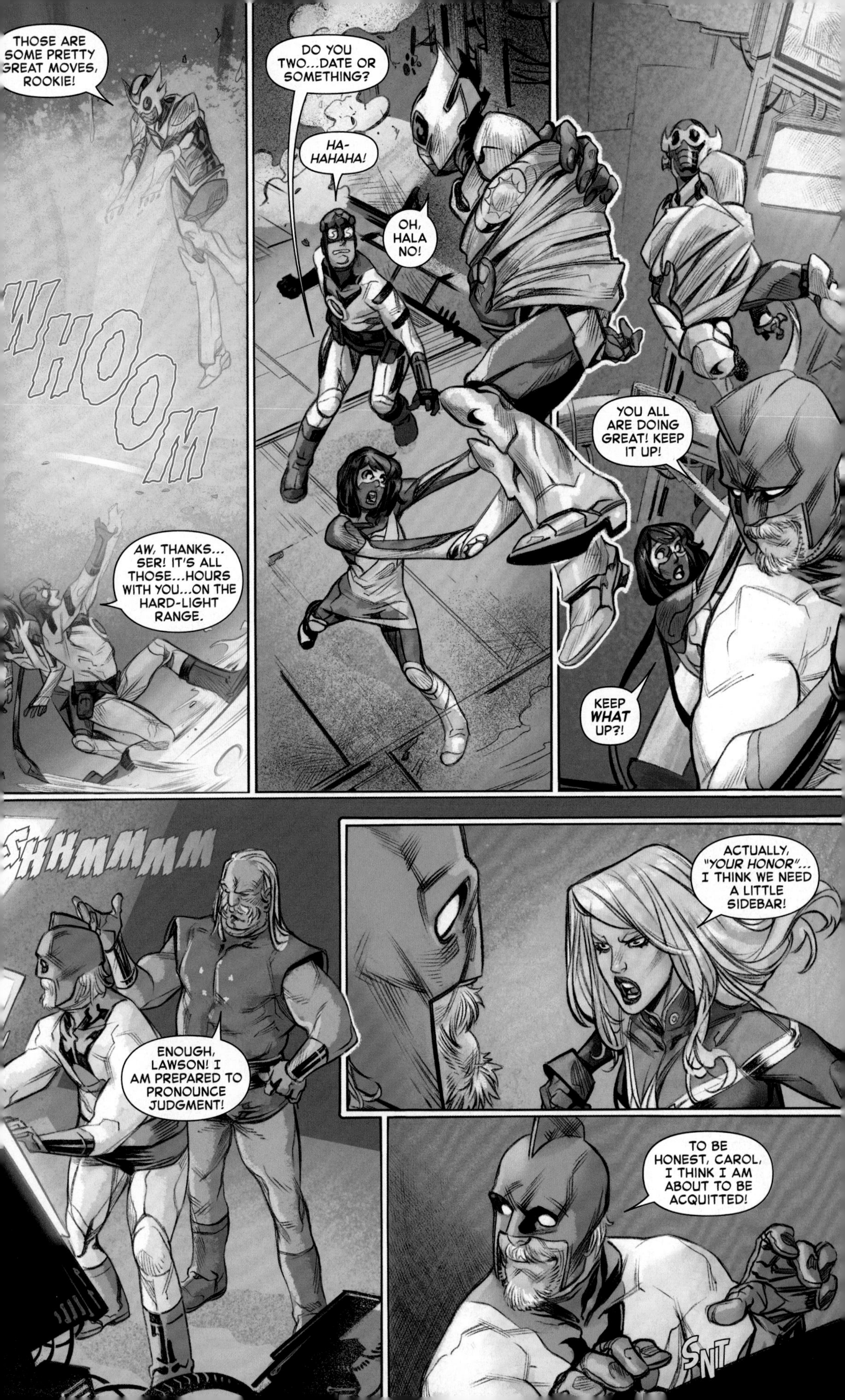
THOSE ARE SOME PRETTY GREAT MOVES, ROOKIE!
WHOOM
AW, THANKS... SER! IT'S ALL THOSE...HOURS WITH YOU...ON THE HARD-LIGHT RANGE.
DO YOU TWO...DATE OR SOMETHING?
HA-HAHAHA!
OH, HALA NO!
YOU ALL ARE DOING GREAT! KEEP IT UP!
KEEP WHAT UP?!
SHHMMMM
ENOUGH, LAWSON! I AM PREPARED TO PRONOUNCE JUDGMENT!
ACTUALLY, "YOUR HONOR"... I THINK WE NEED A LITTLE SIDEBAR!
TO BE HONEST, CAROL, I THINK I AM ABOUT TO BE ACQUITTED!
SNT

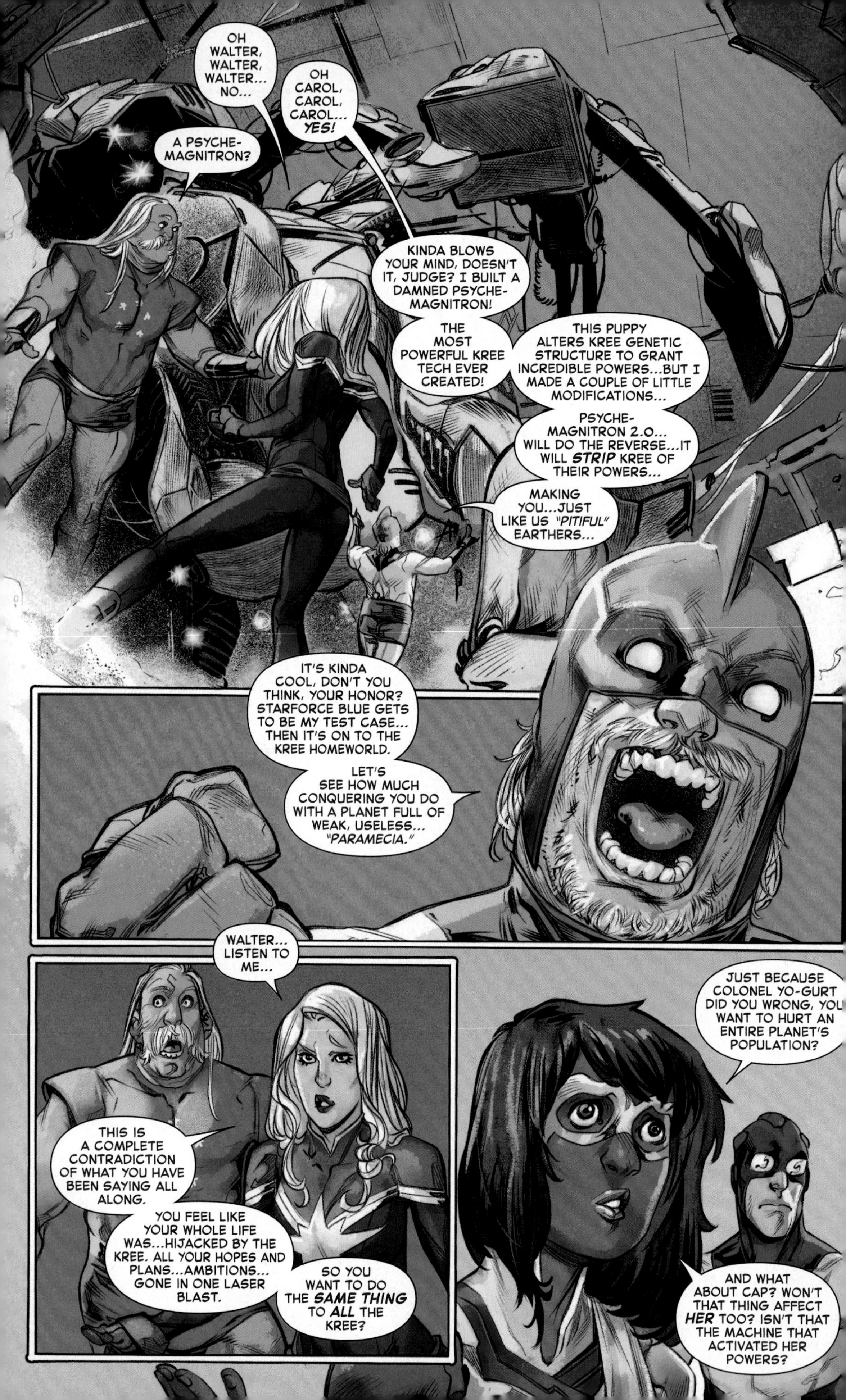

OH WALTER, WALTER, WALTER... NO...
OH CAROL, CAROL, CAROL... YES!
A PSYCHE-MAGNITRON?
KINDA BLOWS YOUR MIND, DOESN'T IT, JUDGE? I BUILT A DAMNED PSYCHE-MAGNITRON!
THE MOST POWERFUL KREE TECH EVER CREATED!
THIS PUPPY ALTERS KREE GENETIC STRUCTURE TO GRANT INCREDIBLE POWERS...BUT I MADE A COUPLE OF LITTLE MODIFICATIONS...
PSYCHE-MAGNITRON 2.0... WILL DO THE REVERSE...IT WILL STRIP KREE OF THEIR POWERS...
MAKING YOU...JUST LIKE US "PITIFUL" EARTHERS...
IT'S KINDA COOL, DON'T YOU THINK, YOUR HONOR? STARFORCE BLUE GETS TO BE MY TEST CASE... THEN IT'S ON TO THE KREE HOMEWORLD.
LET'S SEE HOW MUCH CONQUERING YOU DO WITH A PLANET FULL OF WEAK, USELESS... "PARAMECIA."
WALTER... LISTEN TO ME...
THIS IS A COMPLETE CONTRADICTION OF WHAT YOU HAVE BEEN SAYING ALL ALONG.
YOU FEEL LIKE YOUR WHOLE LIFE WAS...HIJACKED BY THE KREE. ALL YOUR HOPES AND PLANS...AMBITIONS... GONE IN ONE LASER BLAST.
SO YOU WANT TO DO THE SAME THING TO ALL THE KREE?
JUST BECAUSE COLONEL YO-GURT DID YOU WRONG, YOU WANT TO HURT AN ENTIRE PLANET'S POPULATION?
AND WHAT ABOUT CAP? WON'T THAT THING AFFECT HER TOO? ISN'T THAT THE MACHINE THAT ACTIVATED HER POWERS?

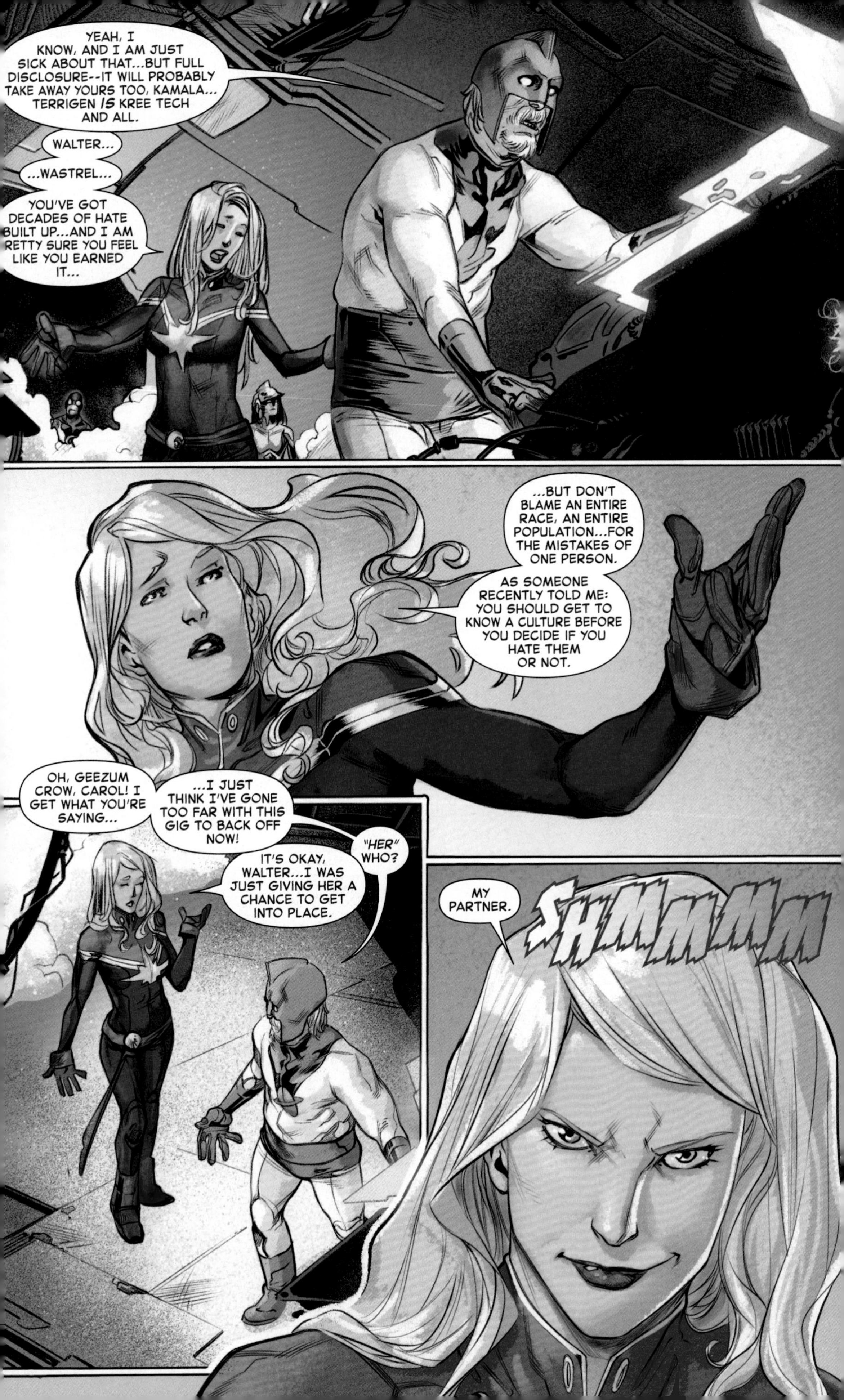
YEAH, I KNOW, AND I AM JUST SICK ABOUT THAT...BUT FULL DISCLOSURE--IT WILL PROBABLY TAKE AWAY YOURS TOO, KAMALA... TERRIGEN *IS* KREE TECH AND ALL.
WALTER...
...WASTREL...
YOU'VE GOT DECADES OF HATE BUILT UP...AND I AM PRETTY SURE YOU FEEL LIKE YOU EARNED IT...
...BUT DON'T BLAME AN ENTIRE RACE, AN ENTIRE POPULATION...FOR THE MISTAKES OF ONE PERSON.
AS SOMEONE RECENTLY TOLD ME: YOU SHOULD GET TO KNOW A CULTURE BEFORE YOU DECIDE IF YOU HATE THEM OR NOT.
OH, GEEZUM CROW, CAROL! I GET WHAT YOU'RE SAYING...
...I JUST THINK I'VE GONE TOO FAR WITH THIS GIG TO BACK OFF NOW!
IT'S OKAY, WALTER...I WAS JUST GIVING HER A CHANCE TO GET INTO PLACE.
"HER" WHO?
MY PARTNER.
SHMMMMM

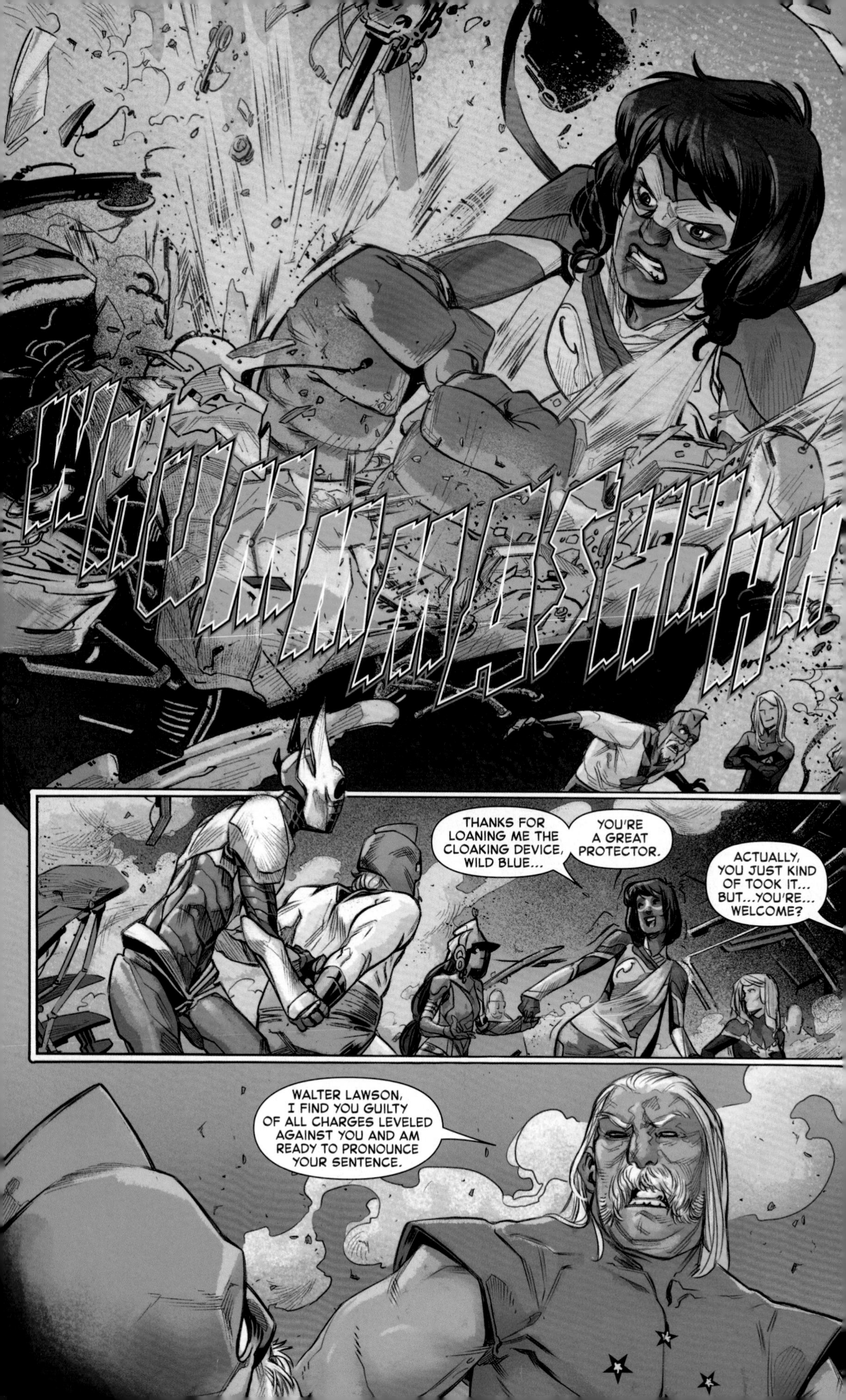
WHUMMMASHHHH
THANKS FOR LOANING ME THE CLOAKING DEVICE, WILD BLUE...
YOU'RE A GREAT PROTECTOR.
ACTUALLY, YOU JUST KIND OF TOOK IT... BUT...YOU'RE... WELCOME?
WALTER LAWSON, I FIND YOU GUILTY OF ALL CHARGES LEVELED AGAINST YOU AND AM READY TO PRONOUNCE YOUR SENTENCE.

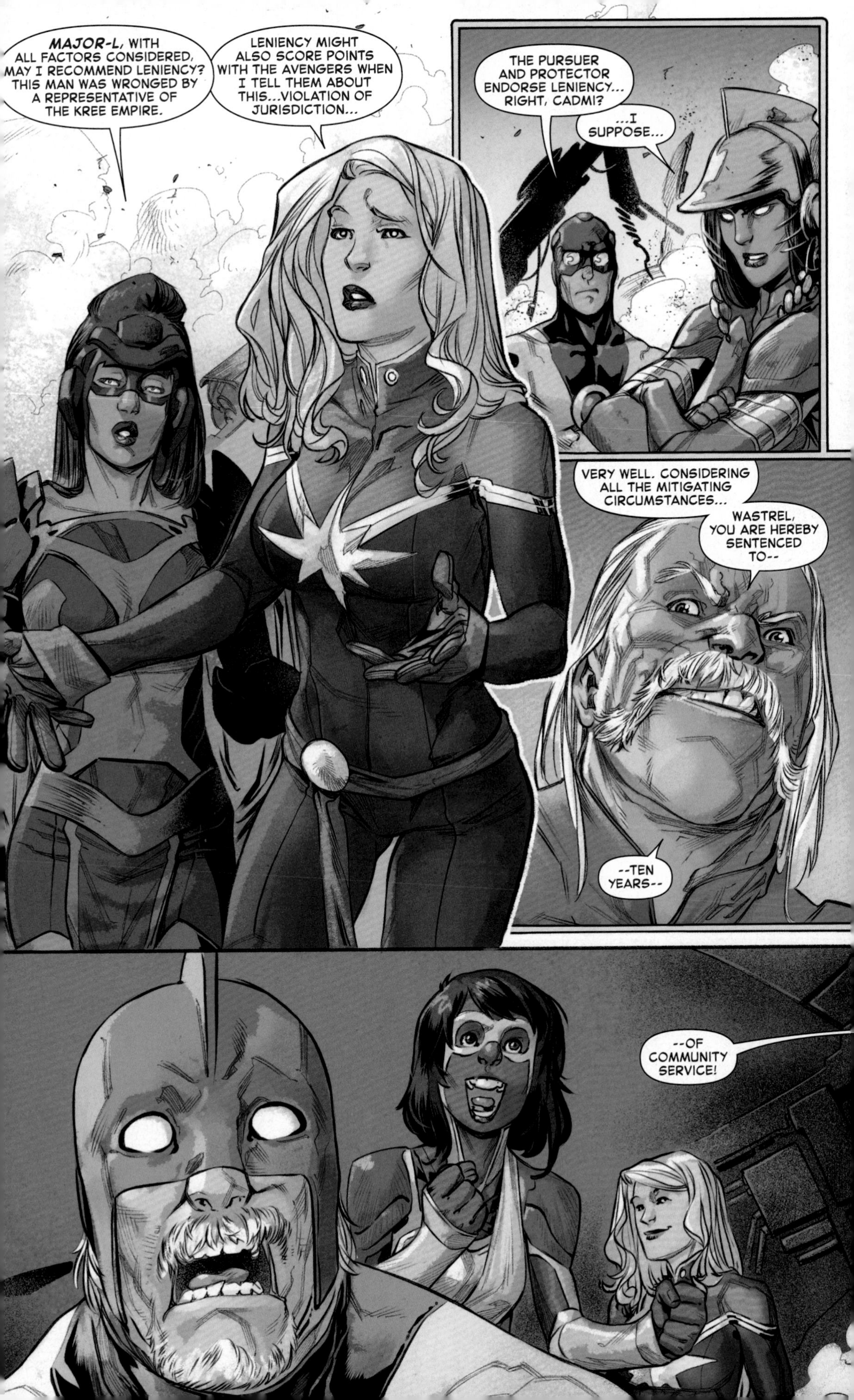
MAJOR-L, WITH ALL FACTORS CONSIDERED, MAY I RECOMMEND LENIENCY? THIS MAN WAS WRONGED BY A REPRESENTATIVE OF THE KREE EMPIRE.
LENIENCY MIGHT ALSO SCORE POINTS WITH THE AVENGERS WHEN I TELL THEM ABOUT THIS...VIOLATION OF JURISDICTION...
THE PURSUER AND PROTECTOR ENDORSE LENIENCY... RIGHT, CADMI?
...I SUPPOSE...
VERY WELL. CONSIDERING ALL THE MITIGATING CIRCUMSTANCES...
WASTREL, YOU ARE HEREBY SENTENCED TO--
--TEN YEARS--
--OF COMMUNITY SERVICE!

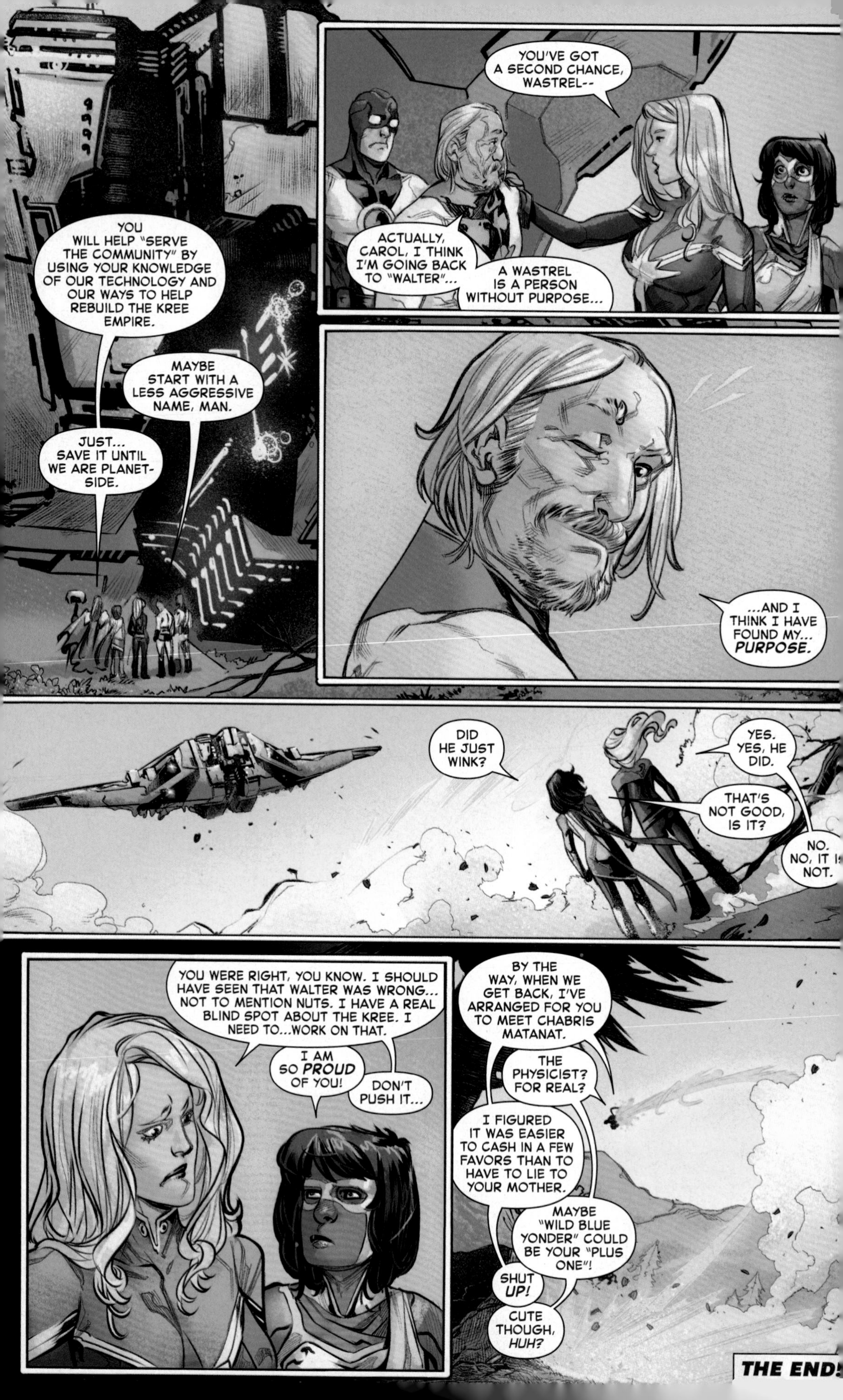
YOU'VE GOT A SECOND CHANCE, WASTREL--
ACTUALLY, CAROL, I THINK I'M GOING BACK TO "WALTER"...
A WASTREL IS A PERSON WITHOUT PURPOSE...
YOU WILL HELP "SERVE THE COMMUNITY" BY USING YOUR KNOWLEDGE OF OUR TECHNOLOGY AND OUR WAYS TO HELP REBUILD THE KREE EMPIRE.
MAYBE START WITH A LESS AGGRESSIVE NAME, MAN.
JUST... SAVE IT UNTIL WE ARE PLANET-SIDE.
...AND I THINK I HAVE FOUND MY... PURPOSE.
DID HE JUST WINK?
YES. YES, HE DID.
THAT'S NOT GOOD, IS IT?
NO. NO, IT IS NOT.
YOU WERE RIGHT, YOU KNOW. I SHOULD HAVE SEEN THAT WALTER WAS WRONG... NOT TO MENTION NUTS. I HAVE A REAL BLIND SPOT ABOUT THE KREE. I NEED TO...WORK ON THAT.
I AM SO PROUD OF YOU!
DON'T PUSH IT...
BY THE WAY, WHEN WE GET BACK, I'VE ARRANGED FOR YOU TO MEET CHABRIS MATANAT.
THE PHYSICIST? FOR REAL?
I FIGURED IT WAS EASIER TO CASH IN A FEW FAVORS THAN TO HAVE TO LIE TO YOUR MOTHER.
MAYBE "WILD BLUE YONDER" COULD BE YOUR "PLUS ONE"!
SHUT UP!
CUTE THOUGH, HUH?
THE END!

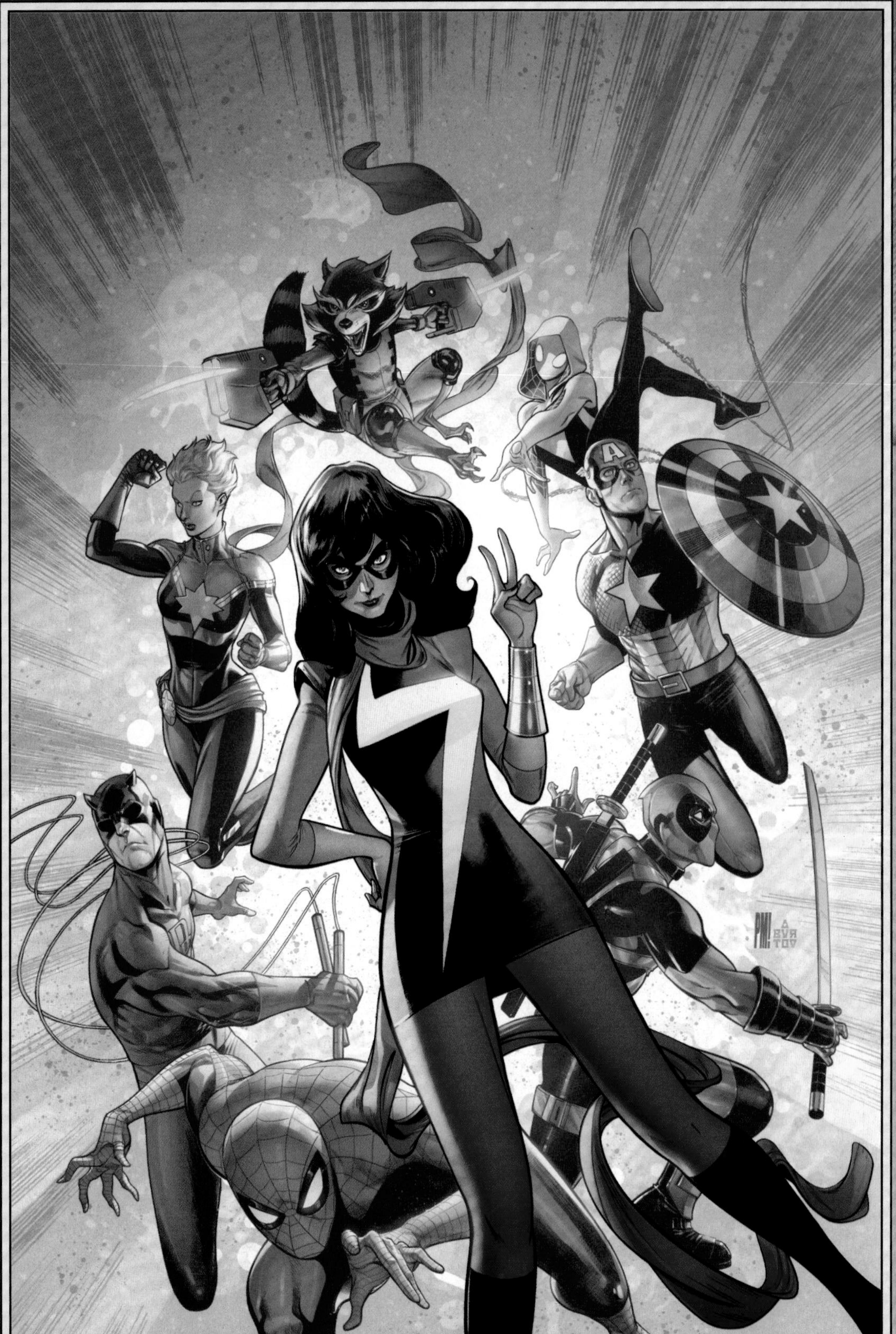

#1 VARIANT BY
PACO MEDINA & JESUS ABURTOV

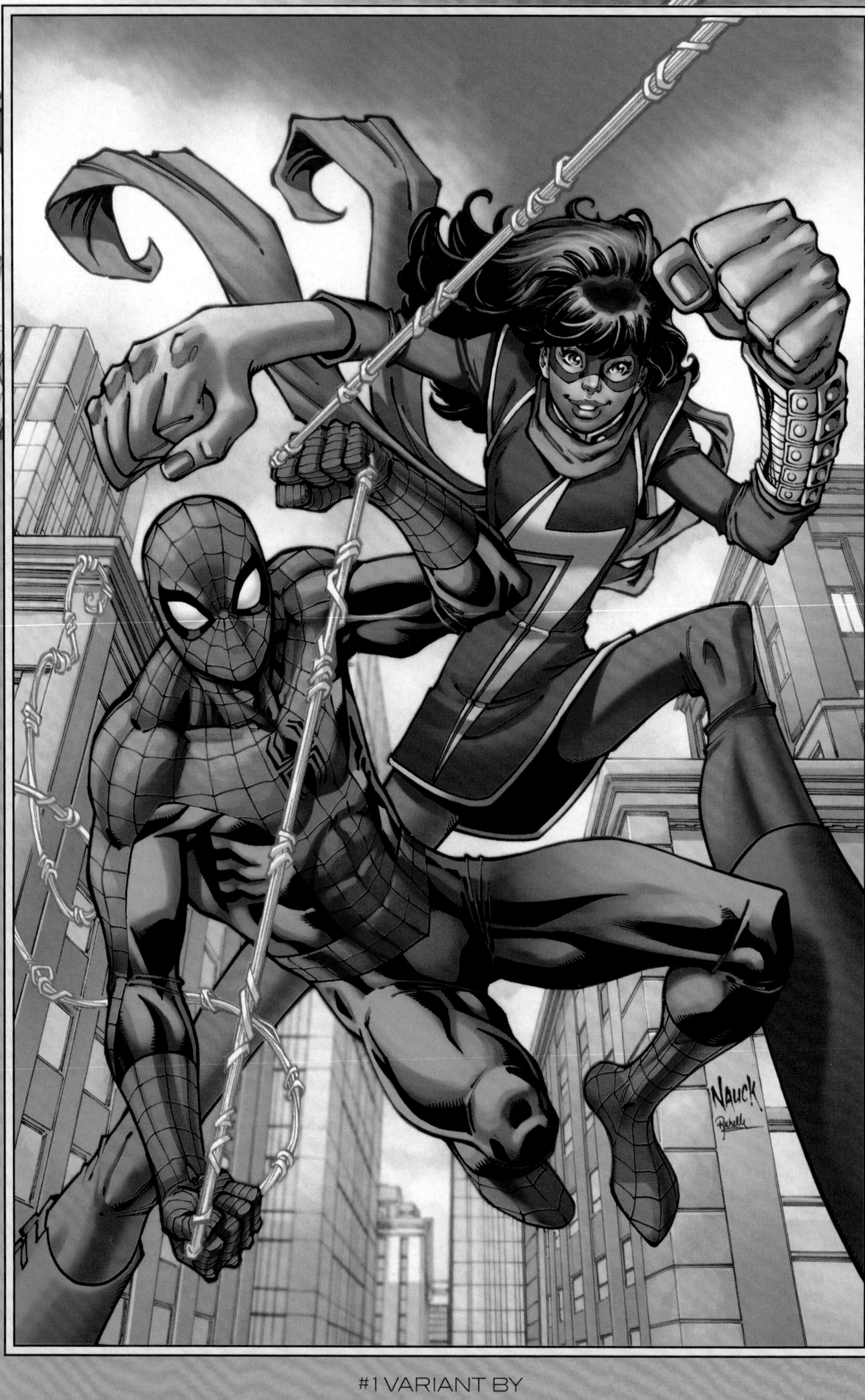
NAUCK
Rachelle

#1 VARIANT BY
TODD NAUCK & RACHELLE ROSENBERG

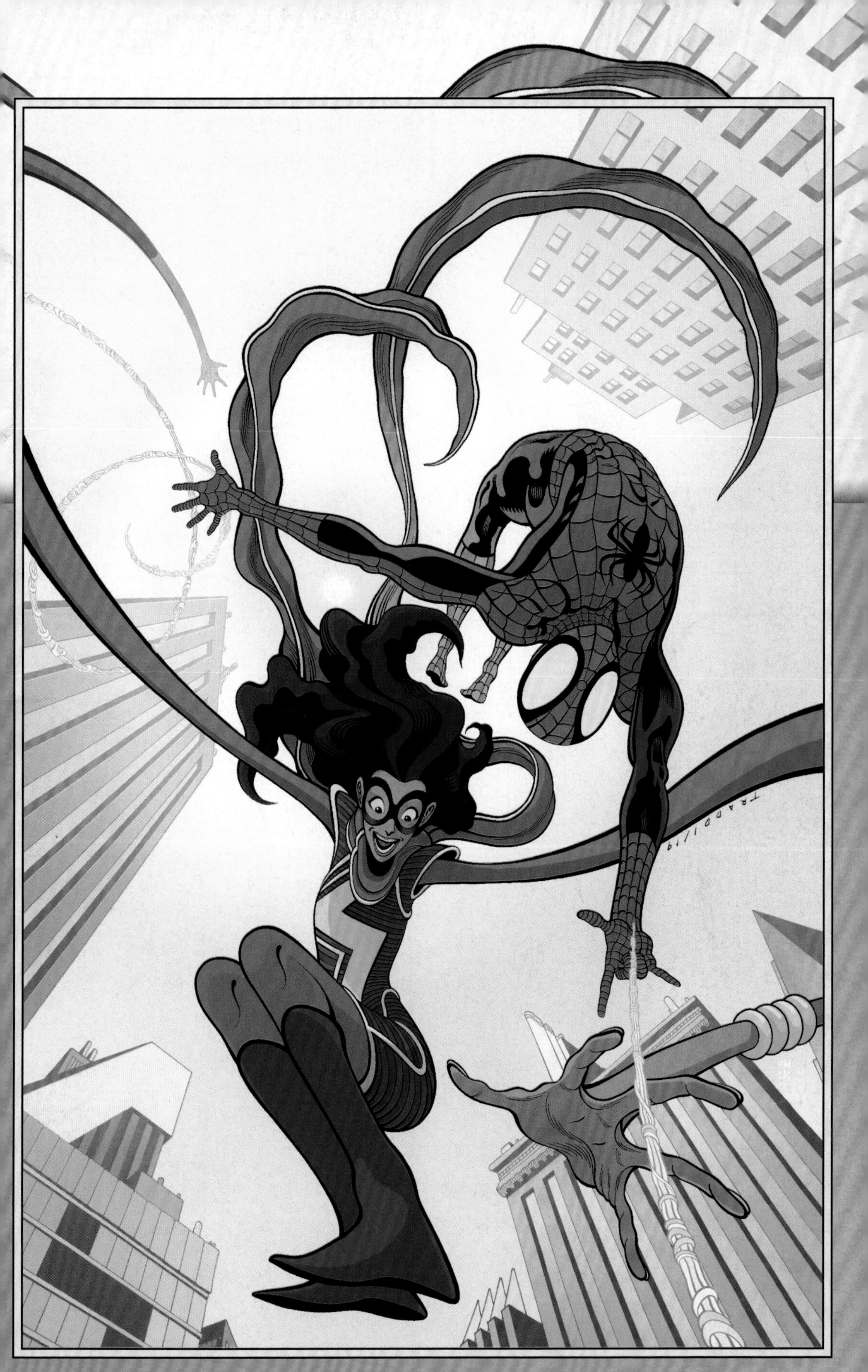

#2 VARIANT BY
TRADD MOORE & HEATHER MOORE

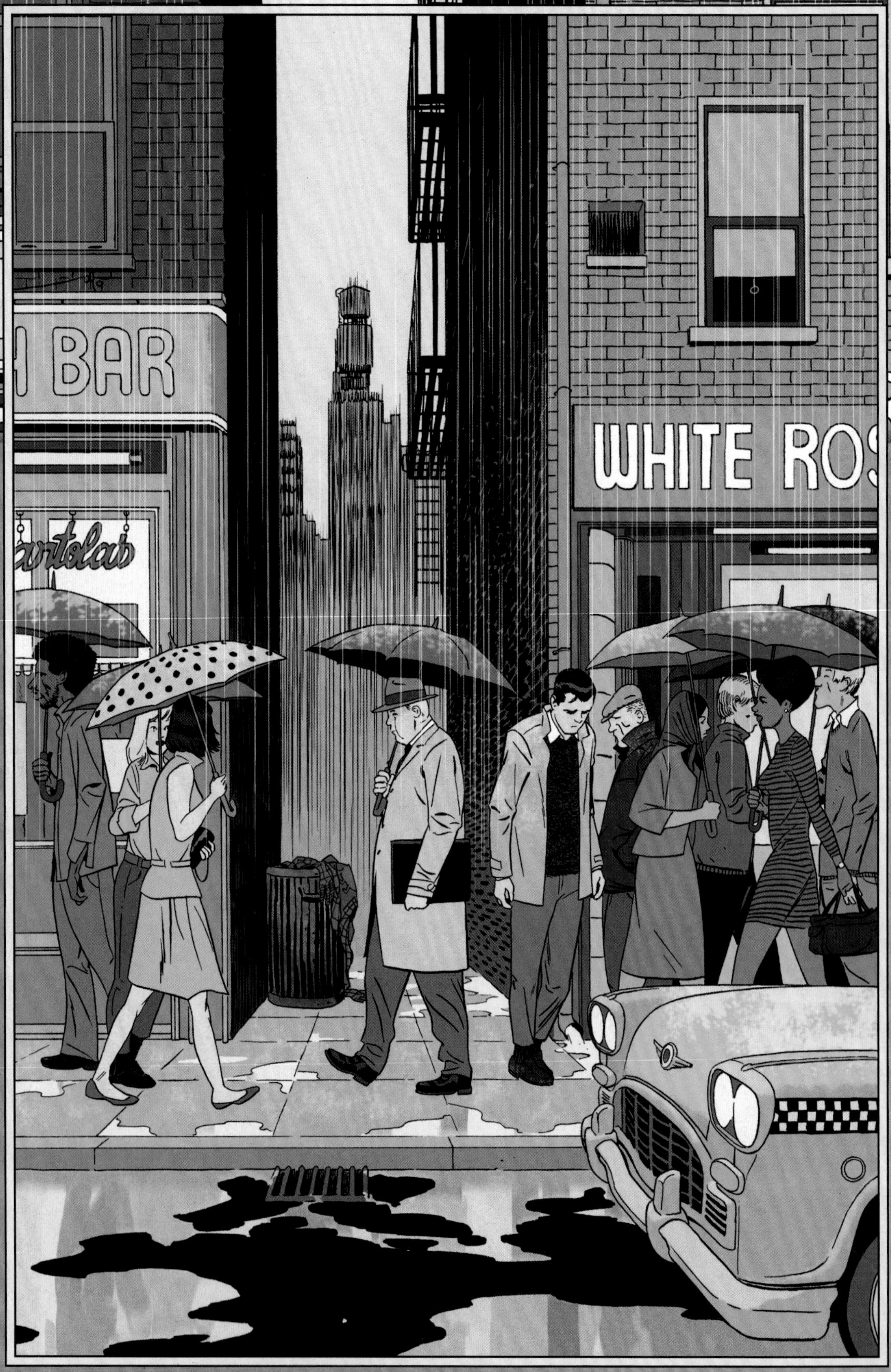
BAR
WHITE ROS
artolas

#3 MARVELS 25TH TRIBUTE VARIANT BY
MARCOS MARTIN

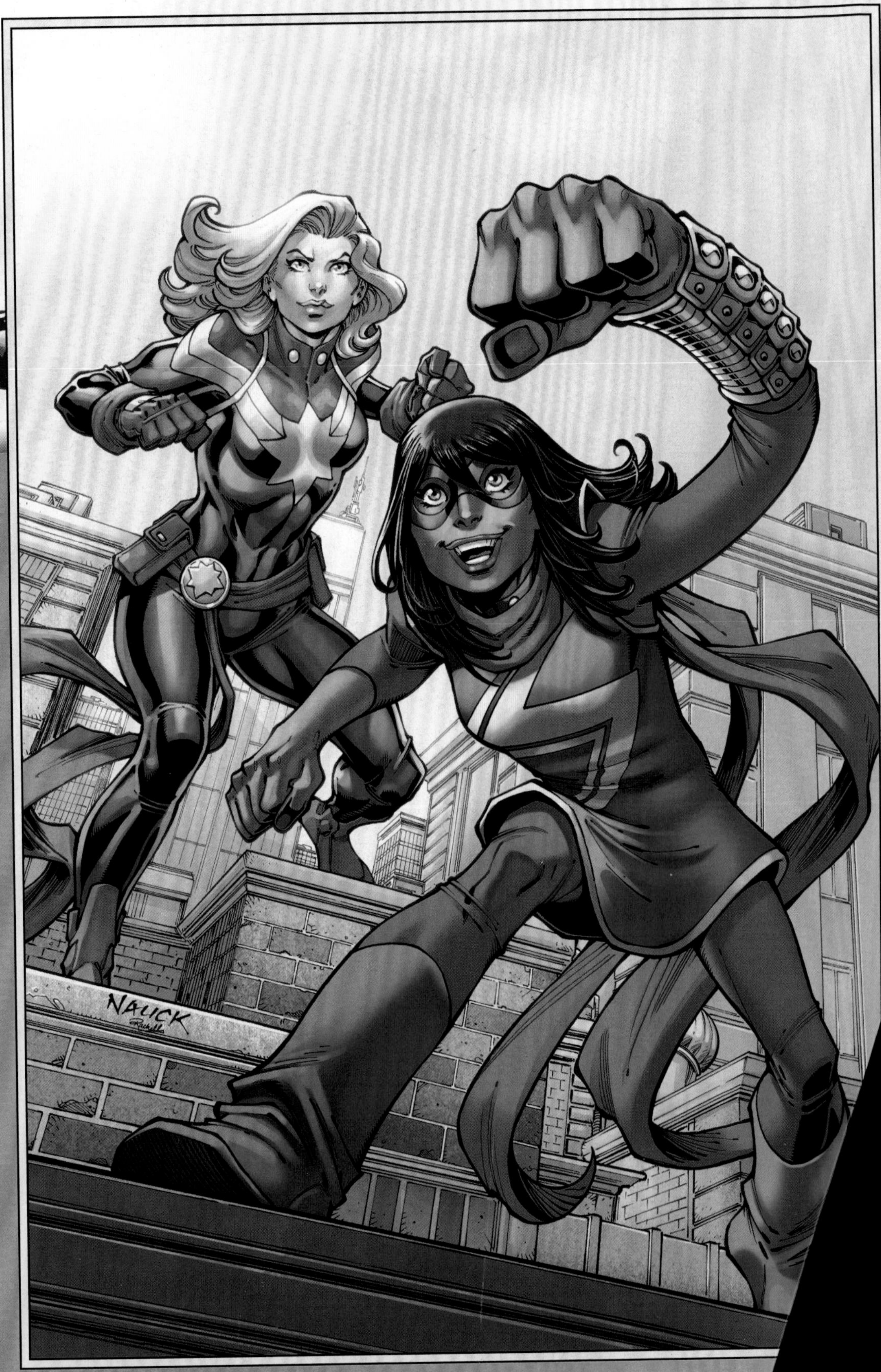
NAUCK

#4 VARIANT BY
TODD NAUCK & RACHELLE ROSENBERG